Paid, Owned, Earned

Paid, Owned, Earned

Maximizing marketing returns in a socially connected world

NICK BURCHER

KoganPage

LONDON PHILADELPHIA NEW DELHI

First published in Great Britain and the United States in 2012 by Kogan Page Limited

120 Pentonville Road	1518 Walnut Street, Suite 1100	4737/23 Ansari Road
London N1 9JN	Philadelphia PA 19102	Daryaganj
United Kingdom	USA	New Delhi 110002
www.koganpage.com		India

© Nick Burcher, 2012

The right of Nick Burcher to be identified as the author of this work has been asserted by him in accordance with the Copyright, Designs and Patents Act 1988.

ISBN   978 0 7494 6562 9
E-ISBN   978 0 7494 6563 6

British Library Cataloguing-in-Publication Data

A CIP record for this book is available from the British Library.

Library of Congress Cataloging-in-Publication Data

Burcher, Nick.
   Paid, owned, earned : maximising marketing returns in a socially connected world / Nick Burcher.
      p. cm.
   ISBN 978-0-7494-6562-9 – ISBN 978-0-7494-6563-6   1. Marketing–Management.
2. Internet marketing.   3. Online social networks.   4. Digital media.   I. Title.
   HF5415.13.B778 2012
   658.8–dc23
                                                                          2011038487

Typeset by Graphicraft Ltd, Hong Kong
Print production managed by Jellyfish
Printed and bound by CPI Group (UK) Ltd, Croydon, CR0 4YY

*The internet boom will return – and it will be bigger
and more profitable than the first time round.
They sound like the views of a web nerd – or a lunatic.
But this amazing assertion comes from respected
US economist W Brian Arthur.*

*According to economists who agree with Arthur,
technology must become so user-friendly that
people do not think twice about it.
In that respect, the internet is being absorbed into
everyday life, despite slow download times and quirky graphics.*

*Once the glitches are ironed out, so the theory goes,
the real money will be made by the players left standing.*

(Graeme Beaton, Dotcom boom 'just beginning',
Mail on Sunday, This Is Money, 3 March 2002)

Contents

About this book

In the past this book would simply have been words on paper, but this text exists as an e-book and a book in traditional format. Furthermore, whilst this book functions as a stand-alone text, each chapter can be read in isolation, and there is a list of key points at the end of each one. Finally, this book also acts as a starting point for further exploration, a gateway to a range of supplementary content that has been created online to support the words you are about to read:

- **www.paidownedearned.com** – expands on some of the themes within the following pages and also contains up-to-date thinking and further content that didn't fit in;
- **www.delicious.com/paidownedearned** – contains all the links referenced through the book, with everything tagged by category and chapter number;
- **www.facebook.com/paidownedearned** – a centre for links, new content and related discussion – please join me!
- **www.youtube.com/paidownedearned** – features an aggregation of all the videos referred to in the coming pages;
- **www.slideshare.net/paidownedearned** – holds a slideshow overview of the following pages and also hosts other related presentations;
- **www.twitter.com/paidownedearned** – will syndicate and aggregate relevant links and will also aim to expand on the themes that follow;
- **Google+** (to be confirmed).

Feedback and discussion through the areas detailed above are welcomed, but above all I hope you find the coming chapters useful, informative and interesting – and thank you to those who put up with me while I put this together (you know who you are!).

Nick

Foreword

In an era of continuously improving technology that is changing the way people behave and communicate, it is time to upgrade and reboot our approach to marketing.

Today, we live in a world of connections enabled by the internet, where people connect to transact, discover, share and express themselves. This network of connections between people, enhanced by social networks and mobility, is profoundly changing how people learn, experience and communicate with and about everything, including a marketer's products and services.

Four key shifts occur in this connected age:

1 *Blurring definitions:* It is harder to compartmentalize marketing into old buckets of analogue and digital, press, television and radio, or above-the-line and below-the-line as digitization and mobility bleed the borders between them.

2 *Facilitation versus just marketing:* Increasingly we are marketing to ourselves as we go online and ask our friends, or do research at marketers' and third-party websites, or plough through forums and compare prices and features. Marketers have to learn to facilitate this self-marketing.

3 *Listening to influential voices matters as much as listening to heavy users:* Focusing on heavy users will always matter, since these segments usually offer the greatest profit. But as people connect with each other and share and express their opinion it is imperative to understand heavy advocates and detractors (who often are different from heavy users).

4 *Real-time response and iteration:* A connected age does not fit into marketing flow charts and schedules. People are sharing, expressing and reacting all the time in a global world. They share and launch conversations about products and campaigns on their own schedule. Marketers must now have

an infrastructure and mindset to incorporate these new behaviours.

Today we need a new framework to think and undertake marketing communications, one that is relevant to changing times and new behaviours. We believe paid, owned and earned is the new framework, and this book is a manual on how to refurbish and retool your mind and your company to this new reality.

Read it. It will make you smarter and possibly could make you rich.

Rishad Tobaccowala, Chief Strategy and Innovation Officer, VivaKi

Introduction

Karen had a problem. She was living in the Danish capital, Copenhagen, with her baby son August, but all was not well. August had never seen his father and Karen had no idea where to find him – and didn't even know his name.

Karen had been out in Copenhagen. She had met a male tourist, ended up having a one-night stand and shortly afterwards found out she was pregnant. Karen went on to have a beautiful baby boy, but was left with an emptiness, a feeling of helplessness, that her son would never know his father.

'Hi, my name is Karen'

In September 2009, with August 18 months old, Karen could stand it no more and decided to take to the internet in a quest to track down August's father. Not knowing his name or where he was from meant that she had nothing to go on. There was nothing Karen could search for, not a single piece of information she could use to start her quest.

The only option was to send out a message and hope that it spread far enough for someone to recognize her and want to get in touch. Under the moniker of Karen26 she created two things. First she created a web page that also doubled up as a blog, documenting her quest and her progress. The second thing Karen created was a YouTube channel on to which she loaded a simple explanatory film featuring herself and August:

> Hi, my name is Karen, and I'm from Denmark, and this here is my baby boy. His name is August. I'm doing this video because I'm trying to find August's father, so if you are out there and you see this, then this is for you. We met one and a half years ago, when you were on vacation here in Denmark, and we met at the Custom House Bar. I was on my way home, and I think you had lost your friends, and then

we decided to go down to the water to have a drink, and that's really embarrassing but that's more or less what I remember. I don't remember where you're from or I don't even remember your name. I do remember though that we were talking about Denmark and the thing we have here with *hygge* that foreign people always ask about. You were really nice, and I guess I decided to show you what *hygge* is all about... I know that this is really a long shot, but if you are out there and you see this, or anybody else who can help me sees this, please contact me. I will put my e-mail with this video, so just write me.[1]

Going viral

The YouTube film became an instant hit. Over the course of just a few days over a million people watched Karen26's YouTube appeal. Karen's story was reported by papers across Scandinavia, featuring prominently in leading titles like *Aftonbladet* and *Politiken*, before news organizations across the world joined in. Bloggers and social media users also highlighted Karen's YouTube video, linking to it, discussing it and embedding it across the web – and the more the news covered it, the more people referenced it, so the more the news featured it.

This was incredible. A simple home-made video uploaded to YouTube had become a destination for people from across the world, attracting wide-reaching coverage across a variety of traditional and new media platforms. It looked like the internet and its mechanisms for sharing were going to bring success. Karen's 'viral video' was about to do the impossible: find August's father!

But there was a problem...

After its Friday release and five days of mass coverage, after five days of internet users forwarding, embedding and discussing Karen's *Danish Mother Seeking* video, it was discovered that Karen was a fake.

Karen was an actor, and the whole story had been created and paid for by VisitDenmark through their media and creative agencies. After a few days both VisitDenmark and their agencies were celebrating the success of the Karen26 film. 'It is the most successful viral advertising ever. We have gotten through the media noise. And it has cost the same as a 30-second advertising spot that will appear a few times on TV2', stated Peter Helstrup from the advertising firm Grey, makers of the video.[2] However, the feeling of jubilation was soon diluted as the backlash kicked in.

The Karen26 video had been distributed using viral seeding. VisitDenmark had paid a seeding company on a per-view basis to get the Karen26 film to critical mass. The video had therefore been pushed out through a number of channels (targeting news organizations and bloggers alike), and the seeding push had been fantastically effective in generating coverage and views.

Once a video or piece of content is established using this route, it can then spread on its own, and Karen spread far and wide. This sort of virality is hard to activate (as we'll see later), but effectively the more coverage that content receives, the more people talk about it, resulting in more people going to view the content and more people talking about it. The whole process becomes self-fulfilling, and this is what saw the view count for Karen's appeal grow so quickly

#unKaren and the spirit of HC Andersen

But Karen was not real. She was played by a professional Danish actor, Ditte Arnth, although this was not acknowledged in the video, and at no point did the film state it was created by VisitDenmark. There was no reference in the script or the video description, no logo or trailing of the video with a VisitDenmark message or tag. From news organizations to bloggers and general YouTube users, people believed the video was genuine. The video views leapt as people jumped at the chance to help, so naturally when it was revealed that the video was a promotional mechanism a large number of those who had tried to help now turned against it.

The initial reaction of VisitDenmark (and their agencies) was to defend the campaign. The VisitDenmark tourist organization called this video 'story telling on YouTube in HC Andersen's spirit',[3] and in Danish newspaper *Politiken* Dorte Kiilerich, CEO of VisitDenmark, was quoted as saying 'Karen's story shows that Denmark is a broad-minded country where you can do what you want. The film is a good example of independent, dignified, Danish women who dare to make their own choices.'[4]

This just stoked the fires more. As Twitter users discussed and linked to the film, '#Karen26' became one of the most used phrases on Twitter – it became a so-called 'trending topic'. Now other trending phrases like '#unKaren' were seen, and in Denmark especially the general reaction was extremely negative, but this only served to drive more views of the Karen video.

Politiken reported that across a single weekend the Karen26 film had been viewed in 153 different countries,[5] and in submitting Karen26 to the Cannes Lions awards in the 'Best Use of Social Media' category Grey revealed that in the five days that it was officially live Karen26 attracted 2,578,961 views across 466 websites in 216 countries,[6] was Googled 83,000 times and made YouTube's top 10 most viewed list.[7] Karen26 was even featured on US TV news.

Denmark's a liberal country, but they're not *crazy*...

In the 'Did You See That?' section of the Fox News show *The O'Reilly Factor*, presenter Bill O'Reilly was joined by Fox News anchor Jane Skinner to discuss the *Danish Mother Seeking* film. Their two-minute conversation summed up many of the issues surrounding the Karen26 video and, after showing an edited version of the film, they concluded their segment with this:

> *O'Reilly:* Look, Denmark's a liberal country, but they're not *crazy*, but they did pull this?
>
> *Skinner:* They did after about four days or so.
>
> *O'Reilly:* Four days! Let me get this right before we move on. Denmark wants people to go visit, so they put up a single mom who doesn't know the name of the father?
>
> *Skinner:* She's an actress. We should point that out, and that's not her real name.

O'Reilly: Right, it doesn't really happen. This is a script. You wouldn't know that, though. This is pretty convincing – but they think that having a woman giving birth out of wedlock, not knowing the father, is going to make people come to Denmark?

Skinner: ... after a drunk one-night stand.

O'Reilly: Excellent, oh yeah!

Skinner: And they pull it, but if you think about it in this day and age...

O'Reilly: Sure, it's on YouTube or whatever tube you're watching.

Skinner: It was linked to 83,000 websites![8]

The Karen26 discussion then finishes and they move on to another hot topic of the day.

You can't put it back in...

The final comments of this exchange sum up the problem. VisitDenmark's Kiilerich (finally) changed tack and said 'I am very sorry that the film has offended many people. That wasn't our intention at all. The goal has been to create positive recall of Denmark and create conversations about Denmark. To prevent offending people any further we have removed the film from YouTube.' However, as O'Reilly and Skinner correctly identify, just because the official version of the film has been taken down it doesn't mean it's gone.

The original *Danish Mother Seeking* video was removed, but the blog posts and comments won't go (at the last count there were over 10,000 related posts), and a Google search for the phrase 'Danish Mother Seeking' now produces a staggering 511,000 results on an 'exact match' search.

Furthermore the *Danish Mother Seeking* video was extensively parodied, remixed and remade by YouTube users. PrinceWorld uploaded a video called *Swedish Father Seeking Danish Mother*,[9] HotGarbageComedy created a video with plastic-baby-holding, cigarette-smoking, vest-wearing Brad seeking a Danish mother under the title *Brooklyn Father Seeking (Parody of Danish Mother Seeking)*,[10] and Mindjumpers uploaded a video called *Danish Mother Seeking (The Father's Story)*,[11] commenting that 'We hope to start a debate about how social media can be used wisely in the future.' There are many, many more with people re-enacting the *Danish Mother Seeking* film, a music track called *Danish Mother Seeking – I'm Not a Bimbo Remix*[12] and even a Darth Vader mashup entitled *I Am Your Father, August*![13]

'My name is Ditte'

The VisitDenmark Karen26 activity was rumoured to be a series of three films, with the hook and reveal planned to come later, but the explosion of negative coverage meant the campaign never got that far. This is given credence by the fact that a supplementary video called *Danish Mother Seeking, Part 2*, featuring Arnth holding a fish and talking about it in the same way she discussed August in the original film, has mysteriously appeared on YouTube (though for some reason the description links to a Danish adult social networking site).[14]

Arnth was also a guest on a prime-time Danish chat show shortly after the *Danish Mother Seeking* video activity broke, and she revealed that she was paid only 50,000 kroner (about £5,000) for her role, but the publicity she has received has made her a household name in Denmark.[15] As with Isaiah Mustafa from the Old Spice advertisements, this exposure can only have helped her career – a YouTube viral video pushing her into the Danish mainstream.

The marketing challenge for tourism agencies in countries like Denmark is in raising awareness, and the insight behind the campaign seems sound, as whenever a destination is featured in world news (sport, politics, entertainment, etc) awareness, and subsequent consideration of it as a tourist destination, tends to increase. One example of this can be seen with Kazakhstan, as after the film *Borat: Cultural Learnings of America for Make Benefit Glorious Nation of Kazakhstan* performed strongly at the box office, Hotels.com 'experienced a 300% hike in searches for hotels based in Kazakhstan thanks to the publicity... despite the fact that the film's fictional depiction of the country is far from flattering and none of the film's scenes were actually shot in the country'(!).[16]

The paid, owned, earned jigsaw

To deliver the impacts and global attention that Karen received would have needed a significant budget if traditional paid media had been used, but instead the Karen26 film perfectly harnessed the mechanics of the social web. It was the reaction to the content itself that caused the issues. Social amplification of the film increased the awareness of Copenhagen as a potential place to visit amongst the desired target audience (young singles and couples without children who would normally look to places like Amsterdam for a city break), but also provoked a large backlash from everywhere else, and herein lies the dilemma. Adding the disclaimers and logos that would have shown that this was an advertiser-funded film would have significantly weakened its viral coefficient. The film spread exactly because these disclaimers weren't present. 'We have to help', 'Is this for real?' and 'Have you seen this?' are all great drivers of virality, but in this case these factors also heightened the size of the backlash.

The paid, owned, earned jigsaw is therefore complex. Rather than being a media channel in its own right, social media has changed everything for everyone. Karen26 is a great example of how, when activated, the so-called 'people's network' of interconnected consumers can contribute to content getting significant reach and coverage, which can then lead to the content becoming newsworthy in its own right. However, Karen26 also shows the need to find a tone of voice that everyone buys into, as well as the need to plan for every eventuality. (The other noteworthy point is that, whilst Karen26 entered global consciousness as a result of earned media conversation, an initial paid media push created the original critical mass of attention.)

The socially connected marketing landscape is based around behaviours and people. Marketers need to understand the new ways in which the public are communicating, connecting, consuming and sharing. However, the socially connected world presents a complex picture that is growing and evolving all the time. There are so many options and so many varying definitions that, whilst the potential upside is large, there is significant risk for confusion and disappointing results too.

Frank Rose sums up the new world in the May 2011 edition of *WiredUK*:

> The 30-second television spot, reviled as it was, served a purpose psychologically. It compartmentalized the advertisement function, tucked it away in its own separate box, allowed us the illusion that our entertainment was somehow unsullied by it – even as it swallowed up eight minutes out of 30. Now that audiences can go anywhere they want and tend to be repelled by any whiff of a come on, that no longer works. The blur of entertainment and advertising doesn't mean no rules, it means new rules: no shouting, please, and if you want me to pay attention to your pitch, you'd better offer me something to make it worth my while.[17]

eMarketer stated in late 2010 that 'some of today's greatest success stories in branding blend ingredients from the three kinds of marketing media: paid, owned and earned',[18] but paid, owned and earned can be used for direct response and performance advertising too. In fact, everything is now linked together, and this book sets out to explore a range of different ideas for getting everything to work together – maximizing returns in a socially connected world.

Welcome to paid, owned, earned!

Chapter One
How the world of paid, owned, earned works

Defining the elements

Marketing and advertising are now being defined by the mantra of paid, owned, earned. This trilogy is made up of:

- *Paid media* – paid placements that promote a product, website, piece of content or anything else that an advertiser wants to pay to draw attention to.

- *Owned media* – any asset owned by the brand. (In the digital space this could be a website or microsite, a social network presence, a branded community, an app or simply a piece of branded content. However, owned media assets are in the real world too – Coca-Cola talk about their trucks and vending machines as owned media, retail stores are owned media, airlines can use boarding passes as owned media, and so on.)

- *Earned media* – brand-related consumer actions and conversations. (These have traditionally only really happened offline, but, as we'll see, more and more earned media is being generated online, and this can be tracked and optimized.)

On the surface this all looks (relatively) straightforward, but the trick is to get all the aspects of the paid, owned, earned jigsaw to work together for maximum effect. This chapter will lay out general principles, and the following chapters will explore specific constituents of the paid, owned, earned landscape more deeply.

The Shannon–Weaver model of communication and paid media – the traditional model of advertising

The long-standing Shannon–Weaver model from 1949 framed the advertising process and worked to the idea that a 'sender' sends a 'message', which travels through a 'medium', and after making its way through various 'noise' (interference and filters) the message is then picked up by a 'receiver'.[1] Communication is broadcast from one entity to another. (See Figure 1.1.[2])

FIGURE 1.1 The Shannon–Weaver model

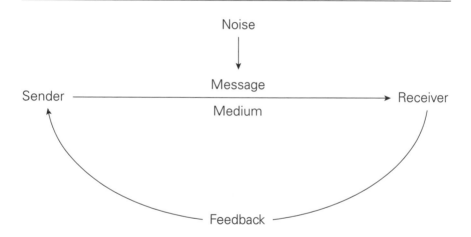

This model applied to both one-to-one communication and communication from one to many. From an advertising perspective the roles were essentially fixed. The sender was the broadcaster or publisher, who then allowed advertisers to pay to place messages around the content that was being sent. The receiver was the consumer audience, and receivers could receive information only at the time it was sent.

The different ways that advertising messages are received and processed

In 1885, Thomas Smith's book *Successful Advertising* laid out a mantra for how paid media advertising worked, recounting how a consumer reacts upon each exposure to an advertisement up to 20 exposures.[3] Smith believed that the first time people look at an advertisement they don't see it, the second time they don't notice it, on the third exposure they become aware that it is there, and so on.

Over the years, thinking became more sophisticated, and Herbert E Krugman refined Smith's ideas further, declaring that in psychological terms the first three exposures were the only ones worth worrying about. He categorized these against the concepts of curiosity, recognition and decision (the ingrained optimal frequency of three). The first advertisement impact raises the question 'What is it?' The second impact raises the question 'What of it?' The third exposure then becomes the key impact, with all subsequent exposures just reinforcing what has gone before. Thus advertising was about sending messages to receivers, with strategy around type and frequency of message resulting in consumers being persuaded.

Moreover, in 1965 in *The Impact of Television Advertising: Learning without involvement*, Krugman further noted that advertising works in two different ways, affecting either active memory (high involvement) or implicit memory (low involvement). He argued: 'With low involvement one might look for gradual shifts in perceptual structure, aided by repetition, activated by behavioural-choice situations, and *followed* at some time by attitude change. With high involvement one would look for the classic, more dramatic, and more familiar conflict of ideas at the level of conscious opinion and attitude that precedes changes in overt behaviour.'[4]

There are therefore two key ways in which the brain can receive a marketing message: 1) advertisements that prompt active processing can lead to immediate changes in perception and spur action; 2) low-involvement advertisements can deliver gradual changes over time. Repeated exposure using standard advertisement formats has continued to be the staple foundation of paid media advertising, but developments in recent years have significantly changed approaches (and this idea of active processing versus low-involvement processing is important at various points in this book).

Targeting active memory and cutting through the noise

In a world of fragmenting channels and ever increasing numbers of advertising messages, getting noticed has become more challenging (and expensive). Furthermore, the differences between products (such as the quality of a supermarket's own label and the brand leader) have shrunk, and in many cases the main difference is now the perception of the brand or product and the related marketing. Advertising has become more important, whilst becoming harder to execute!

As Jean-Marie Dru wrote in *Disruption: Overturning conventions and shaking up the marketplace* in 1996, 'product discontinuities' (where a new product changes or revolutionizes a market or category) are rare. There is therefore:

> all the more reason to look to advertising to create one. To do whatever it takes to bring about a new phase in a brand's life. To make people 're-read' the brand and to help them see it with fresh eyes... discontinuity in advertising occurs when both the strategy and the executions are ruptures with what has gone before, when the planner rejects using a familiar approach and the creative does so as well.[5]

Dru sums up disruption as simply 'breaking with the status quo, refusing given wisdom, and finding unexpected solutions'. His philosophy of disruption was based around the idea of needing to cut through and stand out (in order to target the active memory) and led to the continual 'pushing of the envelope' on formats, with advertisers pursuing extraordinary executions that you simply couldn't miss. Frequency of three campaigns using standard formats did not go away, but were often enhanced with an eye-catching stunt or execution, particularly when a new product launch or brand relaunch was involved.

The feedback loop and the new delivery mantra – relevance

An early revision of the original Shannon–Weaver model saw the addition of a feedback loop, the theory being that the actions of the receiver would provide useful 'data' back to the sender. The sender would send a message and then be able to use the feedback loop to understand more about campaign reception. Feedback came from answers to questions about consumer actions, such as: Did the receiver make a purchase? Vote for the required candidate? Respond to the mail-out? and so on. Measurement surveys and focus groups harnessed the feedback loop to judge the effectiveness of advertising and marketing in fulfilling objectives.

In recent years a further approach to paid media has emerged and makes full use of this feedback loop. Digital advertisements are now tailored to consumer actions in real time, thus improving relevance and potential effectiveness. Advertisers don't have to just buy numbers now; they can buy highly specific audiences. Performance advertising options facilitate everything from micro-campaigns through to large-scale campaigns that are made up of lots of little campaigns, the idea that 1+1+1+1+1+1 etc can be more effective than a generic mass-reach campaign where the same message is sent to everyone.

The feedback loop allows online display advertisements to be delivered using behavioural (based on actions) or contextual (based on relevant editorial) targeting. Search advertisements go even further, as they are served in response to what individuals are searching for at any moment in time, and Facebook advertisements are shown in line with users' interests (with the most recent iteration allowing these advertisements to be served in real time). Relevance is now critical, and the feedback loop provides the information that facilitates this. In the past the feedback loop was analysed post-campaign to judge effectiveness. In today's online marketing the feedback loop is interrogated as advertisements are delivered, allowing for continual tweaking and optimization.

All three paid media approaches (frequency of three campaigns, disruptive executions and performance-based digital activity) are now used and in many cases run side by side and complement each other. In today's world paid media is not the only way of getting marketing messages in front of the consumer, though. There are now a variety of ways of using owned and earned media to send messages too.

Always-on owned media – changing the way that the message is received

The arrival of the internet meant that content could be always on, and the need to consume the message live or on the day of issue effectively disappeared. Additionally, the internet acts as an archive, preserving information, and as a result the volume of digital content has exploded. On-demand mechanics give 24/7 access to content and content experiences, and both publishers and advertisers are utilizing the web in order to be available for consumers whenever they want to interact.

For many advertisers the brand website started out as something of a (limited) online brochure in response to the fact that consumers were using the internet to search out specific information prior to purchase, but, as connection speeds and browser capabilities improved, owned media websites started to evolve into something more compelling. Registration forms were added, dealer and store locators included, customer relationship management programmes implemented, e-commerce functionality made widespread and experiential elements introduced (view the car from any angle, in any colour and so on). Indeed, the importance of a website was highlighted in research published in April 2008 under the title 'The brand effects of adwords'.[6] It showed that, whilst Google advertisement impressions contributed to an 11 per cent increase in unaided awareness, a 59 per cent increase in unaided awareness was seen if the user visited the promoted website.

The concept of owned media has evolved further still, with advertisers now thinking about their assets differently, and self-contained content experiences are being built out on brand properties and/or third-party social platforms. Brands are using these hubs to foster engagement and relationships, with all of this serving to reinforce the idea of advertisers being content marketers, often more akin to a publisher than a seller of products. For advertisers, the importance of having dedicated online assets (website, social network page, etc) has grown immeasurably.

Valerie Lopez at Cision wrote on the *Cision blog*: 'Creating a social hub can serve many purposes and can ultimately lead to the highly sought after Earned Media. Your social hub should serve as a one-stop shop for basically anyone with access to the web. It's here that you can promote and raise awareness of your brand, product and services and at the same time connect with end-users.'[7]

As a result, content doesn't even need to be 'sent' in order for consumers to receive it. Internet users can now directly access brand properties by typing URLs into a browser, find what they need by using a search engine or follow a link suggested through a social network connection. Subscription mechanics enhance this further by allowing marketers to deliver content directly to the user rather than having to spend time, money and effort continually bringing the consumer to the content!

Content and information can now be accessed any time, anywhere, from a multitude of different devices, and the opportunities to develop deeper, more interactive experiences and participation platforms have been embraced by the marketing community. Owned media has helped to shift marketing emphasis from 'push' strategies (where messages are sent to the consumer) towards 'pull' strategies (where the consumer seeks out the content or the brand in question).

In the Google book *Winning the Zero Moment of Truth*, author Jim Lecinski quotes Bob Thacker, who simply says: 'Engagement with the customer today isn't just pouring a message on their head and hoping they get wet. It really is understanding that you must be present in a conversation when *they* want to have it, not when you want to.'[8]

In a number of cases the audience for branded content and advertiser sites now even rivals the audience of traditional publishers. Audi have their own TV channel, and the Pepsi Refresh project was highlighted in the October 2010 issue of *Admap*, with Shiv Singh, Director of Digital at PepsiCo, saying that 'Pepsi's refresh.com website now generates more traffic than [many of] the sites Pepsi buys advertising on.'[9]

The way that the public access information has fundamentally altered, and as a result the purchase pattern against many categories has changed in a number of ways. Not only has e-commerce boomed (notably in areas that have cut out intermediaries – think airlines selling directly to consumers or eBay directly connecting buyers and sellers over large distances), but the reduction of barriers to information access has seen a significant rise in the number of educated consumers, the so-called 'prosumers'.

In early research in this area Vauxhall dealership group Network Q found that, in the car-buying process between 2000 and 2005, average UK dealer visits prior to purchase fell from 7 visits in 2000 to just 1.5 in 2005.[10] In *Winning the Zero Moment of Truth*, Jim Lecinski revealed that Google research had shown that 'the average shopper used 10.4 sources of information to make a decision in 2011, up from 5.3 sources in 2010'. He also highlighted that '70% of Americans now say they look at product reviews before making a purchase', '79% of consumers now say they use a smartphone to help with shopping' and '83% of moms say they do online research after seeing commercials for products that interest them'.[11]

Furthermore, for more and more advertisers, social networks and social media content hubs are in many cases now more important than the traditional website and/or campaign microsite. These owned spaces give brands a presence, but also enable a dialogue to be maintained with consumers 24/7, and are based on mechanics that facilitate interaction and viral spread.

Brand social hubs are facilitating social commerce too, with so-called F-commerce seeing more and more brands selling through their owned media spaces on Facebook, whilst Vivaki Chief Strategy and Innovation Officer Rishad Tobaccowala sees owned media marketing shifting from engagement to utility and advises brands to 'stop elongating the game [and worrying about time spent with the brand and] focus on how quickly and how well we fulfil particular needs'.[12] Rather than a brand just creating a digital experience to extend and fulfil paid media advertising, there are now opportunities to create something of use to a consumer, something that extends the relationship with the brand by being useful instead of simply engaging, and this can dovetail with paid and earned strategy too.

The changing nature of consumers – consumers as senders, consumers as producers – and redrawing the Shannon–Weaver model

Consumer amplification of the message

The evolution of owned media has not been the only change since the Shannon–Weaver model was originally created. Now when a professional sender puts a 'message' into the world it can be amplified and re-broadcast by the receiver and then re-broadcast again by subsequent receivers, and so on, with everyone adding their own thoughts, comments or reinterpretations at each stage. A consumer can receive a message, but through digital channels has the potential to share this with friends and connections, who can then re-broadcast the message again.

In a piece in the January 2011 *Admap*, Tim Broadbent highlights how this resending can help advertisers, stating that:

> Effectiveness Awards campaigns that win both creative and effectiveness awards share two characteristics. First, they are more likely to appeal to the emotions – logic persuades, but emotion motivates. Second, they are more likely to create brand buzz. It is known that famous campaigns create PR for the brand, but in the new communications era of consumer-generated content and social media, this benefit is being magnified. The campaign gets loved in Facebook groups, discussed on blogs, forums and chatrooms, and imitated on YouTube. The result is that the brand is seen as the most authoritative in the category; it defines the category in perception. For the same weight (defined as share of voice relative to share of market), campaigns with this type of 'creative' content were 11 times more likely to be effective. They generated almost six percentage points of market share growth per unit weight on average, while the other campaigns generated only half a percentage point of market share growth per unit weight.[13]

Peer-to-peer sharing can therefore benefit brands, and the fact that receivers can also be senders means that from an advertising

FIGURE 1.2 The Shannon–Weaver model revisited

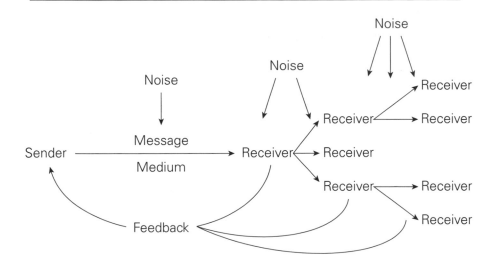

perspective the original Shannon–Weaver model needs to be readdressed. Indeed, the US Congress Office of Technology Assessment thought about this when stating that 'The somewhat passive notions of "message," "sender" and "receiver," draw attention to the problems of effective communication'; the original Shannon–Weaver model has 'problems involved in, or issues about, who gets to formulate, send, and access information; on what basis, and with what objectives and effects'.[14]

The Shannon–Weaver model therefore needs to be revisited and redrawn to show the potential for amplification and resending. (See Figure 1.2.)

How consumer activities are creating earned media

This is not the only complication for the original Shannon–Weaver model, though. Technological advances (digital cameras, internet-enabled mobile devices and so on) have seen everyone become armed with the tools of production, whilst social media channels have given everyone (free and easy) mechanisms for distribution. The role of sender is therefore no longer purely the preserve of publishers or advertisers, and the roles of sender and receiver have even become interchangeable. Jay Rosen, Professor of Journalism at New York University, describes the shift in an article in the *Economist*, stating that the tools of production have shifted to the 'people formerly known as the audience'. The article then highlights a further shift, 'the rise of "horizontal media" that makes it quick and easy for anyone to share links (via Facebook or Twitter, for example) with large numbers of people, without the involvement of a traditional media organisation'.[15]

The ability for the traditional audience (receivers) to pass on or publish through social platforms can result in conversation that drives advertiser content initiatives. Social technology means that information is not just for the local water cooler; the internet enables groups to congregate around common themes, and then work or discuss with each other across great distances, with their labours accessible to the world via search engines.

Consumers can therefore now be both senders and receivers, and so can brands, and so can publishers. Blogs and social sites like YouTube allow consumers to create and distribute their own content, and a huge volume of user-generated content (UGC) is uploaded to the web each day. YouTube has over 7,000 hours of full-length movies and shows on its platform now, but this is a drop in the ocean when set against the fact that 48 hours of content is uploaded to YouTube every minute (and through search or social sharing all of this has the potential to find an audience).

Much of the UGC uploaded to the web consists of people documenting their personal opinions about brands and product experiences. The potential for anyone to be a sender has seen an explosion in the volume of product questions, photos, reviews, experience videos and customer feedback posted online, with brand reputations affected either positively or negatively as a result. Earned media word-of-mouth advocacy has scaled and can now spread over much further distances, resulting in significant enlargement of the feedback loop.

Furthermore, internet users are now thinking about content in ways that have previously been reserved for products and brands in real life. In *Media Studies: The essential resource*, Rayner, Wall and Kruger highlight the first chapter of John Fiske's book *Understanding Popular Culture*, where 'Fiske considers the ideological underpinning of jeans' and suggests that 'when we buy particular brands or styles of jeans we are not just buying jeans, but products that, to some degree, reflect our own sets of ideas and values. The jeans we buy have become in some way a sign signifying how we see ourselves.'[16] Moreover, in *Understanding Popular Culture* Fiske himself states that 'clothes are more normally used to convey social meanings than to express personal emotion or mood'.[17]

Today this thinking is also reflected in how and why people engage with brands online. Sharing content, participating in advertiser spaces, 'liking' brands and connecting to the right people are all methods of self-expression. As Jonah Peretti of BuzzFeed told Web Expo 2.0, 'on Facebook you share things that define you and make you look good'.[18] In the same way that people wear designer label clothing and the emblem becomes a source of pride or a personal statement about who they are, internet users are now attaching virtual badges to themselves by virtue of their online behaviours. Being publicly seen to be a fan of a brand, sharing the latest video clip, installing the latest application to your profile, having a creative avatar and so on are the digital equivalent of offline expression through the culture, labels and brands that people choose. Gaining earned media amplification is therefore not simply about content being passed on; it's about content generating emotional involvement too. People choose to participate or share things because they feel a need to – great brands and great content create this need. The act of engagement and pass-on is therefore a considered and deliberate action, not just something that happens incidentally.

Indeed, Philippe Boutie, writing in *Communication World* in April 1996, argued that, 'in the New Media environment, every brand fan can become an evangelizer [a sender], spreading the brand gospel and influencing other consumers'.[19] Boutie further believed that, 'for marketing-intensive durable goods where peer advice is all-important (cars, hi-fis, computers), a portion of the heavy advertising budget could be redistributed to reward brand ambassadors' – a remarkable prediction given what has happened since!

Marketers can also take advantage of the expanded feedback loop and the richer vein of consumer insight that online earned media provides. In his 2006 book *The Lovemarks Effect*, Kevin Roberts discusses the Saatchi & Saatchi Pathways model for creating Lovemarks, essentially a modern and more involved interpretation of the Shannon–Weaver model. He highlights the increasing usefulness of the feedback loop, writing that it is not just giving 'rational inputs' to the advertiser, but giving 'emotional expressions' too.[20]

Essentially, consumers are not just giving feedback in terms of sales, through their online actions and conversations, but are also giving 'guidance on what needs to be done to enhance the brand relationship'. Advertisers have always been able to listen to consumers using methods like focus groups and surveys, but the scaling of earned media now gives the chance to listen to a much wider group, over a much wider area, in real time. This information can be used to spot trends and gain insights that can fuel product design, customer service, and strategic and creative approach, and it offers the potential to power programmes that drive buzz, sharing and advocacy.

Explaining how paid, owned and earned link together

As the evolved Shannon Weaver model shows, the media landscape has become significantly more complicated in recent years, and the execution of marketing and advertising campaigns has become more challenging. An October 2010 article in the *Huffington Post* saw Kirk Cheyfitz write:

> There is angst in ad land over the complexity of media. Ad planners wring their hands, bemoaning the proliferation of media channels and the unpredictable ways in which consumers jump from TV to Facebook to text messages to Google to foursquare to iPods... and so on. What's a brand to do? Out of the chaos in the media world and the complexity of infinite digital channels, a new way of looking at media is emerging that is simple, useful and strategic. The latest buzz in advertising puts all media in just three categories: paid, owned and earned.[21]

Cheyfitz argues that these labels are useful because, 'No matter what new media channels the geniuses invent tomorrow, this logical set of strategic categories doesn't change.' Paid, owned and earned channels do not exist in isolation, though. They work side by side; they overlap and all affect each other. Sean Corcoran of Forrester in December 2009 put forward some initial thoughts on this. He suggested:

- *Paid* – 'The role: Shift from foundation to a catalyst that feeds owned and creates earned.'
- *Owned* – 'The role: Build for longer-term relationships with existing potential customers and earn media.'
- *Earned* – 'The role: Listen and respond – earned media is often the result of well-executed and well-coordinated owned and paid media.'[22]

In early posts on the subject of paid, owned, earned, Daniel Goodall, a marketing planner at Nokia, detailed the Nokia approach in a couple of blog posts on his *All That Is Good* blog, explaining that Nokia have been using a 'media trinity' of bought (paid), owned and earned and that all Nokia digital activity is attributed accordingly.[23] An important element of his thinking aimed to explain the benefits of each of the three, and he mapped them on to an axis showing 'control' and 'reach'.[24] Owned has the most control but smallest reach, followed by paid, and then earned, which has the least control but the highest potential reach. This is one of the trade-offs in paid, owned, earned thinking; benefiting from the amplification potential of earned media is invariably the result of giving up elements of control. The greater the control of the message, the lower the risk, but the less potential there is for spread. Less control equals more potential for earned media amplification, but more potential for trouble too. (There are no easy answers here, but it is worth thinking about this at the beginning of the process!)

Planning and executing across paid, owned, earned

Traditionally there was little overlap between the three areas of paid, owned, earned, but in digital media, particularly on social platforms, things get more confused. It's not just that things work alongside each other, but that each area drives another too. In a socially connected world every action creates a reaction. My version of the media trinity (Figure 1.3) seeks to express the dynamic interactions of each area to show how paid, owned and earned media work together and

FIGURE 1.3 The media trinity

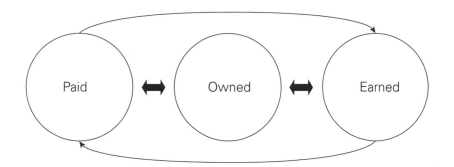

the potential flow of communication between them. The arrows are the key element of this representation, though, as they highlight that everything is linked together and nothing stands alone. (See Figure 1.3.)

- Paid media drives traffic to the owned media destination, the classic 'go here now' advertising, but paid media can now drive owned media engagement *and* create earned conversation. Speaking at the Cannes Festival in 2011, Jeffrey Graham from Initiative 'told delegates that getting the correct mix of paid, owned and earned could transform a low involvement brand into a high one'.[25]

- An interesting owned space or piece of owned content can drive earned conversation, which in turn can drive more traffic to the owned destination, which in turn can drive further conversation and so on. (As we will see at different points in this book, effective owned media content can also help paid media advertisements to work harder.)

- Earned media conversations can highlight owned media spaces and turn them into vibrant communities. Conversations and sharing can also aid the effectiveness of paid messages (for example, the TV advertisement that gets shared on YouTube or the earned media conversations that produce natural search results, which help paid search to work harder and so on) and, as noted earlier, the earned media conversation also provides a feedback loop from which insight can be harvested to inform paid (and owned) strategy.

An intriguing aspect is that some of the newer platforms are seen in all three areas. 'Doing something on Facebook' can sit anywhere within paid, owned or earned, as, like other social networks, Facebook offers a range of different routes for brand involvement. Depending on what it is, Facebook activity is able to deliver against a range of different objectives (from awareness to relationship building and advocacy). A Facebook strategy can therefore take many forms.

Paid advertising on Facebook can work as it does elsewhere on the net (driving off-site to an advertiser destination), but can also be used to promote brand activity inside Facebook. Owned media can be a Facebook brand page or profile, a customized tab on the Facebook page, a Facebook place or Facebook deal, an application that sits inside Facebook, a Facebook event or even Facebook functionality integrated into a brand's main website. Earned media can be Facebook users talking about a brand between themselves, setting up their own group or page about the brand, 'liking' an advertisement or brand page, leaving comments on a brand's page, agreeing to attend an event or inviting friends to participate in a competition or promotion. All of these elements are trackable and provide data and feedback on user actions, allowing campaign elements to be optimized accordingly.

The Facebook landscape is therefore complex, with paid, owned and earned initiatives all possible, and interlinking, on the same platform and sometimes even coexisting in the same advertisement unit! For example, Sponsored Stories are paid placements that can be used to showcase user interactions on the site and on 4 May 2011 Volkswagen ran a paid media Facebook advertisement, with the placement containing an owned media video and earned media ('Like' button) functionality – paid, owned, earned all working together.[26] This clearly gets more complicated once other media channels are factored in and everything starts to feed everything else.

Indeed, at Cannes Graham stressed that there was a need to 'create a virtuous cycle of involvement', with research showing that 'the relationship between paid, earned and owned is not linear. The three types work together in a dynamic way and are most powerful when the consumer is truly involved, driving the relationship.'[27]

So we start to see that everything is linked and nothing exists in isolation any more, especially on social platforms. Rather than replacing the pre-existing media channels, earned media is booming *alongside* them, backing up G Franz's idea that 'the proliferation of new media adds complexity to the media landscape, since these new media channels rarely replace old media. Rather they tend to complement.'[28]

Working with paid, owned, earned – always-on versus campaign

In order to effectively plan and execute across paid, owned, earned, there is first a need to understand the differences between the always-on presence and campaign-based activity.

As discussed earlier, the nature of the web means that consumers expect advertisers to have some sort of permanently accessible, 24/7 presence online, and more and more expect this to be interactive and responsive. Owned media is important in fulfilling against this always-on expectation. The brand website offers information, contact forms and, in an increasing number of cases, e-commerce, whilst social presences on platforms like Facebook and Twitter facilitate frictionless dialogue.

On the other hand, campaign-based activity will tend to harness elements from across the paid, owned, earned trinity and is used to deliver specific messages against specific objectives, normally across a limited time period. Furthermore, whether by design or default, this sort of activity will also have a knock-on effect for always-on spaces, driving traffic, fan numbers and engagement levels (an effect that can be amplified if the activity is effectively optimized).

The variety of executional options now available can therefore be allocated against paid, owned, earned and split out between 'always-on' and 'campaign' (with always-on tending to be a longer-term commitment that crosses multiple departments, whereas campaigns will tend to be more specific and time sensitive). (See Table 1.1.)

The following chapters will cover the above and will group them into nine general areas, with a chapter dedicated to each. These roughly

TABLE 1.1 Executional options

	Always-On	Campaign
Paid	Paid search	Broadcast/display
		Performance advertisements (including paid search)
		Paid seeding
Owned	Website	Microsite
	Social hub (Facebook page, YouTube channel, Twitter account, brand community)	Tactical content (campaign hubs, page tabs, videos, tweets, apps, events, etc)
	(Utility) apps	(Campaign-based) apps
	Social media optimization	Social media optimization
	Customer service	
Earned	Social listening	Blogger outreach
	Community management	
	Customer relationship management	

fall in line with the chronological process for managing campaigns across paid, owned and earned:

- *Chapter 2* – listening (mining the feedback loop for insight and determining objectives and strategy);
- *Chapter 3* – creation and management of social content hubs (creating always-on hubs and starting to participate in conversation);
- *Chapter 4* – creation of (campaign) content;
- *Chapter 5* – social media optimization (optimizing content hubs and content campaigns to enhance visibility and potential for sharing);
- *Chapter 6* – seeding and distribution (for driving advocacy and generating content spread);

- *Chapter 7* – broadcast (using mass-media advertising to generate owned and earned media traction);
- *Chapter 8* – performance advertisements (using performance-oriented paid media advertising to drive fan bases and attention for initiatives);
- *Chapter 9* – responding (conversation strategy and customer service);
- *Chapter 10* – measurement (across paid, owned and earned).

Different strategic objectives require different solutions, and it is rare for all the areas above to be used in the same campaign (though listening and measurement should be used in some form on every campaign and every piece of activity, regardless of the channel or product).

Budgeting and measurement

The final conundrum is around budgeting and measurement. In the past the bulk of the budget would go on paid media, but now that everything is interlinked perhaps one of the hardest challenges is how to allocate budget across the three areas of paid, owned and earned.

Nokia employee Arto Joensuu has written about this on his *Working in Digital* blog, thinking about 'working versus non-working costs' and noting that traditionally, 'on average, companies would invest maybe 10–15% of their budget on the marketing concept creation, another 15–20% on the actual production of the ad and finally, the remaining 65–75% on buying media'. He argues that today 'the media split starts looking more like a 30% concept, 30% production, 40% media buying'.[29] (The rationale here is sound, but this only really thinks about owned media or content and paid media promotion – we need to think about the costs associated with earned media too.)

In principle, though, an increasing emphasis on owned media content and earned media amplification should lead to a lower reliance on paid media, but this is not always true in practice, and the allocation of budget is not easy. Paid media is a known known; impressions and eyeballs are guaranteed (though admittedly this is a guaranteed *opportunity* to see rather than a guarantee that someone will actually see it). The cost of owned media development and hosting is known in advance (though effectiveness is predicted rather than guaranteed). However, earned media is almost a complete unknown; it is inherently unpredictable, as it relies on the actions of the public.

We can try to work this thinking into equations that need to be solved to evaluate the most effective way of executing activity and delivering ROI. For example (purely using figures that are easy to add up and illustrate the point!):

Traditional equation:

Paid 95 + owned 5 = 95 impressions + 0 conversations = 95

New equation with a greater emphasis on content:

Paid 85 + owned 10 = 85 impressions + 15 conversations = 100

New equation with an even greater emphasis on content, plus seeding activity designed to drive conversation:

Paid 75 + owned 15 + earned 5
= 75 impressions + 30 conversations = 105

The equations represent the idea that earned media investment coupled with additional commitments to content can lead to greater returns when combined with traditional paid media. It may then be possible to realize these greater returns on a reduced marketing budget overall.

If all three areas are measured side by side, it is possible to build up learnings over time, and these benchmarks can then make it easier to start to form (and solve) the equations that model different scenarios around paid, owned, earned. There is no magic, one-size-fits-all formula, though. The scale of the conversation will vary by brand, by product and by content and will be affected by everything else that is going on in the world. (Share of conversation is harder to model than share of market!)

The other thing that should not be forgotten or overlooked is that in the traditional equation the output is guaranteed, as paid media delivers guaranteed impressions. With the new equations the output can be more variable – the upside can be significantly higher, but there is a potential downside too. What if the equation ends up looking like this?

Complete new equation (scenario 2):

$$\text{Paid } 75 + \text{owned } 15 + \text{earned } 5 = 75 \text{ impressions } + 0 \text{ conversations} = 75$$

Or worse:

Complete new equation (scenario 3):

$$\text{Paid } 75 + \text{owned } 15 + \text{earned } 5 = 75 \text{ impressions } + -25 \text{ conversations} = 50$$

In these equations the activity results in under-delivery, as the public were not interested in talking about or sharing the content or, in the worst-case scenario, consumers were moved to talk negatively about the advertiser. (It's not just about volume of buzz; it's about volume of positive sentiment – it is unlikely that an increase in conversation will be celebrated if it is all critical!)

When things go wrong the fault is most likely to lie with the insight and idea conception rather than the delivery. Real-time listening can help to amend or refocus campaigns that aren't working as planned, but those who argue that, in time, earned media can completely replace paid media ignore the fact that production lines don't stop and businesses cannot afford to be left with excesses of stock if a campaign doesn't deliver.

Advertising and marketing are invariably used as a stimulant for sales, and the predictability inherent in paid media plans aids business forecasting. Paid media offers guaranteed delivery of impressions (and sales), whereas even with the best owned and earned media planning and execution there is luck involved in instigating cascades, viral effects and sharing. Invigorating earned media is a great way of delivering additional value, but the results can never be guaranteed, and advertisers need to be wary of putting all their eggs in the earned basket.

Ideally, the three areas need to work side by side, but apportioning budget between paid, owned and earned is difficult. The key to getting things right (or as right as possible) is therefore undertaking rigorous research and discovery in the planning stage, setting concrete objectives, clearly defining ownership and roles, being adaptable as initiatives progress, and then measuring and learning over time. In a world where no one knows the (full) answers, a culture of testing and learning will help to build up the knowledge base that will help predict, drive and refine efforts across paid, owned and earned. The equations above get easier to write and answer against this sort of backdrop!

Aligning different stakeholders to deliver across paid, owned, earned

Marketing across paid, owned, earned also travels across a number of disciplines and stakeholders, resulting in the need for significantly more organizational alignment than in the old world. Different departments, from website controllers, to PR people, to legal departments, to customer service departments and product development, need to work closely with media, public relations and creative disciplines to ensure maximum returns. Success in one area potentially amplifies the return in another, whilst negativity in one area could lead to a lowering of effectiveness in another.

Departments that have traditionally been separate and working to different objectives now have to work together for the greater good, for example the customer service and support departments now have an important role to play in generating (positive) earned media. Sharing results within an organization (between departments and across borders) is useful too. In an ever changing marketing world, knowledge and experience provide an edge; shared learnings can therefore help successful activity and techniques to be scaled and underperforming options to be parked.

As Andrew Walmsley wrote in *Marketing* magazine: 'Only brands that can fit the jigsaw puzzle together, creating a consistent presence across bought [paid], owned and earned media, can exploit the synergies that lie between them... until marketers can control these channels in a unified way, customer journeys will be disrupted, inconsistent and often abandoned, costing revenue now and against future relationships.'[30]

Paid, owned, earned is therefore not limited to the advertising or marketing departments; it has implications for how things are done (and the associated organizational structures) across the company. This may be a long-term consideration for many organizations, but those that have been able to adapt have been seeing positive results – we'll look at social media governance and training in Chapter 9.

Most of all, though, working across paid, owned, earned is about consistency and commitment. Campaigns that look to harness paid, owned and earned cannot be done piecemeal or half-heartedly. The most successful activity has been built around strong, unifying ideas that can work across all channels. Owned media promoted with paid media provides an essential base, and earned media (hopefully) delivers additional, bonus attention.

KEY POINTS

- The media landscape is now defined in terms of paid, owned and earned.
- Advertising messages are received through either active or low-involvement processing.
- Advertising can be delivered in three different ways – through repetitive low-involvement (frequency of three), through impactful disruption or through contextual or behavioural relevance at the point of delivery.
- Media is always on, and brands should be too – social hubs are important for this, though we need to recognize the difference between 'always-on' and 'campaign' activity.

- Brands should aim to engage and provide utility rather than just shout.
- Consumers can re-broadcast and amplify messages, but they can also create.
- Content can be social currency.
- Brands need to act like publishers as well as advertisers.
- Everything links together – paid can affect earned and so on.
- It is necessary to think about strategy across all three areas, as each has relative strengths and weaknesses.
- A testing and learning approach will help budget setting and strategy over time.
- Paid, owned, earned is larger than the marketing and advertising department, and different stakeholders need to be aligned accordingly.

Chapter Two
Listening

Soft and yielding like a Nerf ball – an introduction to listening to your customers

Episode 15 of Series 2 of *The Simpsons*, 'O brother, where art thou?', sees Homer Simpson meet his half-brother Herbert.[1] Herbert doesn't live in Springfield, though; he lives in Detroit and is the successful head of a car manufacturer. This episode sees Homer and the Simpson family go to stay with Herbert, and Herbert offers Homer the choice of any of the cars in his garage, but none of the cars presented are to Homer's liking. Herbert is obviously dismayed and on realizing that Homer is a typical American consumer decides to offer him a well-paid consultancy job with the brief to design the sort of car that he (and by definition other average Americans) would really like. Homer is given a team of engineers and gets to work...

Through Homer Simpson's input, Herbert has brought the American public directly into the design process and, whilst we all know how this is going to end, we watch nevertheless. Homer orders various additions like a cup holder, but not a cup holder for 'a little cup, but one of those super-slurpers at Kwik-E-Mart'. Homer proclaims that 'Some things are so snazzy they never go out of style! Like tail fins... and bubble domes... and shag carpeting.' Homer continues, 'I want a horn here, here and here. You can never find a horn when you're mad. And they should all play *La Cucaracha*.' 'A separate soundproof bubble dome for the kids with optional restraints and muzzles' is also incorporated into the design!

The final car retails for $82,000 and is described as 'powerful like a gorilla, yet soft and yielding like a Nerf ball'. Herbert sees the product for the first time at the grand unveiling when it is revealed to him and an accompanying audience of mega-celebrities and journalists. Herbert quickly realizes he has made a terrible mistake. The car is a 'monstrosity', and it forces Herbert out of a job and the company to be taken over.

In 1991 Homer participating in product development made for good comedy and entertainment. However, as is often the way with life imitating art, the passing of time has seen the content in this episode of The Simpsons turn from outlandish comedy to a reflection of the world we now live in. The feedback loop enables businesses to tune into the consumer zeitgeist as never before, and the information gleaned can be used in a variety of areas, from product development through to content creation, advertising campaigns and customer service. Listening data can also be used to augment marketing measurement.

Customer feedback aids understanding and helps businesses evolve to meet the needs of their consumers. Actionable insight can be gained either through directly requesting customer feedback by way of surveys, suggestion boxes, etc or through the studying of patterns in data or conversation online. Indeed, the opportunities presented by earned media online are pushing more and more companies to orientate around customer satisfaction as a key goal, with many also developing initiatives that aim to tap the feedback loop to incorporate customer ideas into products.

Improving product and customer satisfaction through listening

This sort of approach is being adopted across a wide range of categories and has even been the driving force behind an extensive marketing campaign by public transportation providers in Denmark.

In Copenhagen, bus companies Arriva and Movia jointly launched a campaign in June 2008 called 'Jeg vil ha en bedre bustur' ('I want a better bus ride').[2] Starting on lines 150S and 173E, the campaign focused around improving the service and making the bus a more desirable travel option. Passengers have been asked for feedback and suggestions, and many of these have been actioned. The companies are listening to their customers in order to improve their product and increase passenger numbers.

For example:

- In response to a text message that asked for more entertainment on the journey, screens were added to the 3A and 4A lines, with sound accessible through FM radio or mobile phone.
- Via the website someone asked for more information about the places that the bus passed every day, and in response route guides for each bus line have been published in the weekly magazine.
- The 'Better bus ride' campaign has also included drivers. Each week a top 10 drivers list is published, detailing those who have driven in the most environmentally friendly fashion (saving fuel, helping the planet and delivoring a smoother or more pleasant journey). Winning drivers are rewarded and highlighted on the website, again all in response to a passenger suggestion.

Furthermore, across a week at the beginning of May 2010, Movia and Arriva created 'Love Week', a week where a 'love seat' was introduced to each of the 103 buses on five routes, and passengers and drivers were all invited to do nice things. Twenty-one driver birthdays were celebrated, and on 5 May one of the drivers, Mukhtar, was persuaded by a friend not to take a day off for his 41st birthday.

Mukhtar's first journey on 5 May got under way, and a man in black tie got on to the bus and started playing the trumpet; then a woman in the middle of the bus started singing the Danish version of *Happy Birthday*, and other passengers joined in, bringing a smile to Mukhtar's face. The bus then had to slow down and stop as it ran into a demonstration, but this was not an angry mob. The crowd turned round en masse and started singing *Happy Birthday*, waving flags and signs bearing Mukhtar's name. Mukhtar got off the bus, was embraced, given flowers and a present, and was genuinely moved to tears. Someone else then took over the bus driving and everyone ended up happy.

The events of that morning were captured on film, and a video entitled *Mukhtars Fodelsdag* (Mukhtar's birthday) was uploaded to YouTube,[3] where it has now been viewed over 2.7 million times.[4] The customer-centric approach has offered a platform for content development that has generated earned media as it has spread online, but most importantly the implementation of passenger suggestions and the atmosphere that has been instilled on the journeys have seen passenger numbers increase by 21 per cent! The entire ethos of the company has evolved, and encouraging customers to make suggestions, considering them and implementing the best ones has not only improved customer satisfaction, but has also increased company reputation and staff morale.

We don't now need to ask consumers explicitly for feedback, though. The internet is providing a treasure trove of conversation data that can be mined to provide insight that can be factored into product strategy, marketing strategy and customer service.

Using data from Google and Facebook for actionable insight

Traditionally a mix of focus groups, survey data (from firms like Nielsen and TGI), competitive analysis, retail analysis, category research and proprietary information has been used to uncover brand truths and the category state of play from both business and consumer standpoints, but the feedback loop provided by the internet is now offering new sources of information. For example, Google Insights for Search can provide insight derived from what people are searching for over specified time periods, and advertisers can supplement all of this with their own tracking data.

Search engine use gives a good insight into the public psyche. John Battelle in *The Search* describes a search engine as offering 'a place holder for the intentions of humankind – a massive database of desires, needs, wants, and likes'.[5] Tuning into this data can therefore potentially identify patterns and trends that can be interpreted and used in strategy accordingly. Bill Tancer from Hitwise writes in *Click*: 'Watching consumers' actual online behaviour is the surest way to keep abreast of every changing consumer use, and to understand what is important and when.'[6] Whilst he has had mixed success in using search data to predict *American Idol* results, the Google Eurovision Insights widget has twice successfully predicted the winner of the *Eurovision Song Contest* in recent years.[7] This backs up the idea of a 'database of intentions' and, using Google's free Insights for Search tool, aggregated search data can be harnessed by advertisers to spot trends and help garner consumer insight.

It is now also possible to dig into what people are actually saying online, rather than just what they are searching for, and this can improve our consumer understanding still further. An early Facebook listening tool called Facebook Lexicon helped with understanding what people were talking about on Facebook at any moment in time. Lexicon aggregated the occurrences of words on people's Facebook walls and plotted them on a graph to show the correlation in use on a timeline.[8] Some interesting social insight could be gained. For example, it was possible to see that a spike in mentions of the phrase 'party tonight' was followed the next day by a spike against the word 'hangover'. Worryingly, there also seemed to be a direct correlation between occurrences of the words 'tequila' and 'pregnant' (day one 'tequila', day two 'pregnant'), and there was a big drop in the occurrence of the phrase 'Happy birthday' on 29 February! These are all nuggets of insight that could help inform a strategy, and Lexicon helped take the pulse of Facebook users by showing what they were discussing at any point in time.

Lexicon was also useful to advertisers from a measurement perspective, as it was possible to see spikes in Facebook mentions around Facebook promotional activity. Lexicon showed both Dr Pepper and Skittles getting huge uplifts in wall mentions after running Facebook gifting activity inside Facebook, giving visibility into how these paid promotions were also able to generate earned media conversation (a principle that we'll revisit in Chapter 10).

The Lexicon data were interesting, but things have moved on since and the tool has been retired. However, Facebook has a new system called Chatter Count that now takes into account all mentions on wall posts, status updates *and* searches (though this is currently an internal Facebook tool, rather than something that is available for public use). There are other ways to listen to the actions of the users of Facebook, though, and sat nav manufacturer TomTom found an opportunity after uncovering a Facebook group called 'Campaign to get Brian Blessed to do a voiceover for my sat nav'.[9]

The group creators wanted to have the booming voice of the legendary British actor and leader of the Hawkmen in *Flash Gordon* giving directions to them, with Blessed himself even embracing the idea and helping to make a (low-budget) mock-up film in May 2010 to show what a good idea a Brian Blessed sat nav would be![10]

TomTom were listening, and they told the group's founders that if they hit 25,000 members[11] then the Brian Blessed sat nav would become a reality[12] – and when the group reached the 25,000-member target TomTom made it happen.[13] Listening and then embracing the Facebook group led to free exposure for the product (the Blessed version featured in a number of news articles), a range of product feedback from the comments in the group and 25,000 people publicly supporting the brand through Facebook.

This is all about listening to customers and potential customers, understanding what they want, harnessing insight to make the product or service better and ideally then delivering accordingly. But listening is not just about product evolution, though this is clearly an interesting use for it. Listening can provide consumer insight and understanding that can be used to fuel advertising strategy too, and this insight can be harnessed from across the social web, not just from Google or Facebook.

Using listening tools

Stephen Baker writes in *They've Got Your Number*: 'For market researchers, blog posts... open a window onto a consumer's life. Blogs and social networks offer up-to-the-minute intelligence – something marketers have long dreamed of.'[14] There is now no need to rely solely on focus groups. 'It's as if a universe of focus groups is forming online. Tens of millions of people participate. Many write copiously. And from a marketer's point of view many are gloriously indiscreet about practically everything.' Social media sceptic Andrew Keen simply writes in the *Cult of the Amateur*: 'Web 2.0's infatuation with User Generated Content is a data miner's dream.'[15]

Furthermore, whilst many internet users work hard to manage their online personas (as witnessed by the different types of profile pictures – 'I'm single and attractive' versus 'Here I am with my partner' versus 'Here I am with my children'), they still have a tendency to produce an accurate picture of themselves even when they are trying to be someone else. A paper published in the *Personality and Social Psychology Bulletin* in September 2009 analysed the idea of idealized identity and studied the assumptions about personality made by a pool of observers to photos of 123 people that they did not know.[16] The results proved remarkably accurate when compared to reports from close acquaintances. One of the authors, Simine Vazire, stated that 'The research suggests that strangers can know as much about your personality as acquaintances just by looking you up on the Internet.'

This was further backed up by a study on Facebook published in *Psychological Science* that 'found that online social networking sites are not effective for promoting "idealized" identity. Instead, such sites often portray personality quite accurately.'[17] People are trying to manage their online identities, but no matter how hard they try they are revealing detailed information about their actual lives and their true preferences, fuelling the feedback loop for advertisers.

This brings a whole new dimension to consumer research. Focus groups have traditionally been used to gain consumer insight, but they are expensive and time consuming to organize. They also tend to be out of context (often in neutral venues with groups of strangers thrown together for discussion), are difficult to scale and, however skilled the facilitator, are only a representative sample of a target audience. There is also no way of knowing how much answers are influenced by surroundings, other people present or the desire of participants to say the right thing.

Steven D Levitt and Stephen J Dubner write in *Superfreakonomics*, 'There is good reason to be sceptical of data from personal surveys.

There is often a vast gulf between how people say they behave and how they actually behave. (In economist-speak, these two behaviours are known as *declared preferences* and *revealed preferences*.)'[18]

Social listening doesn't necessarily replace the depth of information provided by focus groups or market research. It is skewed towards those who are active online, but it does have access to a much wider pool of participants and the insight is derived from what actual product users are posting to review sites and forums or from what friends and connections are naturally sharing with each other rather than from discussion prompted by a moderator. As Charlene Li and Josh Bernoff write in *Groundswell*: 'Designed cleverly enough, market research surveys will answer any question you can think up. But they can't tell you what you never thought to ask. And what you never thought to ask might be the most important question for your business.'[19]

Moreover, social media information is immediate, it's unfiltered and it's in real time. Listening tools can harvest and present data derived from online conversations, but the real trick is in being able to filter and analyse the information to turn it into something meaningful. The variety of insight that can now be derived from consumer posts and consumer opinions that are published on the web led Kevin Roberts in *The Lovemarks Effect* to explore the creatives' conundrum. He surmised that 'One of the most important things creative people have to do is listen. You'd think that what creative people do best is talk... The truth is, the important step that precedes everything else is good listening.'[20]

The easiest way of starting out is to use some of the free tools. Setting up a Google Alert on a brand name sends an e-mail every time the brand is mentioned. Using Twitter Search will show when Twitter users have mentioned a company or product. Tools like BoardReader, Google Blog Search, BlogPulse, Social Mention and Technorati can also help track what people are saying.

As may be expected, though, the free tools are by no means perfect. The data provided are rarely comprehensive and rarely aggregated, and the information provided tends to be moment-in-time rather than historical data that allow evolution over time to be mapped. Additionally, the information from the free tools cannot be filtered by things like geography, and sentiment scoring or accurate sentiment is rarely included. It is also very difficult if your brand name is a common term rather than a unique name (think of the potential for misleading information around brand names like 'Surf', 'Tide' or 'Bold'), and in many cases it is necessary to listen using Boolean logic query strings with AND, OR, NOT, etc. (This helps to only uncover mentions around a certain product or event, but may rule out useful data at the same time.)

Ultimately, if you only have a small amount of data to collect and if you are only looking for mentions rather than audience insight and brand sentiment then using the free tools to collect data by hand may be acceptable, but if you are basing important business decisions on the findings then a paid tool becomes essential. As Stephen Baker notes in *They've Got Your Number*, the scale of the blogosphere is so large that 'the only way to harvest and file the customer insights streaming from blogs is to turn over the work to computers'.[21] Unsurprisingly there are also now a great number of tools and options for tuning into your customers' online comments. The difficulty is knowing where to start!

Different tools, different capabilities, different costs

There are large price differentials across the available listening tools, yet the most expensive, enterprise-level listening solutions are growing in popularity. Cost is dictated by volume of information, the level of data cleansing that is applied, the complexity of analysis and the level of human involvement. To illustrate the difference we can look at 2011 Super Bowl social media analysis, where a number of different suppliers reported tweet volume around the 2011 game. This raised the profile of the companies in question, but the fact that the volumes picked up by each tool were different may not have helped the sector overall. There was a consensus that Doritos had generated the most tweets, so the takeout was correct. It was just that the volume of tweets identified was different, and in some cases the difference was significant.

The default amount of information harvested by different tools varies. Some tools just pull in a sample of blogs and forums. Others will pull in all the blogs and forums that they can find (including from many forums that require registration or log-in). Some use samples of tweets. Others pay to use the Twitter Firehose, which gives access to all tweets, and so on. In many cases a sample of the data out there will be enough. On other projects it may be essential to get everything (for example, general perception around brand health versus mining for comments about potential side effects of a new drug – sample data versus a need for every mention). Some tools deal only with blogs and forums. Others also present data from mainstream news sources, YouTube, Flickr, social bookmarking sites, Twitter and Facebook. The standard datasets consist of posts or posts and comments. Others will go further and even semantically analyse photographs and videos.

Approach to data is also interesting, especially with sentiment analysis. Should a post like 'great stereo, terrible engine' be classified as positive, negative or neutral? Some tools will break out sentiment at incident level, so instead of just classifying a whole post as positive, negative or neutral, the post will be split out. Splitting out incident-level sentiment means that 'great stereo, terrible engine' counts towards one positive mention and one negative mention rather than contributing towards a 'neutral' or 'mixed' score. This different interpretation is important (particularly to product departments), as people rarely talk about a single point, and in some cases mentions can be weighted (criticism of the engine will be rated more significantly than criticism of the stereo). Blog posts particularly will tend to be an amalgamation of thoughts, and analysis at a post level can see large amounts of information scored as neutral and neglected as a result – even though it might be significant. The other issue is that listening tools tend to treat all posts as being equal even though audience size and influence vary.

Different businesses and different categories will have different requirements of a tool, and as a result some solutions will be more suitable than others, with suitability varying according to objectives and needs. The complexity of approach essentially determines cost, particularly around identification of themes or sentiment analysis, and many companies are realizing the value of using listening data across an organization. (As a result they are also realizing that the cost of listening needs to be funded by the whole organization rather than just the marketing and advertising departments.) Listening is only really useful, though, if it can deliver actionable insight, something which comes only from digging deeply to understand not just what is happening, but why it is happening, and the hardest element of listening is the interpretation of language and context.

Dealing with spam, sarcasm and slang

Spam

The internet is riddled with spam posts, spam tweets, spam blogs and spam comments, with spammers aiming to attract accidental traffic or boost search engine visibility for their sites.

The effectiveness of Twitter Search in driving click-through means that spammers regularly append their tweets with phrases from the Trending Topics list. Including a word (or hashtag or conversation label) from the Trending Topics list in the body of a tweet means that the tweet will show up in the list of tweets that is produced in response to a Twitter user clicking on the related topic or searching for the topic in question. This means that users will see the spam messages as they scroll through the latest news or comments around a popular topic, but may not realize they are spam tweets before they click.

High-end UK furniture chain Habitat tried to harness these Twitter mechanics in 2009 and became caught in a blaze of negative publicity. Habitat's strategy was to use phrases like '#apple' and '#iranelection' in their tweets (for example, '#Mousavi Join the database for free to win a £1,000 gift card'[22]). People in Iran were trying to get the message out about post-election anti-democracy crackdowns, people around the world were retweeting and trying to help, and even more were using Twitter Search to watch events unfold. Habitat (and others) appeared to see this as an opportunity to raise attention for their own ends. Habitat subsequently apologized profusely and explained that it had 'never sought to abuse Twitter' and that the actions were not 'authorised by Habitat' (again earned media effort resulting in the brand going backwards).

Habitat never acted in this way again, but the practice of including a Trending Topic in random tweets happens all day long. Twitter work hard to try to filter out spam, but the actions of the spammers are reflective of the perceived value of being linked to the Trending Topics list (either directly or by association), and listening tools have to filter this noise – spam tweets have to be removed from results to prevent false data being reported.

Search engine rankings are also susceptible to the work of spammers and 'black hat' search engine optimization (SEO) practitioners. Search engine results pages (SERPs) are based on what their algorithms identify as the most relevant sites in response to a query, and a major factor in the judgement of relevance is how many inbound links a site has. Links are generated naturally through bloggers and websites linking to stories they appreciate, but links can also be generated through link farms, spammers creating spam blogs or, more usually, spammers leaving comments on blogs across the web. These comments are normally brief and only vaguely related to the posts in question. The purpose of the spam comment is simply to create a link back to the spammers' own site or the site that they are promoting. These are two word-for-word examples of the wisdom that has been left in the comments on my blog recently:

> Hi Nick!! Great information thanks for sharing this with us. In fact in all posts of this blog their is something to learn. you are Professional Essay Writing. your work is very good and i appreciate your work and hopping for some more informative posts.

> Hey, Its really useful post, i will definitely use and forward to my friends. Online Shopping in Pakistan Send Gift to Pakistan Search Hotels Casual Wear.

The spelling, grammar and punctuation are exactly as they were written, and the underlined words in these comments are links to other sites. Can you spot them? If these spam comments are not filtered out, a listening tool may suggest that my blog features professional essay writing, Pakistan and hopping.

Another annoyance for listening practitioners is the presence of blogs and sites that do nothing other than republish content from other sites (in order to create content that can be monetized through affiliate links and advertising). Twitter robot accounts can also be created to tweet links and content automatically – again producing large volumes of verbatim content that can skew the results from listening tools. Spam content offers little or no insight that is useful to advertisers and, whilst it can be quickly picked out by human eyes, the presence of spam necessitates greater human involvement in listening projects and results in projects taking longer and costing more to complete.

Sarcasm

A rigorous and structured approach to data analysis is needed, and this becomes even more important around sentiment. Accuracy varies between solutions, with much of this down to the level of human involvement. Mechanical sentiment analysis is cheaper than machine-plus-human sentiment analysis, but you get what you pay for.

Even after the spam has been filtered out and the irrelevant mentions removed, the work of humans in listening analysis doesn't stop, as sarcasm and slang also necessitate the involvement of real people. A useful rule of thumb is that 60–70 per cent of sentiment analysis is fairly straightforward; the rest is the hard bit. There is no problem when things are 'great' or 'awful', but when Michael Jackson decided 'bad' meant 'good' then machine analysis would (in all likelihood) have ruled his lyrics to be expressing negative sentiment, whereas he was in fact portraying himself positively. This is where the involvement of human eyes helps further.

For a human brain the comprehension of sarcasm is an interesting process. The left-hand side of the brain deals with the understanding of words and sentences, but the right *parahippocampal gyrus* is the area of the brain that deals with sarcasm interpretation. The right-hand side is therefore needed to understand humour and language that is not literal, for example puns, jokes and sarcasm, so comprehension is derived from both sides of the brain working together. The mental process also involves an element of social cognition, the ability to put yourself in someone else's shoes. It's the idea of being able to experience the context as well as the words (and this sort of intelligence is still beyond most computers and algorithms!).[23]

Slang

Computer programs can follow logical rules and interpret the words, but without human help they struggle to comprehend fully. Once youth-speak and slang are factored into the mix it gets even more complicated. The *Daily Telegraph* reported the work of Lisa Whittaker from the University of Stirling, who studied the language used by teenagers aged 16–18 on Bebo and Facebook in Scotland. She found that:

- 'Young people often distort the language they use by making the pages difficult for those unfamiliar with the distortions and colloquialisms.'
- 'The language used on Bebo seems to go beyond abbreviations that are commonly used in text messaging, such as removing all the vowels.'
- 'This is not just bad spelling, which would suggest literacy issues, but a deliberate attempt to creatively misspell words.'
- 'The creation and use of their own social language may be a deliberate attempt to keep adults from understanding what is written on the page.'
- 'By doing this they are able to communicate with their in-group and conceal the content from the out-group. This further adds to their online identity.'[24]

Not only are machine-based analysis systems having to deal with the difference in interpretation of words like 'sick' (great if it's in association with a new piece of technology, bad if it's used in association with a hospital patient), but they are now faced with an ever changing youth-speak, deliberately designed to confuse observers and those who aren't part of the club!

To get a feel for how difficult this is, consider this example of a poster from Haringey Council (local government) in north London. They are encouraging young people to get tested for the sexually transmitted disease chlamydia, and as part of the campaign they have created a poster based on a Facebook-type profile for an invented site called Baitbook.

The posters are displayed in places like youth centres and show fictional character John 'Bad Boy' Brown updating his status with:

'I Think I Have Chlamydia – But Who Cares? Dis Man Will Still Get Gal... Don't Watch Dat!'

In response his friends reply with a selection of comments including:

'Narrrrsty, any gal dat sleeps wiv u now is nasty or will have somefink worseeee! Get tested blud!'

'WAT DA???? Cuz, u cant be seriously finking dis is kool?'

(And so on.)

At the end of the comments John 'Bad Boy' Brown reappears to sign off with the comment:

'Oh Ma Dayzzzzzz! Proper hype, safe peepz I'll Do It 2mo now get off my page!'

This poster is part of a campaign that has been created by Haringey Youth Services and seeks to connect with young people in north London by using their own language. (The first phase of the campaign saw a 34 per cent increase in the number of tests requested.[25]) This is a good result, but the campaign also serves to show the problems of handing text analysis and sentiment interpretation to machines. The exchange above has been created by a local government department to emulate teen-speak and, as Lisa Whittaker notes, this sort of slangy English is deliberately designed to be confusing and impenetrable for older generations – but it's impenetrable for machine-based sentiment analysis too!

To highlight how hard this can be, listening provider Converseon noted in a recent white paper that 'There are an estimated 1,000 new words added to the Urban Dictionary daily. Google reports that 20% of searches in a particular month have never been searched before. This is because human language is not static – it's highly fluid.'[26] Indeed, the most used phrase on Facebook status updates in 2010 was 'HMU' (hit me up), a phrase that barely registered in Facebook status updates in 2009 and a phrase that I was unfamiliar with prior to the publication of the Facebook report![27] Accurate sentiment scoring can only really come through machines and people working in combination.

The problems with allocating language and location

The other problem facing listening tools is the attribution of language. French people tend to write on domains that end .fr and they write in French, but if you are running a listening project in Canada how do you keep Canadian French comments whilst effectively filtering out French French comments – especially on a global platform like Twitter? English speakers confuse things even more, as they are just as likely to publish to a .com domain as they are to a local version. The machines that power listening therefore have the difficult challenge of deciding which part of the English-speaking world posts and comments are from. IP addresses, spelling (eg 'colour' versus 'color') or references to local context can help, but effectively the machines require further human intervention to help them categorize – and even then it's extremely hard to identify that it was an Irish user who left a comment on a US website, to correctly attribute the tweet of an Australian living in London or to segment the activity of New Zealanders living in Hong Kong! This is all made especially complicated by the global village, which now sees brands and products being present in multiple markets.

This is not so much an issue for the US market because of scale (the volume of verbatim content from other countries does not necessarily skew US results), but results in smaller English-speaking markets like the UK, Ireland, Australia and Singapore can be significantly distorted by US 'pollution' (or hampered by a lack of scale around volume of identifiable results). One of the only ways to address this comprehensively is to build up a pool of sources from the ground up. Starting from a base of sites or profiles where location is detailed, further sites and users can then be manually tagged and added to the listening database. Rather than crawling everything and trying to attribute location, the tools only crawl sites that have had location previously determined. This reduces the potential scale of the conversation that can be analysed in the short term and is a labour-intensive process, but where in many cases we are looking for a representative sample of data this is a preferable approach to pulling in everything and misattributing as a result.

In fact there's only one thing worse than having no information and that's having the wrong information. As the plethora of online social listening tools continues to increase, it's worth looking at more than just price – approach to data, scale of data and the quality of the data analysis provided are key elements. Buying in a cheap system and then acting on bad data will be more expensive in the long run than investing in a machine-plus-human solution now. With human involvement (from people who understand the business and what to look for), machines can learn over time; with no human sense checking, machine-only sentiment analysis may not ever get to the point where it can be truly reliable and useful.

The complex nature of data cleansing should not act as a discouragement to using listening, though, and listening can be applied in a number of areas. From insight for product design and strategy, to identifying the voices around a brand, to risk management, to acting as a customer service and crisis management solution (we'll look at responding in Chapter 9), to measurement (covered in Chapter 10), social listening taps into the feedback loop, and the results produced can drive real business performance.

How Cadbury used listening to bring back a classic chocolate bar

In the 1980s Wispa was the second-largest brand in the Cadbury portfolio, but, with fading sales, Wispa was delisted in 2003. When Facebook and YouTube really came to prominence in 2007, consumers started spontaneously using these platforms to demand the 'return of Wispa'.[28]

A case study article in *Admap* highlighted that Cadbury used a listening system provided by Market Sentinel to tune into this buzz, as Cadbury needed 'tangible numbers to fully understand the demand' and the 'intensity' of the conversation. Using listening tools Cadbury were able to understand:

- who was talking about Wispa and where they were saying it;
- what was being said about Wispa (was this a fad or was there really a demand?);

- the impact on Cadbury as a brand (were the conversations Wispa specific or did they have a wider impact on the brand as a whole?);
- data on participants (how many people were involved?).[29]

Cadbury found that thousands of people were involved and that the existence of this online Wispa discussion had a benefit for the Cadbury brand in general. This 'proof' helped to sell the concept to internal stakeholders (the potential of this sort of finding covers many departments) and prompted Cadbury to bring back Wispa for a trial period in late 2007. Listening data fuelled the product thinking, but also helped in the formulation of marketing and advertising strategy, with nostalgia identified as a key theme to play on.

Twenty-four million trial bars sold out in only six weeks, and as a result Cadbury brought back Wispa on a permanent basis. Wispa sold 1.2 million bars in a single week and generated a total of £25 million in sales for Cadbury in 2008, meaning that Wispa had gone from an unwanted or 'delisted' product to a product that transformed Cadbury's fortunes, seeing the company record a 30 per cent increase in annual profits, with Wispa as the star performer.

Instead of having a blank sheet of paper, there was a huge pool of consumer information to tap into, and Cadbury used this to drive business results. This type of listening analysis can be used to look at buzz around an owned brand, buzz around a competitor or buzz around a category. Listening can also be used just to provide useful insight into the lifestyles and cultural consumption of a target audience. Instead of having to second-guess wants and trends, listening gives a route into the consumer psyche that can then be used to develop products, offerings and marketing campaigns.

Using listening data to power an owned media space and drive advocacy

A key area for Wispa was the Facebook page, and subsequent advertisements in numerous channels promoted the page, using psychological nudges to further grow the fan base. Straplines such as

'Sean Morgan – join him and the 810,280 others at facebook.com/wispa' or 'Sam Henne – join her and the 810,280 others at facebook.com/wispa' were featured on newspaper advertising, and they utilized the idea of 'social proof'.

Put forward as one of the six principles of influence by Robert Cialdini, social proof is about following others. It can be 'used to stimulate a person's compliance with a request by informing him or her that many other individuals, perhaps some that are role models, are or have observed this behaviour'.[30] Additionally Cialdini noted that social proof is most influential under two conditions – uncertainty (when people don't know what to do they will look to follow others) and similarity (people will follow those who they believe are similar to themselves).

Not only was Wispa using offline media to promote its Facebook page, but it was using one of Cialdini's ideas of influence to encourage even more people to sign up – the implication being that everyone was doing this and you'd be missing out if you didn't too.[31] This is a key idea in earned media advocacy, but, where Wispa was using social proof in paid media advertising copy, UK telephone and online bank First Direct are using social proof on their (owned media) website.[32]

Advocacy has always been important to First Direct, and they have traditionally emphasized happy customers in their TV advertisements. These lacked true authenticity and credibility, though, as paid media spots offer only limited airtime and as a result only positive customer experiences were highlighted. This idea has evolved, and First Direct are now using their owned media (website) to showcase all customer comments about the brand, using social listening to power everything.

On their website First Direct proclaim: 'At First Direct we don't shy away from feedback, we thrive on it – it shapes the way we do things around here.' First Direct still use customer testimonials to highlight their service, but now source them directly from social media, using a social listening tool to aggregate comments and sentiment that are then posted directly to the First Direct website.

The First Direct site declares: 'This website streams live what's being said about us in online blogs and forums. A black and white perspective. Take a look and then tell us what you're thinking. We welcome your opinion, whether you're a customer or not.' The implication is 'Why not join them?'

The First Direct site also features 'Talking Point', which is a discussion forum for customers, an 'Impressions' widget that lets people hook up a webcam and record their thoughts directly on to the site, a tag cloud showing the most used words associated with First Direct, and a 'live feelings' stream of sentiment from the internet (which is then aggregated to show percentages of positive, neutral and negative).

Around the launch of this initiative, *Blogstorm* wrote: 'Parting the dark clouds that have surrounded the British banking sector since the beginning of this recession is not an easy thing for those trying to market them. Cutting through the mistrust that surrounds them requires personal relationships with customers, something that many of the bigger banks had lost interest in.'[33]

The transparency of the First Direct approach gives authenticity and allows the bank to harness its fans and advocates. The approach of allowing all feedback (positive or negative) to appear creates an image of trustworthiness, which acts as a category differentiator in the eyes of both current and prospective customers, reinforced through complementary executions in offline media. Rather than listening being used to fuel product or campaign development, First Direct have put listening at the centre of their owned media activity and have built everything else around it.

Few (if any) other banks would dare pursue this sort of initiative in their marketing, but, *Blogstorm* add, 'in showing its human side First Direct has reconnected with current and prospective customers and reinforced one of its USPs – industry-leading, personalised customer service'.

Other banks have launched customer service campaigns (witness NatWest publicly declaring that they wish to become 'Britain's most helpful bank'), but First Direct highlighting consumer conversation takes things further – using a combination of social listening, earned media customer advocacy and owned media to drive both consideration from prospective customers and loyalty from existing ones.

Using listening in crisis management

The feedback available from social listening can be used as an early warning system too. Via digital connections and search engines, one consumer's problem can now be visible to a wide audience, but using a listening tool to track consumer sentiment and specific product mentions means that brands can spot potential problems early and deal with them while they are small problems rather than full-blown crises. Forums are particularly valuable for this and host huge amounts of product-specific conversation. If people are posting about a specific problem then this might be indicative of a wider issue that can be explored and dealt with before it becomes a major issue playing out across mainstream media headlines. (Chapter 9 references the organizational set-up and policy structure that need to be in place to facilitate this.)

Listening therefore has a number of use cases, but with so many different ways of using it the challenge is often not in agreeing to listen, but in deciding which area of a company should own or fund it, how the information will be disseminated and what it will be used for. Again there is the potential or need for many different departments and agencies to work together, and the ability to construct a unified approach across markets and disciplines is therefore vital to avoid duplication of effort and cross-purposes. Client and agency leads need to be established to maximize the benefits of listening across an organization and to have the authority to push the findings into multiple areas of the business.

Depending on the tools used or the quality of analysis the data can be variable, though, and at times it can be difficult to draw out meaningful conclusions. However, listening powers execution across paid, owned and earned (for example, it fuels seeding, responding and measure-ment). Everything starts with listening, and without some form of listening it becomes difficult, if not impossible, to operate in the earned media space – it's also worth paying for quality!

KEY POINTS

- Listening can be used in a variety of ways – from product design, to advertising strategy, to influencer identification, to customer service, to measurement.
- Listening data are semi-real-time and at scale, a useful complement for focus groups and surveys.
- To use listening effectively actionable insight is needed, not just data.
- Google Insights, Twitter Search and other free tools can all provide useful (but basic) information.
- Different tools (with different levels of cost and complexity) are available to help with listening – with costs varying accordingly, though it's worth paying for rigorous data approach and actionable insights.
- Watch out for spam, sarcasm and youth-speak.
- It is difficult to allocate or split out location for popular languages – have a strategy for this before starting a listening project.
- Listening is vital during times of crisis.

Chapter Three
Content hubs and communities

Building an owned media content hub

In an always-on world, brands have to be accessible to consumers around the clock. The traditional internet face was the website but, whilst this is still important, the social network profiles of brands are regularly sought out by consumers. Traditional web publishing (such as website or microsite creation) saw advertisers creating and then having to work hard to attract an audience, whereas official presences built on a social site can take advantage of ready-made building blocks, existing mechanics and the existing audience – creation is easier and audience can be built more quickly on a social network than on the wider web.

As a result, an owned media social destination is now a key pillar in marketing strategy or social strategy. Traditional advertising tends to be based around bursts or campaigns (on and off), whereas a social profile allows an advertiser to be always on and always available for interested consumers. The social presence is more than just a content repository for current and historical campaigns, though. It is a go-to destination and, most importantly, it's a venue for two-way conversation and one where like-minded individuals can congregate.

Clay Shirky writes in *Here Comes Everybody*, 'Media is increasingly less just a source of information as increasingly more a site of co-ordination because groups that see or hear or watch or listen to something can now gather around and talk to each other as well',[1] whilst Mark Earls writes in *Herd* that the key to this sort of approach 'appears to be feedback loops, participant–participant as well as host–participant... Without this the essential power of interaction and co-creation is either hindered or unfocussed (in which case continued participation is often seen to be costly and is therefore abandoned).'[2]

The feedback loop in the Shannon–Weaver model of communication was added as an afterthought. Now it has to be central to owned and earned strategy and for many a social hub is a critical component. A custom hub, a Facebook page or a YouTube channel can be created, but there is a difference between establishing a presence and having an active community.

Developing a community around an owned media social hub

Infrastructure is created, but community or institution evolves and builds over time with etiquette and norms derived from shared experience and history. In 'The social construction of reality', Peter L Berger and Thomas Luckmann describe in detail how institutions and communities are formed. They describe individuals as having 'habitualised actions' and institutions as the product of 'a reciprocal typification of habitualised actions by types of actors' – essentially the institution is created from the shared actions and learnings of participants. Institutions and communities grow gradually ('reciprocal typifications of actions are built up in the course of a shared history, they cannot be created instantaneously, institutions always have a history of which they are the products') and 'institutions also, by the very fact of their existence, control human conduct by setting up predefined patterns of conduct, which channel it in one direction as against the many other directions that would theoretically be possible'.[3] Communities have rules and boundaries that define behaviour, and these rules evolve over time from the actions of participants.

Internet communities differ from communities of the past, though. James J Sempsey and Dennis A Johnston published research that they had conducted into the social and psychological aspects of multi-player online gaming in their paper entitled 'The psychological dynamics and social climate of text-based virtual reality'. They found that players would 'often indulge in, and be able to keep track of, several separate conversations at a time (often with individuals from outside the present group) without the confusion and noise that would normally result from such activity in the real world'.[4]

This ability to participate in multiple conversations or multiple communities was also one of the threads explored by Cova and Cova in their treatise 'Tribal marketing' in 2001. They noted key differences between the tribes (communities) of the past and the tribes of today, arguing that, where people in the past were members of a single tribe, tied in by language, geography and family, in today's society, particularly virtual society, people are freed from these confines and restraints. The modern consumer is not limited by distance and can now participate in multiple communities that can be based around more esoteric concepts, feelings and '(re)appropriated signs'.

Additionally, Cova and Cova interpreted their theories on tribes into a marketing context and suggested that 'Today consumers are not only looking for products and services that enable them to be freer, but also products, services, employees and physical surroundings which can link them to others, a tribe.'[5] Advertisers that can facilitate this sort of connection or that can add value to an existing environment therefore stand to benefit.

Marketing to communities

Community-based marketing is not easy, though. As Henry Jenkins *et al* write in 'If it doesn't spread, it's dead', 'Knowing that the community pre-exists the brand or franchises engagement with it means corporations need to legitimate their entrance into this space.'[6] You can't just go crashing in and expect participants to welcome you.

Indeed, Martin Czerwinski at SparkLinx, ZenithOptimedia's social division in Germany, says 'Social media ist eine Cocktail-Party', effectively comparing behaviour in social media and community marketing to the way you would behave if you were attending a cocktail party.[7] I presented a similar idea at a conference in 2008 under the heading 'If you are going to gatecrash the party...' and offered nine thoughts around this party-crashing concept:

1 Know why you are going before you get there.
2 Think about the sort of entrance you want to make (quiet or loud).
3 Respect the hosts.
4 Be helpful and useful.
5 Don't stand in the corner expecting people to come to you.
6 Slowly get to know the attendees one by one.
7 Engage in conversation (talking and listening).
8 Stay for the evening, not just the first five minutes.
9 Aim to be invited next time!

Marketing through owned and earned media is therefore more than pushing out a sales message. In a world of connected communities the advertiser needs to think about facilitating and helping too. This could be through participation within a particular community (often offering rewards), or it could be that advertisers create their own community hub, but to pursue this route it has to be an always-on, long-term commitment, and community management and moderation need to be worked out before activity starts.

Community and group collaboration is thriving in the social gaming sector that has been built on social networks, particularly on Facebook (with knock-on effects for the providers of these games – witness the size of Zynga's proposed initial public offering!). Indeed, the scale of these new social games means not a day seems to go by without someone requesting help in their Mafia Wars or updating friends on progress in managing their farm, town, zoo, etc.

One of the most successful games has been Zynga's *Farmville*. Players assume the role of farmer and '*Farmville* is a game where you can farm with your friends.' In 2006/07 the buzz was around virtual worlds like *Second Life* and the ability of participants to create their own spaces, but the flaw with these was that the audience size did not match the hype – the numbers inside *Second Life* at any one time tended to number in the thousands or tens of thousands rather than in the millions, and for the same reason Google's foray into this space, *Lively*, did not last long. These virtual worlds did not scale in any meaningful way, but within 12 months of launch *Farmville* was attracting 83.1 million monthly active users, with 28.7 million tending their farm and their crops on a daily basis![8]

Social games are self-contained communities; the playing all happens within the application or game, but actions are amplified to all social network friends regardless of whether they are registered game players. This amplification brings attention to the game hub, drives additional users and also creates a compelling advertising opportunity, but marketing to these audiences has to happen within the game environment. Bertrand Bodson, co-founder of *Bragster* (a community based on daring other users to do things), wrote in *iMedia Connection*, 'For this [sort of community engagement approach] to work, brands need to be willing to go beyond short term obvious approaches and invest time upfront to establish credibility towards often-skeptical online users.'[9]

In March 2009 Microsoft's search engine Bing engaged the *Farmville* community, aiming to drive the number of people who 'liked' Bing on Facebook. Working inside the game, they offered *Farmville* virtual currency ('three farm cash credits') to those who 'liked' the Bing Facebook page. Instead of advertising to a mass audience across the web, Bing focused on a single environment and offered incentives that were relevant and useful. Promotional messages were sympathetic to the *Farmville* environment ('Whether you want to buy a horse or a tree, Bing can help you decide'), and the offer was highlighted by social gaming blogs, whilst *Farmville* fans syndicated this information through their own social presences. This targeted activity saw Bing add 400,000 Facebook fans in just a few days![10]

There are other interesting examples of advertisers reaching into *Farmville*-type communities. In January 2011 Toyota launched its new line of Prius cars at the Detroit Motor Show and at the same time debuted the new Prius in the *Car Town* social game, showing off the new models to *Car Town*'s 7.2 million users (and demonstrating a real world USP, with the Prius cars having a greater fuel economy than other cars in the *Car Town* game). Additionally, Toyota asked game users to visit the Prius showroom and vote in the 'Prius Goes Plural' campaign, with voters eligible for a virtual T-shirt with their name on it (those who voted for the winning name 'Prii' then received an extra reward once the competition had ended).[11] Furthermore, anyone buying a 2011 Prius could collect 1,000 gold coins every 24 hours from a Prius money tree that appeared post-purchase outside their personal garage.[12]

Three additional Prius models were released into *Car Town*, the 2012 Toyota Prius Plugin, the 2011 Toyota Prius V and the Prius c Concept, and owning more than one Prius would increase the amount of gold coins offered by Prius money trees.[13] Again this is more than just advertising within a community. This is about weaving a brand narrative into a social game and supporting the existing players. Justin Choi, President and CEO of *Car Town* parent company Cie Games, used some enlightened words at the Prius launch, saying that '*Car Town* is more than just a game; it's a media platform.'

Building bespoke, brand-specific communities

Advertisers are now establishing their own community and media platforms too. These have taken a number of forms, from loyalty areas (such as BMW's Drivers Club for BMW owners in China) to self-help customer service forums (like HP's customer support forum) through to innovation communities that allow brand fans to give feedback and make suggestions (such as My Starbucks Idea). Perhaps the most commonly referenced example is P&G's Being Girl, a community that gives advice to teenage girls around a range of topics whilst also providing specific information relating to feminine care.

Both specialist services and media owners now offer advertisers the ability to create communities. There are some topics that people feel a desperate need to connect on and discuss, but these are often not suited to generic, reach-based social networks. This was a core principle of Google+, with the Circles feature allowing users to segment their friends into different groupings and manage or restrict sharing accordingly, and this kind of segmented approach is particularly useful around health topics.

Health is highly personal, and participation and discussion in a topic-specific community is generally the preferred route. There are for example a large number of different cancer communities (from those suffering through to those who have survived), and in China ZenithOptimedia helped birth control pill Marvelon to create a community with leading Chinese web destination and search engine Baidu – the 'Marvelon Healthy Contraception Centre'.[14]

Although China's National Population and Family Planning Commission have said that less than 40 per cent of the population is subject to the 'one-child policy', since 1978, when the policy was introduced, citizens (particularly women) have borne a huge responsibility in the area of family planning.[15] Additionally, birth control in China is a sensitive subject, and there is a reluctance to discuss this topic, so Marvelon faced a difficult task in reassuring Chinese women and promoting product usage in a highly regulated advertising category against a backdrop of Chinese women who are averse to discussing the topic.

Marvelon opted for a custom community solution that saw the development of a considered and educational dialogue through a safe communication platform, a private destination built out around the topic. This consisted of a question-and-answer community anchored on the Baidu Knows section of Baidu.com, where participants were able to discreetly share knowledge and experiences with one another. Community members also had the opportunity to address more intimate questions to an online Marvelon expert for a personalized response.

Paid media support promoted the community, and Marvelon educational messages ran on TV shows and in magazines. Whilst the paid media advertisements did little other than promote the Marvelon and Baidu hub, they succeeded in attracting a large number of people who were keen to get more information and discuss the issues within the online hub.

Total community views reached 637,612 in the first six months, 3,700 questions were asked, and 150,000 visits were driven from the community to the main Marvelon website. Furthermore, Marvelon became market leader, with 62 per cent share and 64 per cent brand awareness, whilst product usage over this period increased. By creating a hub based around Baidu, Marvelon created a safe space for conversation and dialogue, which gave Marvelon the opportunity to interact with consumers and consumers the opportunity to interact with one another. As this example shows, if promoted and developed in the right way, communities can provide an interesting approach for advertisers, offering both a rich feedback loop of insight and the ability to help and engage brand fans. Again, though, this doesn't happen overnight, and needs commitment and support if it is to flourish.

The importance of brand profiles and content hubs

Brands targeting wider reach can create owned spaces on social platforms too. In 2007 YouTube launched an offering called YouTube Channels. This allowed users to create a basic content hub for their videos, but also allowed advertisers and organizations to create professional channels with an appropriate look and feel (in exchange for advertising commitments).

Individual videos still exist as individual videos, but are also aggregated on branded YouTube channels. Showing how widespread the use of channels is, in December 2007 the UK monarchy launched a royal channel (which hosted live streaming of the 2011 wedding of William and Kate), in January 2009 Pope Benedict XVI launched a dedicated YouTube channel, and in November 2009 even the Iraq government created an official YouTube presence! Broadcasters have also been able to launch YouTube channels that offer long-form content to YouTube users (all rolled up into a specific YouTube section called 'Shows'), and there are a huge number of advertiser channels now on the platform.

YouTube has further social functionality around the video window, and the YouTube comment area provides a platform for debate around content. Large volumes of posts and user interactions can be witnessed on many videos, user-generated responses or parodies can be posted to main videos as a 'video response' (with this enabling users to draw attention to their own creations), and all of this benefits the search ranking of the official content. The official video can therefore act as a kind of linking gallery or entry point for all the other related content, which is then easily accessible through the YouTube channel. With YouTube now the world's second-largest search engine, having content that is visible and easy to find is important.

Brands are able to create custom channels and pages, but in many cases they are being pushed into establishing official presences on social networks, as if they don't do this willingly then the potential for 'ridiculously easy group forming' is enabling users to establish brand presences unofficially – with many spectators unaware of the lack of official involvement.

The original community functionality on Facebook was based on Facebook groups. Anyone could set up a Facebook group, and some of the most popular original Facebook groups were set up around random topics, for example 'When I was your age Pluto was a planet', 'If this group reaches 100,000 my girlfriend will have a threesome' and 'I secretly want to punch slow walking people in the back of the head'. Facebook users were also setting up groups around brands, some of which were complimentary, some of which weren't. It is unlikely that Crocs would have been pleased to find that in November 2007 membership of the group called 'I don't care how comfortable Crocs are, you look like a dumbass' stood at 676,483, but on the other hand low-cost fashion retailer Primark were pleased to hear that the Primark Appreciation Society had a membership of around 100,000.[16]

The Primark Appreciation Society originally seems to have been set up as a kind of ironic homage to the newly opened Oxford, UK store in 2006 by an Oxford Brookes University student, but more and more people joined.[17] As word of the Primark Appreciation Society group spread, the original foundation of irony was lost, as new joiners were joining because they genuinely loved Primark (illustrating Berger and Luckmann's point about the meaning of an institution evolving over time and being defined by the actions of the actors within it). There are now 550 photos and over 546 discussion threads on the Primark Appreciation Society Facebook group, with discussions and wall posts ranging from random spam to group members discussing Primark product ranges, uploading photos and talking about Primark experiences. There are suggestions for new lines, comments on existing products and fashion-based discussions around looks and outfits. The Primark Appreciation Society group is therefore full of useful feedback, but whilst this feedback is publicly visible it is effectively being directed to a member of the public rather than the company in question.

The group members are proud to be members (and seen as being members) of the Primark Appreciation Society. They are actively talking about Primark every day, but this presented a dilemma for the brand. Should they set up an official presence, co-opt or embrace the existing group or clamp down on the unofficial nature of it? In 2007 a spokesperson for Primark's parent company, Associated British Foods, clarified their position, saying, 'An independent Facebook group launched by our customers is of far more value than anything we could do.'[18] At this time many brands were unsure about jumping into Facebook, but the launch of Facebook Pages in late 2007 changed the landscape dramatically.

Facebook groups are accessed from inside Facebook (and are still popular with users), whereas Facebook pages tend to be accessible to any internet user, whether they are logged in to Facebook or not. Mass, advertiser-based groups are now less in evidence, as many brands have created an official Facebook page as an always-on hub. The appeal of Facebook pages was further enhanced in June 2009 when Facebook launched Facebook Usernames, as this allowed brands and individuals to have their own custom URL, meaning that the address of a specific Facebook page could be easily promoted through other media and marketing touchpoints.

Like websites, social hubs can host photos, videos, updates and links, but they also allow for brand-to-user, user-to-brand and user-to-user conversation, and this is the key difference. A website tends to be one-way and provides information; it is rare for websites to have community functionality. On sites like Facebook and YouTube it is second nature. People join for many reasons, but a key element is the fact that they can talk to the brand and also converse with other like-minded individuals who have chosen to gather there. The brand social hub provides a platform for community, as users can like, comment, share and even post their own content.

The mechanics of the social graph

This mix of users, advertisers and content means that social networks are based on a complex system of interlocking connections. Facebook call this 'the social graph', and the whole site is based around this premise: the idea that each Facebook account represents the sum of the user's interests and relationships. Facebook users are friends with other users, and comments and actions are shared. Virality is built in; if I make an update or like something, then my friends receive a notification in their Facebook news feed showing my action, and vice versa. I can also choose to share content from other sites with my friends; again, posting to my profile syndicates the content to my friends' news feeds, and many applications (like Spotify) now offer the chance for users to automatically share actions with their friends via Facebook or Twitter.

Any updates from Facebook pages that I have liked also appear in my news feed, and any actions I take on the page (liking, agreeing to attend an event or leaving a comment) are also broadcast to my friends. Updates from brands and friends therefore appear side by side in a user's news feed. My personal Facebook experience is a combination of messages from friends and advertiser connections. (Twitter works in a similar way, as Twitter users can follow both friends and brands, with tweets all mixed together and served up in a continuous stream.)

The always-on nature of social hubs means that they need to be continually refreshed with new 'conversation currency', things that people can talk about and talk back to, though social hub strategies are not just about those who engage. In a 2008 paper entitled 'Online communities and their impact on business', Rubicon highlighted that 'Online discussion is a poor way to communicate *with* the average customer, because average customers don't participate, but it is a great way to communicate *to* them, because average customers watch and listen.'[19]

Indeed, this taps into Forrester's Technographics ladder, which offers a framework for mapping out target audiences against a collection of different segments defined by action. The categories are represented by the labels of creator (content creators), conversationalist, critic (comment leavers), collector (those who use RSS and tags), joiner (social networkers), spectator (readers and watchers) and inactive. The figures overlap (ie people can be in more than one bucket), but in the second quarter of 2010 a study of the US results showed that 23 per cent of the internet audience were creators, 31 per cent were conversationalists and 33 per cent were critics, compared to 68 per cent who were spectators. (These proportions were similar in other parts of the world too – in the EU it was 14 per cent creators versus 54 per cent spectators, in China 41 per cent creators versus 73 per cent spectators, and in Japan 36 per cent creators versus 75 per cent spectators.)[20]

For every one person creating content or leaving a comment, on Forrester figures there will be two or more people who see it. This will clearly vary by audience and by sector, but it makes the point that many more people spectate than create or comment. Furthermore, whilst the content inside Marvelon's community was essentially private, in many other cases forum and community posts will also show up in search results, driving further exposure to content and allowing even more people to spectate (even if they don't join in!).

Configuring and managing Facebook pages

Options and settings

The default option for a Facebook page is for it to be seen by every- one, and it can be seen whether users are logged into Facebook or not. Pages can be restricted, though, so that only people of a certain age can see them (eg over 18 or 21 to view pages from alcohol brands) or can be restricted so that only people in certain countries can access them – and the ability to limit country access is useful for multinational advertisers. Some advertisers want the brand impact of a huge global page; others are more practically minded and want individual pages for each region, each market or each language. There has traditionally been no right or wrong approach here (and there has been an ongoing debate between those who favour one global page and those who favour language- or country-specific pages), but, with such widespread use of Facebook now and an ever increasing percentage of interaction happening in the news feed rather than on the page, a portfolio approach with individual pages addressing individual markets may be the most sensible approach (if the resource to manage them can be put in place). Naming pages consistently can then help in managing a global Facebook page portfolio and help users find the right one (for example, PageUSA, PageUK, PageIndia and so on), whilst Facebook page settings can be used to lock them to the appropriate markets, reducing the opportunity for messages and conversation to cross borders or contaminate different markets. (Wall posts on a global page can also be geo-targeted.)

There are a number of other settings to explore (whether everyone should be able to post to the wall, whether the default wall view should be posts by everyone or just posts by the page, and so on), but some of the most important settings and techniques are the ones associated with getting Facebook users to click the 'Like' button.

Encouraging liking

Facebook pages offer the opportunity to develop a fan base of sub-scribers, with page owners (brands) then able to push out regular messages to these fans. The 'free impressions' served to fans are valuable in a number of ways, and encouraging liking is therefore a primary objective.

A welcome tab can be created on the Facebook page and used as the landing page when users first arrive. This creates a better first impres-sion then just sending someone straight to the Facebook page's wall, and it also helps to encourage people to like the page, as messages of encouragement can be displayed on the welcome page tab. A recent study of the Facebook campaign of 'a major brand' by BrandGlue showed that landing on a specific welcome tab gave a 47 per cent conversion to 'Like', whereas landing on the wall gave a (significantly lower) conversion to 'Like' of 23 per cent.[21]

This strategy is noticeably deployed by some of the most successful Facebook pages, with Red Bull perhaps the least subtle. Visitors to the Red Bull Facebook page land on a tab that simply shows a fizzing can of Red Bull with multiple arrows pointing to the 'Like' button and a bold message stating 'LIKE OUR PAGE. HINT, HINT.' Getting visitors to engage is arguably the most important thing. It's not just about having someone visit the page; it's about getting someone to visit and like it while they are there.

Page tabs can be further used to drive engagement for the page with a variety of content, graphics, video or even applications and features like polls and quizzes that can be used to encourage interaction. Facebook content management systems from companies like Buddy Media, Vitrue, Involver and Wildfire can then facilitate easy tab management through the use of pre-configured modules (from sweepstakes to discussion boxes) that are easy to design, add and manage. This sort of approach helps to build the fan base, encourages fans to spread the word, gives reasons to revisit the page after fanning and also provides useful analytics data around users and their actions.

An additional incentive to like can be offered by setting up pages or content that can be seen only by those who have liked a page. If users want to watch a video on the Lady Gaga page they have to like the page first, while advertisers such as Absolut, Nike and various others have promoted interesting video content, but have also allowed Facebook users to watch it only after they have liked the page – clicking the 'Like' button offers rewards. This plays to another of the six principles that can be used in the creation of influence relation-ships laid out by Robert Cialdini in his book *Influence*.[22] The rule of reciprocity is based around giving something to get something in return, and in this case it's a question of 'We'll give you cool content if you click the "Like" button.' Competitions, sweepstakes, free sample offers and coupons are therefore all further examples of what I call 'like bribes'.

Facebook marketing is conversation

To maximize the appeal and effect of a Facebook page it has to be updated regularly (ideally daily). The majority of interactions with a brand on Facebook happen in the news feed, though, rather than on the page itself. PageLever analysed a dataset of 400 million fans and found that on average daily unique news feed views were over double those of daily unique page views (7.49 per 100 fans versus 3.19 per

100 fans). In respect of pages with more than 1 million fans, PageLever found the difference was even more pronounced, 2.79 daily unique news feed impressions per 100 fans versus 0.15 daily unique page views per 100 fans.[23] Comscore research entitled 'The power of like' reached similar conclusions when discovering that in May 2011 'Starbucks delivered 156 brand impressions throughout Facebook for every one page view on its Fan Page.' (Comscore found that for Southwest and Bing the ratios were not as pronounced but still significant – 42 to 1 and 45 to 1 respectively.)[24]

For users, Facebook advertiser updates are mixed with updates from friends when they appear in the news feed, so advertisers need to start acting in new ways when updating their pages. It is fine to have the occasional sales-type message (for example, breaking a new TV spot or announcing a new promotion or product), but the bulk of advertiser Facebook updates should look more like updates from friends than updates from someone trying to sell something. *The Cluetrain Manifesto* pushed the idea that 'markets are conversations',[25] and on Facebook this is absolutely true.

In November 2010 an article in *Advertising Age* entitled 'When it comes to Facebook, relevance may be redefined' had the subheading 'To create conversation, simple, random and banal may be a brand's best bets'. The article highlights that one of BlackBerry's most effective tweets in 2010 marked Star Wars Day and simply said 'May the 4th Be With You'. The *Advertising Age* piece goes on to state:

> Relevance has long been a central tenet of effective advertising, but the rise of Facebook and Twitter are forcing a redefinition of the term. As it turns out, many people in social networks don't want to talk about your product, they just want to talk. We've long known that inserting brands into social-media channels requires a conversational touch, but many are surprised by just how conversational.[26]

Another study of company behaviour on Facebook, 'Socially awkward media' by AT Kearney, noted that they 'found that the most successful sites [pages] used a few simple techniques better than their peers – all of which involve creating emotional connections with consumers: invoking nostalgia, engaging in product discussions, and rallying around common causes'.[27]

The Betfair Poker Twitter account takes this to new levels, but has attracted over 11,500 followers as a result. Examples of some of the tweets from @betfairpoker are:

- 'Teach a man to fish and he responds: "I live in Chad. It is totally land-locked. Fishing is of no use to me. But thanks anyway."'
- 'On my way to work I am approached by a well-dressed badger, "You must arbitrate in our dispute with the crows," he says.' (Over the following 30 minutes 13 more tweets continue the story.)
- 'Raising wolves is a lot like raising humans. They still spend most of their time playing Call of Duty and eating the neighbour's chickens.'

As Twitter user Jastrow75 said when recommending the Betfair Poker Twitter account to friends, '@betfairpoker Virtually nothing to do with poker. Everything to do with life, the universe and pigeons.' Indeed, Betfair Poker International PR Manager Richard Bloch told the Business Diary section of the *Independent*, 'It took us a while to work out how Twitter worked – we realised people don't want to be bored with links to the website and bombarded with marketing, so we had to mix it up and provide information as well as something interesting.'[28]

The Betfair Poker Twitter account is popular and retweeted or replied to extensively. It challenges us to think about social messaging differently. Traditionally, creative tension was seemingly always about how big the product shot should be; now it seems that maybe we shouldn't have one at all! Betfair are not the only company to be using this technique to run a social account, and some of the most successful Facebook pages employ similar strategies. Comparisons between posts highlight the benefits of posting in this way.

Skittles post a mix of product-related status updates and random status updates on Facebook and, again, randomness always seems to win through. An update announcing a (professional-looking) Skittles competition to win a Skittles vending machine gained 6,235 likes and 611 comments. These are impressive numbers, but pale in comparison when compared to the 22,251 likes and 1,752 comments that were left on another Skittles (official) page update that simply said 'If a hibernating bear has a nightmare, does he just have to deal with it for months?' The considered, brand-related promotion got 28 per cent of the likes that a random comment from the brand gained! This is not to say that promotional and on-brand messages should not be distributed, but it does highlight that on social platforms engagement comes from thinking about the user first rather than thinking about the brand first.

This sort of irreverent brand updating is very different to the polished content traditionally created by advertisers, and addresses the two different audiences, the active and the passive. The random or funny comments encourage the passive audience to subscribe (and remain subscribed), but also keep the active audience engaged and prompt them to act – they like and comment.

Maintaining a consistent, regular dialogue is not easy, though, unless a structured approach is applied. Working out a tone of voice and topics to talk about is important, helps to keep the conversation going and makes sure that nobody within an organization is surprised by what the company is doing in social media. A good example of this is Malibu rum, which has been running a series of TV commercials that feature fictional radio presenters DJ Bernhard and MC Wonder Full broadcasting their Caribbean pirate radio show. A whole host of content initiatives have seen this campaign and the characters extended across different channels and platforms. In the UK the characters have been fully fleshed out, and Publicis even created a music video for MC Wonder Full, with him performing a specially created track called *Let Me Get That Boom Boom*!

There was an extensive process around this activity, and Tom Ewart of Publicis gave *Creative Review* insight into how the characters were brought to life:

> Online films like *Give Me Some of That Boom Boom* were co-created by Publicis and Great Works in a 'writing room' we hosted here in London to generate a consistent narrative for Radio MaliBoomBoom across all media channels. We wrote a full history of the DJs from birth to present day, which included how the guys met and Wonder's

first (slightly questionable) music video. This ensured that wherever the DJ's perform, and wherever the content appears, it is true to the characters and the idea. Writing rooms are the future of integration.[29]

Popular pages with a defined voice that they stick to means it's like receiving updates from a friend. This is an important aspect of a successful social strategy and one of the reasons why these profiles are popular. Continuity of voice and a consistent tone help people to relate to a brand, and this is another of the six principles that can be used to create the influence relationships described by Robert Cialdini in his book *Influence*.[30] He calls it 'commitment and consistency', the idea that acting in a consistent way and committing always to act in that way lead to the establishment of trust and influence. Understanding the audience can then ensure that the voice stays in tune.

Different brands have to act in different ways, though. Obtuse up-dating is not appropriate for everyone, but the principle of eliciting feedback and encouraging response applies widely. For example, asking topical 'What do you think?' questions is better than posting closed statements. If you give people encouragement to talk about themselves or their thoughts then they invariably will, and the engage-ment level of the page is positively affected as a result.

The EdgeRank algorithm and the importance of engagement and interaction

Facebook has changed news feed functionality in recent times by introducing a number of mechanics that control what gets posted or highlighted. Users no longer see everything (as shown by the PageLever figures above), as Facebook filters what is actually seen, and understanding how these filters work is a key element in Facebook marketing.

A Facebook user's Feed is optimized by a Facebook algorithm called EdgeRank.[31] EdgeRank acts to highlight the updates that it thinks users will find most interesting (creating Top stories) and in determin-ing relevance the EdgeRank algorithm takes a number of factors into account. EdgeRank looks at number of Likes, number of comments, recent history of engagement with the poster or page and recency of information. The content that EdgeRank highlights will therefore be from the pages or people that users interact with the most plus the posts that have secured most interaction from friends (and users can give feedback on what they do and don't like, EdgeRank learns user preferences over time).

This type of noise filtering will undoubtedly become more prevalent (and sophisticated) across social sites. This is important for brands as it's therefore not just about getting fans, but also making sure that fans see what the Page is posting. On Facebook EdgeRank prioritizes and gives visibility to posts from Pages that have the highest interaction rates (other platforms are also heading in this direction too, for example the default view on Twitter Search is (prioritized) 'Top Tweets' rather than 'All Tweets' that have been posted).

Generating Likes and comments therefore not only helps in spreading content through networks of friends, but also is a key contributor to visibility of activity in the first place! Pages with low engagement gain low visibility for updates which produces further low engagement and further reductions in visibility. The only real way to turn things around is therefore to invest in Paid Media, for example on Facebook targeting advertising messages to 'Fans of page' to prompt re-engagement or through using Facebook's 'Sponsored Stories' advertising solution (more about this in Chapter 6).

Studying Facebook Insights data and Twitter Analytics can help to optimize conversation strategy. To show the complexity involved with successful conversation management, AllFacebook.com reported on a study by the Facebook Data Team that showed that 'positive words in status updates garner the most Likes', 'positive emotional words in updates get fewer comments', 'updates with pronouns get more comments and Likes' and 'longer status updates get more comments and Likes'.[32] Using Facebook Insights or Twitter Analytics to continually 'listen' to see which posts have worked better than others is a good way of optimizing Facebook conversation activity – do more of the stuff that fans appreciate and less of the stuff that they don't. Chasing fans is one thing, but chasing engagement should be the priority!

Using a content calendar to plan and manage updates

Once the objectives or goals have been set and the tone and voice have been agreed, then pre-planning of posts and content is a good idea, as it prevents haphazard, ad hoc updates and helps to develop focus. I used to be involved in running university events, and before each year started we used to draw up a rough plan for theme nights across the year. As the year started we would already have a Freshers' Week party, a Halloween event, a Christmas event, a Valentine's event and a summer party pencilled into the diary. A similar kind of approach is useful when running the conversation on social channels.

From time to time there will be socialized campaigns and content initiatives to announce, and when and how these will be introduced to the social hubs should be planned in advance (conversational status updates can be used to keep the page ticking over in between initiatives). You don't have to create spectacular content every day, but an approach of 'Do one great thing every month' is a good starting point, and executions like polls, competitions and applications can all drive further engagement.

As its name implies, a content calendar is about creating a rough game plan in advance. A rolling 30-day advance plan is a good idea, listing all significant forthcoming milestones (a new TV advertisement, content release, a new product launch, etc) and also noting dates that offer opportunities for topical posts, like BlackBerry's 4 May tweet or posts around events like Valentine's Day, April Fool's Day, Facebook's birthday (4 February), International Talk Like a Pirate Day (19 September) and so on. These always seem to generate conversation, as they are things that people are thinking and talking about anyway, and related brand updates can piggyback pre-existing interest.

Google's Doodles (where the Google logo is changed to reflect a topical event) are exactly in tune with this idea.[33] The Google logo changes across the world in honour of dates such as Jules Verne's 183rd birthday or New Year's Day, but from time to time is also changed on a local level to mark country-specific events such as Australia Day or, in Japan, the birthday of Kenjiro Takayanagi. The

Google Doodle appears regularly and always captures the imagination – especially when it surprises people, such as the playable Pac Man Google logo or the Les Paul Google guitar logo tribute. Google scour the calendar to find quirky excuses for conversation and then deliver accordingly, and this is exactly the kind of mindset needed when maintaining an always-on Facebook page or Twitter account.

Topping up conversational updates with things of interest to fans is important too, but content can come from anywhere. Conducting a content audit is therefore a useful exercise, as content that can be used in social spaces can be sourced from a wide variety of places. It's all about understanding the assets available, which could include bespoke content, the latest TV advertisement, interviews, information that gives deeper insight into the organization, links to posts by consumers, or an opportunity to reprise content from the archives.

The Scandinavian Airlines (SAS) Facebook page has a regular feature called 'Flashback Friday'. For example, it posted an old photo along with the question 'How many different aircraft types can you see in this aerial photo from Copenhagen Airport from the late 1960's?' Saks Fifth Avenue use this kind of content too and run 'Saks Archive Fridays', with one of the early wall updates setting the scene: 'We went digging into the Saks Archive to find old catalogs, advertise-ments and even employee newsletters from years past to share with you. Every Friday we will be adding a new picture or two to this album to show you fun things that are part of the Saks legacy!'[34]

Neither of these required a new production budget. The Facebook page allowed old content to be brought back to life and used in new ways. Specific, tailored content is also appreciated, and the efforts of page owners to say thank you when they pass page number mile-stones is noteworthy (for example, passing a million fans has been celebrated by many, from Tourism Australia creating a video with a talking kangaroo saying 'Thank you'[35] through to Porsche printing a top-of-the-range car with the names of all one million Porsche Facebook fans[36]). Engagement is a key objective when running a Facebook page, and using content from across the organization, coupled with regular interesting updates, is the best way of driving the community and growing both fan counts and interaction levels.

Mapping hubs and content connections

Further benefits can be gained through thinking about how different social aspects link together, and content auditing should think about this too. How are things set up? What asset lies at the centre of the always-on structure? How can activity on different platforms all come together as a big picture? A content calendar will specify dates and targets. Mapping the structure of the whole brand-related social ecosystem helps in understanding how to bring everything together to maximize effects.

An illustration of how social platforms can be used effectively in this way was provided by Jonas Tempel and Matthew Adell, CEO and COO of dance music download service Beatport, when they presented at the International Music Festival in 2010. They highlighted how the band Swedish House Mafia had promoted their first single *One*. The release went to the top of the Beatport charts in a matter of hours and marked the culmination of a range of activity that had run through Swedish House Mafia social properties. The Beatport case study highlights the timeline and how the different elements were used and integrated:

- *23 February:* Swedish House Mafia member Sebastian Ingrosso's dog tweets about a new track.
- *12 March:* Swedish House Mafia release a teaser video on YouTube for their participation in the Ultra music festival. It features a clip of the new track, but doesn't draw attention to it.
- *27 March:* The track is debuted at the Winter Music Conference in Miami (with the stage swept for recording devices to ensure no pirating, although the track still leaks to YouTube, albeit with the wrong name).
- *16 April:* The worldwide premiere on BBC Radio 1 takes place.
- *17 April:* The release date is tweeted to fans.
- *23 April:* Swedish House Mafia are interviewed by BBC Radio 1, and the track is described as the 'hottest record in the world'. This interview is combined with a clip of the track, posted to YouTube and Facebook and then tweeted by all three band members.

- *25 April:* One day before release a short promotional video is uploaded to YouTube and syndicated through the Swedish House Mafia website, Facebook, Twitter and MySpace.

- *26 April:* The track is released and goes straight to number one.

This is very different to the traditional way that dance tracks moved into the mainstream, and the *BeatPortal* post that discusses the Swedish House Mafia case concludes with the following thoughts:

> You can take away the power of anybody who controls the front door of their store. You are driving your community, your network, and your fans directly to your products [and you no longer have to rely on an intermediary for promotion]. We see this happening, in terms of growth, every month. Every month there are new social networks that link people directly to content. And the traffic from users who come directly from Facebook Pages, tweets, etc, is constantly growing. People are magically appearing in front of individual tracks instead of getting shuffled through the 'front door' of the store. And I really believe that this is evidence of the Internet's democratizing properties – giving you the power to sidestep gatekeepers and drive fans straight to your records.[37]

Always-on Facebook pages and Twitter accounts (and so on) clearly need commitment and resource to keep them up to date, and in managing social spaces advertisers now have to think and plan like publishers, but doing so can reap rewards in terms of numbers of fans and levels of consumer engagement. Furthermore, publishing tools can be used (effectively content management systems for the social web) to make updating and responding easier and more efficient. These can be used to publish simultaneous updates across different platforms, manage page and tab content, manage conversations and track analytics around numbers and engagement.

Once always-on social hubs are established, every opportunity should be taken to drive their additional visibility by including their addresses (eg YouTube channel, Facebook page, etc) on every available company touchpoint – advertisements, business cards, letterheads, e-mail footers, point of sale and so on. If anything, this is more important than promoting a website address, as the subscribe, follow or like mechanics embedded into social spaces can turn the casual visitor into someone who is exposed to the brand's content on a regular basis. Once subscribed, fans, followers and subscribers automatically receive content as it is created, even if they don't keep coming back to the page in question.

The greater the number of fans, (in theory) the less that advertisers have to push people to the post. The post goes to the people, as users are automatically updated with new content and conversations, which makes it easier for them to share content with their friends too. (The same can be seen with apps, where web content is pulled into desktop or handset applications and, once apps are installed, updates such as new versions are pushed directly to the user.) This changes the flow of communication. Internet users can now manage their relationships with friends *and* brands in the same space, and brands don't have to pump money continually into paid media to send messages to them.

Furthermore, once people have chosen to follow they tend to stay followers, an example of what William Samuelson and Richard Zeckhauser described as 'status quo bias'.[38] In *Nudge*, Thaler and Sunstein repeatedly reference the magazine subscriptions that Sunstein wants to cancel, but never quite gets round to doing, stating: 'One of the causes of status quo bias is a lack of attention. Many people will adopt what we call the "yeah, whatever" heuristic.'[39] Fans and followers display similar traits, as once people commit they tend to stay committed. This is either because they appreciate the content or because unfollowing takes more effort than many are prepared to bother with (especially as Facebook tends to make 'Like' buttons large, prominent and ubiquitous, whilst the 'Unlike' function is present only on the page itself and even then only in light text on the bottom left!).

The creation of a social hub is therefore a key component of digital and all media strategy. It is always on and provides a hub for content, highlights new initiatives, fulfils latent demand created by campaigns in other channels and maintains a two-way dialogue with fans.

KEY POINTS

- Social hubs can fulfil the need for brands to be always on.
- Hubs can be created as stand-alone entities or can be embedded into social networks.
- Global versus local is a key consideration.
- The majority of Facebook interaction happens in the news feed rather than on the page – but even then only a low percentage of people see posts and interact.
- A conversational approach is the key to generating interactions and involvement. Especially on Facebook, learn from others and act like a friend rather than an advertiser.
- Facebook's EdgeRank controls visibility. Interactions improve the likelihood of content being shown.
- A community grows over time and may not necessarily evolve in the way that the brand anticipated.
- Some people will create and participate, but many more will be spectators watching from the sidelines.
- A plan for moderation is important.
- Content calendars can help to structure conversation strategy.
- Content can come from anywhere – hub mapping and a content audit can help in understanding what assets are available.

Chapter Four
Content

TV advertisements as branded content

Traditionally, paid media was the primary (and generally only) mechanic for distributing advertising messages at scale. However, aspects of paid media advertising could still persist and permeate into culture. This pre-internet version of earned media manifested itself through aspects of advertising creative spreading; catchphrases and catchy straplines could enter everyday conversation, and TV advertisement soundtracks became best-sellers (for example, Levi's advertisements created a string of hits for a diverse group of artists from the Steve Miller Band to Babylon Zoo to Flat Eric!).

In the 1990s Guinness were experts at producing iconic TV advertising, and a 1994 advertisement called 'Anticipation' took things further. The 1958 Perez Prado track *Guaglione* was used as the soundtrack,[1] and throughout the advertisement the centrepiece of the screen was a pint of Guinness that was being 'slow-poured', with a 'Guinness man' dancing around the glass and throwing crazy shapes to *Guaglione*. The advertisement finished with the simple strapline 'No time like Guinness time'.[2]

The soundtrack, *Guaglione*, was close to being a Top 40 hit when it was originally released, but after featuring in the 'Anticipation' advertisement the track went to number one in Ireland for two weeks in September 1994 and then number two in the UK in the summer of 1995 (when the advertisement was released in the UK market). The track sold so well in record shops because the 'Anticipation' advertisement prompted a craze for 'Guinness man' imitation, and the music became a staple for nightclubs, bars and student spots, with attendees imitating the moves. The TV advertisement therefore succeeded in driving the music and the dance into mainstream culture, particularly in venues where it was important for Guinness to be front of mind, but the 'Anticipation' advertisement was then adapted so that it could work in other areas too.

At this point in time Guinness didn't own the **www.guinness.com** brand domain, but in 1994 they were forward thinking enough to have a website at **http://www.itl.net/guinness**. Guinness created a screensaver featuring the Guinness man and *Guaglione* and allowed internet users to download it from their site.[3] However, in 1994/95 internet access was limited, with slow dial-up connections the norm. The file size of the Guinness man screensaver was 1.3 megabytes, so different (non-internet) means of content distribution were sought. Carl Lyons, Assistant Brand Manager on Guinness at the time, recounts the solution on his blog:

> In the end, we branded up hundreds of 3.5" floppy discs and put the file on there (it *just* fitted, thankfully). We seeded a few to friends and colleagues and suddenly the requests came pouring in. By letter! I had a box under my desk and spent most of my day stuffing envelopes. People would take the discs and pass them around friends and colleagues. People loved having beer imagery in their workplaces. There was a point in 94/95 when it seemed every office had screens saved to [Guinness man] Joe McKinney dancing round a pint.[4]

Guinness 'Anticipation' was arguably one of the first TV advertisements to be executed as digital 'branded content'. Distribution challenges made it difficult but, as Carl Lyons says, the Guinness TV advertisement not only spawned silly dancing in nightclubs, but it was able to morph into something that became part of people's everyday computing experience. He adds that, 'as a format, screensavers went on to be hackneyed quite quickly, but at the time [the Guinness "Anticipation" screensaver extension] was wildly original' and attracted attention and created engagement as a result.

'Anticipation' showed that there was clearly potential for content to be used as a key element of the marketing mix, especially if distribution mechanics could be improved. Chapter 7 will look at strategies for extending paid media into wider content initiatives that can work across multiple channels. The current chapter is dedicated to how brands and advertisers can develop content marketing initiatives that can work as both stand-alone content and fuel for the always-on content hubs. In today's connected world, the ability to send a message is not dependent on the advertisement breaks offered through the networks of traditional publishers and broadcasters, and content is a critical area.

Weaving brands into the narrative rather than the advertisement break

Advancements in technology have allowed viewers and listeners to filter and avoid paid media advertising, with consumers able to skip through commercial breaks and even use internet tools to block advertisements. As a result the practice of weaving brands and products into content narratives is becoming more and more popular. The programme content rather than the advertisement break around it delivers the message and delivers it *in situ* rather than as an incidental.

This practice is not new (in 1986 Run DMC reportedly received $1.5 million from Adidas in return for endorsing the brand in their track *My Adidas*[5]), but as product placement regulations are relaxed the lines between mediums are blurring, particularly as artists and producers seek alternative monetization routes. Prominent musicians, chefs, athletes, sports stars and so on are now considered 'brands' rather than just excellent in their niche, and the scope for commercial transactions using experts and celebrities like these is growing.

Hollywood productions have actively pursued placement dollars, with Patricia Williams from Wharton highlighting that 'the James Bond film *Golden Eye* was effective in promoting the BMW Z3'.[6] (She also noted that 'a later Bond film, *Die Another Day* – featuring a host of official brand-name products including vodka, a watch and make-up – was dubbed "Licence to Shill" by critics'.) McDonald's further provoked a press response in 2005 when the *Independent* (amongst others) reported that they were offering 'rap artists a fee of up to $5 for every time a song mentioning the Big Mac was played on the radio'.[7] The pay-per-play performance element was designed to encourage the production of hit singles that had Big Mac references within them, but also served to exacerbate sensibilities over where the line between editorial and advertising should be drawn.

In his book the *Cult of the Amateur* Andrew Keen argues that, 'Given our mistrust of traditional commercials, the challenge for marketers in the Web 2.0 democratised media is to advertise without appearing to do so – by creating and placing commercial messages that appear to be genuine content.'[8] Keen sees this as a negative, seeing advertisers moving towards a world where they are furtively seeking to distribute messages to unwitting consumers. However, whilst Keen notes that this has to be 'authentic' for it to work, and subsequently argues that 'such authenticity is utterly contrived', examples such as the 'Guinness man' show that intriguing content appeals to consumers. They have a choice as to whether they engage or not, and the volume of sharing is often such that it appears that (clear) advertiser involvement is not necessarily off-putting.

Additionally, internet users are now conditioned to understand that for many useful services and interesting pieces of content the pay-off is advertising association (from free mobile apps, to advertising supported free music on Spotify, to advertiser subsidized or funded events like the iTunes Festival, to Google advertisements in Gmail, to viral videos). The 2010 USC Annenberg Digital Future Study analysed the attitudes of consumers around paying for content and revealed that in fact 55 per cent of internet users would rather see web advertising than pay.

The study quotes Jeffrey I Cole, Director of the Center for the Digital Future at the University of Southern California's Annenberg School, saying 'Consumers really want free content without advertising, but ultimately they understand that content has to be paid for – one way or another.'[9] However, given a choice between a brand shouting untargeted sales messages in their personal spaces and a brand giving them something useful, entertaining or fun, internet users are voting with their clicks (so long as it is authentic and marked in some way as advertiser content).

There may now be strict disclosure rules laid down by the Federal Trade Commission in the United States and equivalent bodies in other parts of the world, but the main deterrent to a brand acting surreptitiously should be the potential for negative backlash if consumers feel that they have been tricked – the brand goes backwards rather than forwards. For advertisers, creating content and experiences that are worth participating in and sharing is now regularly a more worthy (and ultimately more productive) pursuit than creating underhand content that tricks users into participation or messages that just indiscriminately shout. Today's consumers are acclimatized, realizing that in many cases the content they appreciate cannot exist without advertiser involvement.

Developing content – collaborating with the new producers

One of the most popular ways of producing content is to work in collaboration with a partner. Traditionally this has seen brands working with established media owners to create packages based around editorial or multi-platform solutions, but online there is a much wider pool of talent to collaborate with.

The 'former members of the audience' are able to create content now, and there are notable examples of people managing to build up large followings by distributing their creations through social platforms. Flickr allows for distribution of photography, blogging platforms allow writers to gain attention, and a whole host of new 'celebrities' have emerged through YouTube. Savvy brands have been able to reach out to these new producers, with many succeeding in gaining authentic placements in high audience content. LonelyGirl15 was an online series that saw many brands getting involved, Canon persuaded a whole list of different YouTube personalities (from Chad Vader to the 'Numa Numa' guy Gary Brolsma) to participate in their Battle of the Internet Superstars campaign, and Moxie Interactive worked with MysteryGuitarMan Joe Penna to co-develop some highly viewed, innovative videos that featured Garnier hair products.

This is all about taking advantage of the audience that these new producers have developed whilst integrating products into a low-clutter, credible environment. Furthermore, new channels are spawning new media powerhouses. After launching *Angry Birds* on an unsuspecting public in December 2009, Finnish mobile game developer Rovio has become a force to be reckoned with. Since then there have been 250 million downloads of the game across all formats and devices, an estimated 125 years of *Angry Birds* is played every day, and *Angry Birds* has become so popular that spin-offs such as soft toys, cookbooks (with recipes mainly based around eggs) and even a Hollywood movie have been mooted.

Rovio got a taste of Hollywood in March 2011 when new version *Angry Birds Rio* launched. Marking a tie-up between *Angry Birds* producer Rovio and 20th Century Fox, *Angry Birds Rio* was a fusion of *Angry Birds* and the theatrical release *Rio*. Sixty levels were on offer at launch and have been subsequently augmented with further-level releases such as 'Beach Volleyball' and 'Carnival'. The game promoted the film, and the film marketing was tagged with details of the game. Again, rather than developing their own content outright, Fox partnered with an established property in order to attract attention and engagement and bring the film to life. Moreover, the approach appears to have been a great success as, according to *Mashable*, the *Rio* version of *Angry Birds* received 10 million downloads in the first 10 days,[10] whilst *Box Office Mojo* report that *Rio* achieved a total worldwide box office of $471 million (on a production budget of $90 million).[11]

Working with the new producers may be a more credible (and viable) alternative to working with traditional players, though they can still offer innovative solutions. Essentially it's thinking about not just what content to develop, but how to develop it (stand-alone or through a partner) and where the audience is going to come from.

Developing content to match search behaviour

In the following chapters we'll look at search engines more deeply, but for any kind of content (from articles published by traditional news outlets through to blog writing and video) a huge volume of traffic comes via search. Search engines match users with specific information, and developing content in line with search behaviour can deliver a 'free' audience, reducing the need to use paid media to create attention. Indeed, Chapter 2 thought about how to factor findings from Google Insights into strategy, and developing in line with search trends can be an astute move (so-called 'analytical commissioning'). Jim Lecinski notes in *Winning the Zero Moment of Truth* an example from the White House: 'In the midst of the health care debate, the Obama White House started monitoring what questions people were asking online about the health care bill and they determined that the #1 most searched question was simply "What's in the health care bill?"'[12] In response the administration published an explanation post on WhiteHouse.org titled 'What's in the health care bill?', and this post remains number one on Google listings against this query. Lecinski states that:

> What I love about this story is that you have a team who understand how the web works, how people use the web to seek information, and they used their website to their own advantage. And the best part is that it cost nothing. It cost nothing other than the time it took to actually have that person type up that blog post.

This sort of approach can be adopted for brands too, and one of the most innovative examples of this was provided by Converse and their 'Domaination' strategy.[13]

Converse believe that Google is the 'new gateway to culture', and marrying this to an understanding about how people search led Converse to decide to be 'the first brand to build a campaign around low-competition, low-cost searches that connect us directly to our audience'. Instead of trying to sell something, though, Converse used search to be conversational and created and promoted super-relevant pieces of content for particular moments in time.

Over a period of months Converse launched a whole series of random web pages and web videos that each tied into a concept identified from search data trends. Each piece of activity had its own URL, allowing it to show up against relevant searches (there were 75 different URLs in total), and each piece of activity was also linked to the others in a hub, which created a huge interlinked ecosystem of Converse content.

'Out of your league girl' gave teenage boys advice on seduction tips in response to relevant searches. A page that simply showed 'YES, IT IS' was served in response to people typing 'Is everything going to be OK?' into search engines, and further topical work matched queries such as 'First Day of Summer' or 'Heavy Metal Holiday'. There was even a Converse Spelling Bee (offered up as the only paid search advertisement to people who were searching for 'Scripps Spelling Bee').

The Spelling Bee video told internet users to go to Google and spell a particular word. If they spelt it correctly they were offered a paid search advertisement that led them to part two of the Spelling Bee. This video then asked another question, which pushed the player back to Google in order to enter the answer to question two, and so on. There were five rounds in total, and all of the words in the test were based on low-cost, obscure search keywords. The activity did not need mass paid media to promote it, as highly specific advertisements derived from Google Insights for Search drove awareness, which then spread through word of mouth.

Developing content in line with trends

The Converse opportunity was drawn from building out against search trends, and content creation can also work well when it is in line with wider cultural trends. Instead of targeting the topics of searches, we can target the topics of conversations. We saw in Chapter 3 how Facebook conversation marketing can be more effective when aligned with news, events or specific dates in the calendar, and the same principles can be applied to larger initiatives, listening to the conversation in order to generate topical content that can spread through earned media.

In late 2010, 22-year-old American Ashley Kerekes (@theashes on Twitter) suddenly found herself getting lots of attention as the England cricket team started their 2010–11 series against Australia, with the teams engaging in a long-standing, biennial cricket battle to win the Ashes trophy. Twitter cricket lovers started following @theashes on Twitter, posting messages and questions to her. Ashley's responses made it clear that neither she nor her Twitter account had anything to do with cricket ('I am not a freaking cricket match'), but this only stoked the fires more!

In response Twitter users, including a number of prominent cricket commentators, came together to start a hashtag conversation around the topic '#teachtheashestotheashes'. This public tweeting was visible to the world and aimed to try to explain the rules of cricket to @theashes, a person who really wasn't that interested. Ashley received thousands of messages on this theme, and it was quickly followed by another mass, spontaneous Twitter conversation '#gettheashestotheashes'.[14]

Australian airline Qantas were listening, had seen these hundreds of Twitter users posting messages to @theashes and decided to step in. Qantas answered the call to 'get the Ashes to the Ashes' and flew Ashley and her boyfriend on an all-expenses-paid trip from the United States to the final match at Sydney, where she was given a tour of the ground, lunched by Australian cricket legend Steve Waugh, interviewed the Australian prime minister and appeared on the BBC![15] This feel-good story was picked up across a range of media outlets, provided positive PR at an important time for Qantas and attracted many followers to the newly launched Qantas Twitter account.

Someone else starts the meme, but quick-off-the-mark brands can capitalize by getting involved and associating themselves, either by helping to further the narrative or simply by supporting creators or key actors. The conversation is already happening, and participation can result in coverage and exposure that (far) outweighs the fixed costs involved. The Qantas example was a very specific, timely example that reacted to a real-time happening, but trend watching can feed content initiatives in other ways too.

In 2009 Jill and Kevin made a video of their wedding entrance. The *JK Wedding Entrance* video showed the wedding party, the groom and the bride entering the church and proceeding to the altar. Eschewing the traditional method of walking to the altar with the bride entering the church to traditional wedding entrance music, Jill and Kevin did something else. To the sound of Chris Brown's *Forever*, a choreographed routine saw members of the bridal party dance two by two into the church and, as the routine reached a crescendo, Jill, anything but a nervous bride, danced up to the altar to complete the performance.[16]

The *JK Wedding Entrance* video accumulated 10 million views in a week and grew even more to become one of 2009's most watched videos. Jill and Kevin became the darlings of US daytime TV, recreating their dance for the *Today Show*, whilst another US TV show remade the video with Jill, Kevin and posse dancing into a mock courtroom under the title *JK Divorce Entrance*.[17] Internet mashups featuring different music (from the *Benny Hill Theme* to *Carmina Burana*) also added to the conversation around Jill and Kevin's wedding and drove even more views to the original – which currently has a view count of over 68 million!

In 2011 another wedding, the royal wedding in the UK, was all across the news, and T-Mobile decided to create content to capitalize on this. They reprised Jill and Kevin's *JK Wedding Entrance* video, using 'a host of Royal Wedding lookalikes' and East 17's *House of Love* as the soundtrack. Released on 15 April 2011, the film received 2.6 million views in the first 48 hours, reached 10 million views after seven days and by day 20 had broken the 20 million barrier. A prime-time show on the non-advertisement-carrying BBC then showed the majority of the video and name-checked the brand, whilst bloggers and social network users across the world linked to the video and embedded it on profiles. It was also noteworthy (and no doubt pleasing to T-Mobile) that around 25 per cent of the YouTube views for this film were delivered through mobile devices.[18]

A quirky film that followed the formula of a previous viral hit resonated with the zeitgeist and saw widespread amplification through the actions of the audience. There were even a host of UGC remixes of the T-Mobile film, including a YouTube user re-cutting it using the original *JK Wedding Entrance*/Chris Brown song and various remixes where a 'dirty' grime/dubstep soundtrack replaces East 17. All of this delivered awareness for T-Mobile and the message of 'Life's for sharing', whilst this video also had a knock-on effect of driving further subscribers to the T-Mobile YouTube channel and the T-Mobile Facebook page.

Developing content: harnessing the people's network

The actions of the audience drove T-Mobile views, but the original response to user-to-user sharing and remixing on the internet was 'Cease and desist'. In 2000 Metallica protested (and launched a lawsuit against Napster) about the fact that Napster users were illegally sharing their songs,[19] and in *Wikinomics* Don Tapscott highlighted the example of Wind-up Records, where 'Fans have spent at least a quarter of a million hours producing and sharing more than three thousand [user-generated] music videos.' Tapscott mournfully recounts that 'The company promptly asked for the videos to be removed from the [video-sharing host] site, despite the fact that some fans' videos took up to one thousand hours to create.'[20]

Chris Anderson discusses the short-sightedness of this type of approach in *The Long Tail*. When commenting on dance music remix culture he writes:

> In contrast to record-labels that spend more and more time on litigation to enforce copyright infringement, house music producers (and underground producers in general) have long realised that opening up their goods to being remixed and tweaked has beneficial economic consequences. A house record that does well often attracts remixes from other producers; it becomes a kind of platform. Because these remixes are usually hyperspecialised for different microgenres, they're complements to the original track. As the number of complements increases, the value of the platform track snowballs.[21]

Henry Jenkins *et al* agree in 'If it doesn't spread, it's dead', commenting that 'The repurposing and transformation of media content adds value, allowing media content to be localized to diverse contexts of use', further noting that 'Those ideas which survive are those which can be most easily appropriated and reworked by a range of different communities.'[22] It's not enough just to make great content; it's a question of producing a piece of content that lends itself to conversation or reinterpretation and then allowing others to play with it (and obviously the easier it is to share the better!).

Copyright infringement can now even open up alternative monetization streams for publishers and copyright holders. 'Illegal' content
doesn't have to be removed; it can be harnessed for promotional
purposes and can even deliver new revenue streams. This was well
illustrated with the *JK Wedding Entrance* video. Jill and Kevin did not
have permission to use the Chris Brown song as their soundtrack,
and uploading to YouTube meant that the *JK Wedding Entrance*
contravened YouTube copyright policy: it infringed on the rights of
Chris Brown and his record label.

In recognition of the issues around copyright YouTube have now
developed a solution to rights infringement, giving the 'victims' a
number of options. Rights holders can have videos removed or muted,
but can now also pursue alternative options around monetization, and
these alternatives were used by Chris Brown's record company with
regard to Jill and Kevin's video. They allowed the video to remain on
YouTube, but used YouTube monetization tools to automatically add
click-to-buy overlay (display) advertisements to the film. When people
watched the *JK Wedding Entrance* video an advertisement appeared
for Chris Brown, and these advertisements allowed fans to click
through to Amazon and iTunes, where they could buy *Forever* (the
track used), with all proceeds going to the record company rather than
to Jill and Kevin. User creativity got to remain on YouTube, but the
artistes involved benefited too.

Indeed, from the moment that the *JK Wedding Entrance* was uploaded,
'Chris Brown' searches started to increase quickly. Jill and Kevin's
wedding drove awareness of, and interest in, Chris Brown, and the
view count of the official video for Chris Brown *Forever* started
increasing rapidly too. The percentage of users clicking on the Chris
Brown overlay advertisements that were added to the *JK Wedding
Entrance* video was then seen to be substantially higher than the
YouTube average for this format at the time (approximately double).
Furthermore, after the *JK Wedding Entrance* video was published, the
click-to-buy overlay advertisements on the Chris Brown official video
for *Forever* saw a 2.5 times increase in advertisement clicking.

Views of the *JK Wedding Entrance* drove clicks and led to sales for the
featured Chris Brown track. Even though Chris Brown's *Forever* had

been released the previous year, it became a chart hit again – with no promotion other than the fact that it featured at Jill and Kevin's wedding. The viral wedding video drove so much attention that *Forever* climbed to 'number 4 on the iTunes singles chart and number 3 on Amazon's best selling MP3 list'. By allowing 'unauthorized' content to remain on YouTube, Chris Brown and his record company were able to generate additional sales without doing very much. YouTube mechanisms made it easy both to identify copyright infringement and to monetize it.[23] (YouTube now shows permanent links for tracks and artists alongside videos that include them, promoting iTunes download links for the tracks in question and tour ticket links where appropriate too.)

For their 2009 comeback album *Invaders Must Die*, the Prodigy actively embraced a huge variety of social platforms and further illustrated their understanding of the social media world by adopting an innovative approach to content by encouraging fans to play with and distribute their music – earned media became an important part of their marketing strategy.

The Prodigy created a YouTube video covering 'New Album Fan Guidelines', a series of text slides set over pictures of the band and set to a soundtrack of the latest single:

> It's often difficult for fans and YouTubers to fathom what is allowed on YouTube as regards copyright material and, just as importantly, what's not... to help, here are some official, Fan guidelines from Cooking Vinyl, Take Me To The Hospital, The Prodigy and Web Sheriff as to what you can post.
>
> Do's – it's cool to post clips/audio of... *Omen* (new/second single from the album), *Invaders Must Die* (title track/1st single from the album – but NOT full album of the same name!!), Live/Concert Footage (of tracks from the new album), Older Material (from previous albums).
>
> All of these should include the following, simple credit at the very beginning of your text description of your clip:- '*Copyright recordings, music and lyrics reproduced by kind permission of Take Me To The Hospital/Cooking Vinyl – for original performances by the Prodigy, check-out the official channel at **www.youtube.com/prodigychannel**.*'

Don'ts – It's uncool to/please don't... Post any material from the new album (apart from *Omen* and *Invaders Must Die*/title track), Post any unofficial mixes of *Omen* and *Invaders Must Die* (until after the album is released on 23rd Feb).

Big Respect for following these Fan Guidelines and, for info on The Prodigy's new album and 2009 shows check-out **www.theprodigy.com**.[24]

This again plays to the rule of reciprocity, as the Prodigy are effectively saying: 'We have encouraged and allowed you to play with lots of our content. In return we ask you to respect us and don't play around with the new stuff.' As a result Prodigy content spread across the web (used for everything from advertising agency case studies to *Lion King*/*Doctor Who* mashups), as users felt empowered to use Prodigy music as soundtracks to their own content. Awareness of the Prodigy's music grew as a result of allowing anyone to use their tracks. Moreover, the Prodigy's approach of encouraging spread has opened up numerous sales windows across YouTube: every video that features one of their tracks has an automatic link to a sales page, and Prodigy tours get expansive free coverage!

The increase in the volume of Prodigy content on the web also delivers an SEO benefit through the distributed links and the information that is included at the start of the video descriptions on fan mashups (earned driving owned), and these efforts help the Prodigy look futuristic and caring, whilst potentially dampening piracy and unofficial remixing of their new album. Loyalty, advocacy, sales and 'link juice' are all created through being nice and co-opting rather than ostracizing fans.

This is all very different to the 'cease-and-desist' knee-jerk reaction. Internet users are willing to spend time creating and distributing, and if the mechanics can be put in place to encourage and collaborate then everyone can win. Fans get interesting content and recognition, whilst the brand or advertiser in question can foster a deeper relationship and drive awareness and sales.

User-generated content competitions: the trade-off between earned media and control

Bringing the public into the marketing process can be helpful in building buzz and awareness, but it is also unpredictable. People can come from anywhere and, whilst consumers can help content to spread, they have a habit of not quite doing what they are told and often move in unexpected directions. For brands involving users in the creative process there is effectively a trade-off. As Dan Goodall noted, earned media has the highest potential reach, but it offers the least control.[25] One of the key determinations for advertisers in planning a campaign of this nature is therefore deciding on the level of control that they wish to hand over.

In 2005, as England's new Wembley football stadium in London neared completion, the London Development Agency (LDA) and Transport for London ran a competition to find a name for the main pedestrian footbridge as part of the promotional campaign to build buzz. The bridge into the stadium is a prominent, well-known feature and, with Wembley hosting national events such as Cup Finals, England football matches and major concerts, the 'people's stadium' saw the bridge naming as an opportunity to give the public a say in the final design.

A polling process was undertaken to allow the public to suggest names for the new Wembley bridge and, as it's an international stadium, the Football Association (FA) enabled nominations to come from anywhere in the world. The German public decided to take advantage of this, though, and have some fun at England's expense. To quote Jan from football site *The Offside: Bundesliga*:

> Normally this is the type of news that would have passed me by completely unnoticed if it wasn't for an e-mail a friend send [*sic*] to me and to the rest of his address book. This e-mail offered you the chance to pick on the English, outlined the competition and provided a link to the LDA website where you could send in your suggestions. It also asked you to suggest the name 'Dietmar Hamann Bridge'.[26]

Dietmar Hamann was the last person to score at the old Wembley in 2002, but he was a German and scored for Germany in a crucial World Cup qualifying match. England lost the encounter 1–0, the English manager Kevin Keegan resigned shortly after the end of the game, and English football was (temporarily) thrown into chaos – not the sort of occasion English people wanted to have memorialized in the naming of a significant feature of the new stadium!

Back to Jan: 'Now of course I felt obliged to honor the German–English football rivalry and voted for Dietmar Hamann Bridge. Though I wasn't expecting that this little campaign would have any serious impact on the competition. As it turned out Hamann was the most nominated name "by some distance".'

According to the LDA the first round of nominations saw 670,000 people make suggestions and 'millions more logged onto the site'. Furthermore, 'The bridge's name became the subject of Parliamentary motions in both Westminster and Edinburgh, and people have even demanded details under the Freedom of Information Act.' This was all picked up by mainstream media. A simple PR campaign based around the naming rights for a part of the new national stadium created sizeable coverage both online and offline.

In a post-campaign evaluation the LDA referenced the German activities on their official site, noting that 'many from fans in rival countries [were] seeking to hijack the competition', but the LDA had not handed total control for the naming rights to the public. The rules of the competition gave the FA a get-out, as there was a second stage, which involved a panel of FA-nominated experts trawling through the public suggestions to produce a shortlist of five that would then once again be opened up to public vote. The most popular choice from these five would then be adopted as the name for the new bridge.

LDA Executive Director Tony Winterbottom argued that sportsmen who were 'nominated for what they've done against England sides' were nominations with negative connotations. 'For something this positive and this important, we need a name that celebrates success', and the shortlist framework allowed this to happen. The LDA were therefore able to state that the panel 'were unanimous on excluding the most-nominated name: Dietmar Hamann. The shortlist is therefore likely to infuriate German fans, as well as those in Scotland, Australia, Ireland, Wales and New Zealand, where fans also ran concerted campaigns to promote their heroes.'[27]

The final decision, chosen by public vote from the shortlist, was in favour of the 'White Horse Bridge' (in memory of the 1923 FA Cup Final where 200,000 fans watched Bolton versus West Ham and white Metropolitan Police horse Billie was on the pitch trying to control the people who had spilled on to the grass). This whole bridge-naming campaign energized a huge amount of people and created international buzz around the forthcoming opening of the new stadium. The many attempts to hijack the voting increased the attention levels, but serve as a warning of how things can potentially get out of hand or head in unwanted directions if some sort of 'editorial' control is not maintained. Ultimately the existence of a panel meant the final name could only be chosen from a controlled shortlist (though I personally think the 'Wayne Bridge Bridge', after the footballer, should have been on the list!).

To see how things can go awry we can look at a 2008 Dr. Martens UGC product design competition, where control over a final shortlist was not factored in.

Artists from around the world were encouraged to create unique designs for Dr. Martens boots using a boot template provided by the site, and designs were then uploaded back to the Dr. Martens campaign hub. Site visitors were able to vote on the designs (limited to one vote per day), and a point-scoring, rating system was implemented so that 'Love It' counted as three points and 'Hate It' counted as minus one. Winning designs, one selected by a panel of experts and one selected by public vote, would then be manufactured and put on global sale as part of the Dr. Martens new range. The competition generated earned media attention, as designers were pushed to encourage their friends to vote for them, and added functionality allowed visitors to embed designs into their own sites and social profiles.

The expert panel selected a design called 'Colour Puddle Jump' as their winner, an attractive fashion boot created by Danielle Meder, a fashion illustrator located in Toronto, Canada.[28] This boot design featured a splash of different colours (reds, yellows, pinks and more) and, in judging this design, Jen Ford, Fashion News Director from *Lucky*, wrote: 'Combine a bold colour on a chunky boot and more likely than not it'll overwhelm any outfit. But this sort of New Wave watercolour effect is a perfectly wearable, feminine option – and very springy. A great spring boot.'

The other winner, the design selected by public vote, was the 'Snowboot' by Noah Dreyfuss. On the Dr. Martens competition site Noah introduced himself and his design:

> I enjoy Snow, Robots, Eggs, Beards, and Penguins for their Squeakyness. I like football (The American kind), American made cars, and detest light beer. Anyway, with my designs, I try to show the serious mood captured in life. That's why I chose a penguin in a snowstorm. I bring an intensity to boot design that can only be rivalled by the intensity of a middle linebacker. Unlike other's who may have used this as a platform for their artistic talents, I just want to make people think about their lives... and the penguins. When it comes down to it, life is just Shamrocks and Hand Grenades.[29]

Dr. Martens had no shortlist for the public to choose from. The competition allowed the public to vote on any design submitted – with the very public pledge from Dr. Martens that the design that won the public vote would then be made and sold across the world. The success of the 'Snowboot' was not the result of artistic brilliance, though; the victory was derived from an orchestrated campaign to get it to win.

Users of the *Something Awful* forum asked forum users to go to the Dr. Martens site and vote for boot designs made by forum members every day. A post describes their mission:

> The original idea was to win the contest with an awful boot, not an awesome one. This was in order to show Doc Martens that it's a bad idea to leave these decisions to the internet. Obviously some of us think Snowboot is truly awesome, while others maintain that it's awful. Either way it's not the sort of boot that would've won without us, nor is it the sort of boot you'd actually expect to be properly marketable, so I think we did what we set out to do.[30]

The final top 10 of the most popular designs in the Dr. Martens competition, as voted by the 'public', were all designs created by *Something Awful* members. The open internet vote had been corrupted by subversive internet users, something that Dr. Martens learnt from when launching a subsequent T-shirt design competition where the terms and conditions were revised to state that 'A team from Journeys and Dr. Martens will pick the winner from the 50 designs with the most votes.'

This was one of the earlier UGC internet vote competitions and, whilst Dr. Martens should be applauded for being willing to embrace the new opportunities presented by UGC, they saw at first hand that sourcing crowd opinion to help *inform* expert decision is arguably preferential to leaving the choice completely open to internet users.[31] (With this style of design competition, brands also need to ensure that appropriate moderation procedures are in place.) Public votes can be easily manipulated when groups of internet users decide to campaign to skew results and, if product development (like the 'Snowboot') is tied directly to these votes, a marketing initiative can cause issues for production and sales strategy.

A user-influenced shortlist rather than a user-selected outright winner maintains an element of control for the marketer and is now more prevalent than completely open voting, though in this example it was a double-edged sword for Dr. Martens. On the one hand they ended up with a design that they didn't want, but on the other received far more brand exposure online than they would have done if there had been a conventional winner. The buzz around the T-shirt design competition was tiny compared to the volume of conversations around the boot design competition.

As with Karen26, the conversation spread was driven by factors that probably did not appeal to the instigator, but Dietmar Hamann, the 'Snowboot', Karen26 and so on were responsible for a volume of nominations and visits far in excess of forecasts. A bit of scandal, controversy or subversiveness drives interest and coverage, but the important thing for marketers is either to find a way of making the unacceptable acceptable (handing control over to the public in exchange for earned media) or to find a kind of middle ground that works for everyone (letting go a bit and getting a bit of earned media in return). Without some elements of control, though, you can end up with a German footballer honoured at your national stadium or a big picture of a penguin on an expensive leather boot![32]

Just make great stuff!

The above sections outline a number of different approaches to content development, but in generating earned media the most important thing is to create assets that both engage or entertain the audience and encourage them to share. Jonah Peretti, now of BuzzFeed, sums this up in Bill Wasik's book *And Then There's This*, saying that things 'spread when they speak to the particular relationships between people. There needs to be a social hook to the media... social imperative makes you want to share it with other people, because you want to talk to them about it.'[33] Or, as Greg Verdino writes, 'You earn attention by making people care – by giving them a reason to stop what they're doing and take notice. And you make people care by giving them something they can care about. This could be a great product, a stand-out customer experience, a noteworthy new approach or something to talk about.'[34]

There are a lot of things for consumers to discuss or share now, though, and for advertiser content to feature in these conversations it has to be excellent, visible, well thought through, relevant and noticed. Chapters 5 and 6 will outline strategies for optimization and distribution respectively, but, as industry cartoonist Hugh MacLeod captioned one of his *Gaping Void* cartoons, 'The trick to marketing is to have something so cool, you'd want to talk about it EVEN if you weren't in the business'![35]

KEY POINTS

- TV advertisements can turn into branded content when taken online.

- Brand messaging cannot be skipped if it is woven into the narrative.

- Users will accept 'advertising' or 'advertiser content' in return for value.

- Content campaigns can be developed with the 'new producers', not just the established media players.

- Developing in line with trends (both search and cultural) helps content to gain visibility.

- Embracing the 'people's network' can see content spread further.

- With user-generated content there is a trade-off between reach and control.

- Always maintain final control through the mechanics of a shortlist.

- Innovation and being first are important drivers of attention.

- The key is in making great stuff!

Chapter Five
Optimization

Discovery strategy and the principles of search engine optimization (SEO)

The internet and the growth of search engines have changed the way publishers have to think about electronic publishing. With the majority of online content free, traditional publishers have evolved their models and methods, primarily to attract traffic that can then be monetized with advertising. The content itself, rather than the publisher brand, is now responsible for huge volumes of readers Michael Wolff noted in the January 2011 British version of *GQ* that 'Even a brand-name site like the *New York Times* gets as much as half its traffic from SEO [natural search results].'[1]

Optimizing content for search engines is therefore critically important, and if brands are now acting like publishers then they need to pay close attention to their strategy for content discovery too. The discipline of search engine optimization (SEO) is based around three key pillars: technical optimization, editorial optimization and linking.

SEO – technical optimization

Technical optimization is based on how a site is structured and set up. The site coding and programming language used, the site structure, the way a site is hosted, the load speed, the URL formats, the tagging and a whole range of other technical aspects contribute to how a site shows up on a search engine and, more importantly, where it shows up in the search engine rankings. This isn't about what the content is; it's about how easy it is for search engine spiders to crawl and index it.

SEO – editorial optimization

The second element is editorial optimization. Search engine results are served in response to what a user has entered into the search box, with search engines scanning articles for appropriate keywords before serving up the content that they deem to be most relevant in fulfilling the query. The way that content and articles are written therefore contributes to how much traffic they get and, as a result, copy has changed, as journalists now write both for search engines and for the people who will be reading it. On his *Yoast* blog Joost de Valk believes that journalists (and copywriters) being trained to use optimal keywords in their copy is important,[2] and Malcolm Coles on the *Online Journalism Blog* highlighted how this has changed online journalism when he posted about the online content policy adopted by UK quality newspapers in response to the death of Patrick Swayze. He writes:

> When news breaks, if you want to do well in Google for relevant searches, publish early, publish often and put your keywords at the front. From an SEO point of view, the more stories you can pump out targeting different (or even the same) keywords, the more chance you have of appearing at the top of Google's search results – and scooping up the traffic.[3]

To illustrate how publishers are building their perceived authority around a topic by publishing multiple articles and different viewpoints, Coles notes that on Tuesday, 15 September 2009 the *Guardian* website published 15 web stories on the death of Patrick Swayze, whilst the *Telegraph* published 10 Patrick Swayze stories.[4] This is obviously an extreme example, but the point is still the same – focus on the topic you want to rank for and build out editorial around it.

Furthermore, the title given to web pages and posts is closely analysed by search engines and helps to persuade them to rank content highly – a fact not lost on the *Telegraph* when reporting on Patrick Swayze's death, as 9 out of the *Telegraph*'s 10 articles started with the words 'Patrick Swayze'. This reflects the importance of focusing on the right keywords in titles and body copy when creating with search engines in mind. Michael Wolff also noted this in his *GQ* article:

All written information hastens to conform to the rules, as we have come to understand them, that dictate who comes up first in a Google search... Henceforth, this is the formal structure of how information must be presented: spell out locations (not just the Thames, but the THAMES IN LONDON, not just Paris, but PARIS, FRANCE), lavish great attention and specificity on proper names (not just Barack, or Obama, but as often as it doesn't seem silly, BARACK OBAMA; not just the Queen, but Queen Elizabeth II, Queen of England), eschew pronouns, cultivate repetition (the more times you repeat a word or, even better, set of words – the budget deficit – the better).[5]

Essentially it's about unlearning everything about how to write nicely. It's about keeping search engine spiders happy, but ensuring that the text remains readable for people too. As Wolff says, 'If you follow the rules of SEO, the results are astounding. Google gives you an audience of a size and at a cost almost never before dreamed of. It's like turning on a hose. But you must follow the rules.'

SEO – linking

The third key pillar of SEO is linking. Search engines aim to serve the most authoritative relevant results, and their decision making is based on the volume and quality of outbound and inbound links (this network and link mapping is the cornerstone of the PageRank system that Larry Page and Sergey Brin conceived and used as the basis for Google).

There are various techniques that can be used to gain additional inbound links, and the opportunity for link building has been extended by the extraordinary growth of social networks and the ever greater amount of online content. There are many more places to get links from (blogs, forums, social platforms and so on), and specific content can be created in order to try to encourage linking from others (witness the current spate of infographics). Moreover, brand assets should all cross-link, press releases and outreach should be keyword optimized and contain the correct links, and every opportunity should be used to push out the relevant www address.

These three pillars of SEO all help to drive natural search traffic from search engines. This is important, as once users have been brought to a piece of content it may be possible to get them to re-broadcast it and share it with their friends. There is also an opportunity to get these visitors to view additional content, and it may even be possible to convert them into regular visitors or subscribers.

The rules of social media optimization (SMO)

On social media platforms similar principles apply to the search functions, with Google Blog Search, YouTube search, Twitter search and Facebook search all guided by ranking factors, perceived authority and algorithms to some extent. On social sites other aspects like engagement levels also affect results and results ordering: it's not just a question of how often something is linked to, but also how often people interact and how often they share.

There are ways of optimizing social content so that it both ranks highly and is shared more regularly. Rohit Bhargava's *Influential Marketing* blog is credited with coining the 'social media optimization' phrase in a post in August 2006, laying out five rules of SMO, which have since been expanded to 16 rules after others contributed thoughts.

The original five rules were:

- Increase your linkability.
- Make tagging and bookmarking easy.
- Reward inbound links.
- Help your content to travel.
- Encourage the mashup.[6]

The further 11 contributions are:

- Be a user resource, even if it doesn't help you.
- Reward helpful and valuable users.
- Participate (join the conversation).
- Know how to target your audience.

- Create content.
- Be real.
- Don't forget your roots; be humble.
- Don't be afraid to try new things; stay fresh.
- Develop an SMO strategy.
- Choose your SMO tactics wisely.
- Make SMO part of your process and best practices.

There is no disputing the value of thought across the expanded list. These are all good practices for operating in the social space, but things have changed a lot since the list was written, and in its current form I believe it confuses the issue around SMO. There are things in this list about insight, things about distribution and things about tone of voice to adopt in social spaces. The extended list now represents a mix of thoughts about how to operate and engage across the whole range of paid, owned and earned. It's now a list about everything that can be done across socially connected media rather than a list of specifically how to *optimize* social content.

SEO is primarily about optimizing sites for search engine visibility. SMO should be about (technically) optimizing paid and owned content to maximize the viral coefficient and best enable things to spread. 'Being humble' and 'rewarding helpful and valuable users' and so on are admirable goals for a (social) media campaign, and pursuing the list of 16 will help to deliver success, but we should have a more precise focus. The aim should not be to use social media optimization to fulfil all 16 criteria. We should boil everything down to a single focused concept: 'Maximize visibility by making sharing easy.' Having this simple concept as a mantra will help to maximize the potential for earned media impressions and the chances of success.

Maximize visibility by making sharing easy

Jeremy Liew on the *Lightspeed Venture Partners* blog discussed the concept of viral coefficients in a blog post from September 2007.[7]

Liew highlighted how online services can grow through referral and illustrated how small things can make a big difference. This concept of a viral coefficient can be applied to social content and earned media too.

Liew writes: 'If the viral coefficient (the number of additional members a new member brings) in a population is less than one, it grows but eventually hits a ceiling. But if the viral coefficient is greater than one, it grows unbounded.' He shows the difference between viral coefficients of 0.6 and 1.2. With the 0.6 coefficient 10 members invite a further 6 people, making a total of 16. These additional 6 people invite a further 0.6 people each, making a total of 20. These additional 4 people invite a further 0.6 people each, moving the total to 22 until, after a few more stages, growth stops with a total of 25 people. In contrast a viral coefficient of 1.2 sees growth from 10 to 22 to 36 to 54 to 74 to 99 to 129 to 165 to 208 to 260 and so on, with growth getting steeper and steeper at each stage as each new person invites 1.2 new friends.

If the viral coefficient is above 1 it grows exponentially; below 1 it fizzles out and eventually stops. If we apply this viral coefficient logic to content pass-on, it's about making sharing as easy as possible and motivating each receiver to pass something on to 1-plus contacts. As we'll see in Chapter 6, large chains of pass-on are rare and unlikely. However, the principle of making something easy to share through optimizing the content is important, if not vital, when trying to tie together paid, owned and earned. It may be a mass of 100 people sharing to one friend each rather than the actions of one person spreading through a massive chain to 200 people, but optimizing content so that it is easy to share is an important part of generating incremental reach and additional value through earned media sharing.

Another way of looking at our mantra of 'Maximize visibility by making sharing easy' is therefore to think of it as being about creating the highest possible viral coefficients – and, regardless of what we think we know, the 'test and learn' approach is the only way of knowing what approach will work best.

Conversion optimization and the approach of 'test and learn'

In March–April 2006 Sendhi Mullainathan told *Harvard Magazine* about the work he had done with a bank in South Africa that wanted to increase the amount of loans that they were giving.[8] They mailed letters to 70,000 previous borrowers with an offer but, in order to test creative, the offer was randomized so that recipients saw different interest rates, different pictures, different tables, different incentives and so on.

All of these elements changed response rates. Rational thinking would suggest that the interest rate and monthly repayment would be the most important factors, but 'Interest rate may not even be the *third* most important factor.' Indeed, Mullainathan found that 'A woman's photo instead of a man's increased demand among men by as much as dropping the interest rate five points!' It's easy to make assumptions, but when things are tested they often throw up surprises.

Former Google employee Dan Siroker was part of the Obama election team and followed this type of testing regime for the Obama campaign websites. Conversion optimization of the Obama web properties delivered significant improvements in site performance and, whilst much has been written about how the Obama campaign used social media and the web to organize people and source donations to the campaign, the contribution of conversion optimization tends to be overlooked – and this played a significant role in the performance of the online activity.

The mybarackobama.com page was central to the Obama campaign efforts online, and every aspect was run through the Google Website Optimizer tool. This allowed every element of site content to be tested and retested in order to provide optimal conversion, and using the Google Website Optimizer tool gave feedback on the actions of visitors, meaning that the effects of different combinations of creative could be evaluated side by side. Barackobama.com was configured in different ways so that alternatives could be assessed. Six different assets were tested as the main 'image': a picture of Obama surrounded by placards; a headshot; a family picture in black and white; a video from Obama; and two other videos, 'Sam's video' and 'Springfield video'. Alongside these, four different buttons were tested: 'Sign Up', 'Sign Up Now', 'Join Us Now' and 'Learn More'.

The results of this were both extraordinary and surprising. The headshot resulted in 3.85 per cent more people signing up to support the campaign, whilst the family shot resulted in 13.1 per cent more people joining the website, compared to those who saw the original picture. For the buttons the results were also intriguing. 'Join Us Now' produced 1.37 per cent more clicks than the original 'Sign Up' wording; 'Sign Up Now' produced a drop in clicks of 2.38 per cent; but 'Learn More' produced a significant increase, 18.6 per cent more clicks than the original 'Sign Up' button.

When the family image underneath the headline 'Change We Can Believe In' was coupled with the button text 'Learn More', conversion levels were seen to be a 40 per cent improvement on the original version! Barack Obama raised $500 million through his online site. Statistically it would be inaccurate to imply that 40 per cent of the total revenue raised was down to conversion optimization, but there is no doubt that optimization of content on the site contributed to the effectiveness of the campaign.[9] (This may also explain why online destinations now seem to talk about 'joining' and 'learning' rather than 'signing up'.)

In a *New York Times* article about business school adoption of social media, London Business School professor Dan Goldstein stressed that one of the aspects of the course is around this kind of empiricism, which is essential, as there 'is little known for sure about what works, in terms of marketing strategies, on the internet... It's about testing things, and not about *Mad Men* style intuition.'[10]

Whilst conversion optimization tends to be a discipline more associated with e-commerce, the principles of 'test and learn' or continual optimization can help us with content distribution strategies too. Slight tweaks can make big differences in how internet users respond to and choose to interact with messages. In a world where user distribution and sharing are an important contributory factor to the success or failure of a campaign, then optimizing content and making it as easy as possible to redistribute are important – and 'test and learn' has to be baked into the implementation process. In post-campaign evaluations, great content that is hard to share may well be found to underperform versus less compelling content that was easy to distribute.

How content travels through subscription mechanisms and RSS

Enabling content to travel is therefore critical. Disaggregating site content so that it is available in lots of different places is an important part of this, and the backbone to much of the content flow around the web is a technology called Really Simple Syndication (RSS).

RSS changed the dynamics of how digital content is consumed. It is now rare to view content or visit a website without being encouraged to subscribe, like, follow, etc. Much of the time (though possibly now less in the face of the omnipotent Facebook 'Like' button) this is via a clickable orange box with curved white lines resembling waves of transmission, the RSS button.

The best way of visualizing RSS is to think in terms of how traditional radio works. A radio station broadcasts a signal, and this signal travels through the air and can be picked up on a radio if it is tuned into the correct frequency. Listeners do not have to go to the radio station in person in order to hear the music; it comes to them over the airwaves. It is a similar principle online. A website with an RSS feed will now effectively broadcast a signal across the web, and RSS readers, social network profiles, iGoogle and so on can be tuned into this signal, enabling the internet user to receive and enjoy the content without having to repeatedly visit the source site or page in question.

The major difference, though, is that a radio can listen to only one station at a time in real time, whereas an RSS receiver can receive simultaneous signals and archive what it receives, so content from multiple sources can be picked up and collated all in the same place and displayed in chronological order. Rather than having to visit every individual site, a reader can aggregate content from a range of sources, pulling together a variety of things in one place for easy consumption.

RSS has to be configured on a website, but is pre-installed on most blogging and social networking platforms. However, this is basic RSS, and more advanced services like Google's FeedBurner[11] can now be utilized for RSS distribution. These tools allow the publisher insight into how many subscribers a piece of content or site has and how many of these subscribers click on each piece of content (useful data in understanding which content works best). These tools can also offer functionality such as e-mail subscription to feeds (so that the latest posts are e-mailed) and auto-posting to Twitter, whilst FeedBurner even offers the ability to incorporate Google advertisements into the signal that is produced.

RSS (or the principles of RSS) can be seen everywhere on the web. The idea of consuming site content without having to go to the site itself is now widespread, and RSS plays an important role in helping content to flow across the internet. This is also the principle of apps, and tuning into the signal to receive content rather than going to the site has become so widespread that in 2010 this is what prompted *Wired* Editor Chris Anderson to pronounce the 'death of the web'[12] (though it is worth noting that his pronouncement was a case of RIP the web that involves visiting websites through an internet browser, rather than the death of the internet!).

How social networks refer traffic and boost audience

Referrals from social sharing buttons

Mechanics like RSS help content producers to distribute content across as wide a range of channels as possible, and users are then spreading it further. Articles and campaigns can travel and gain additional impressions through earned media amplification, but this campaign content is also driving traffic back to the always-on websites and social hubs, meaning that referrals generated from 'the conversation' are becoming more and more noticeable. In a blog post in 2009, Hitwise analyst Sandra Hanchard published figures that showed that in Australia social networks had become the most important drivers of traffic across many vertical sectors. She concluded:

> The increase in referrals from Social Networking websites has been largely at the expense of other traffic drivers, including Email Services, Portals and News and Media websites. The implication here is that Social Networks will increasingly become the preferred online channel for organisations to distribute their PR; and in particular, traditional News and Media websites face an uphill battle with Social Networks in providing the most immediate, if not relevant, third-party source of information on organisations.[13]

Since this post this trend has been repeated across the world, and social network referrals have come to take on an important role. A study by TextWise of 8.9 million tweets in early 2010 showed that almost 2 million (22 per cent) of the Twitter messages analysed contained a URL that linked to a piece of external content.[14] Again, anyone can post any link to their Twitter (or other social network) account, but the inclusion of social bookmark buttons in and around content makes sharing easier and more likely. Including 'Share this', 'Tweet this', 'Like', '+1', etc buttons helps content to travel. Social network users simply need to click the share button in order to pass on the content to their friends and increase its viral coefficient.

A study by BrightEdge in July 2011 found that 10.8 per cent of the world's 10,000 largest websites used the Facebook 'Like' button, but also noted that the second most popular share button was Google's '+1' button, even though it had been available for only a short while. The research found that 4.5 per cent of these websites were using the Google button and that this had increased by 33 per cent in the weeks following the beta release of Google+.[15] (The Google '+1' button pushes content into the Google+ universe, but also positively affects the content's presence in search listings.)

Automatic publishing

The viral coefficient also increases if content is already on the platform in question. It is generally easier to reshare (for example retweet) than it is to go through the effort of posting to the platform yourself. Having content inside the sharing universe is therefore also a good practice, and auto-submit features allow site owners to have their content feeds automatically added to social sites through the use of an automatic syndication tool like Twitterfeed or the Google FeedBurner tool.

A Twitterfeed account receives the RSS signal and can then publish content links to Twitter, Facebook and a number of other services automatically – effortlessly maximizing visibility by instantly distributing content across a range of platforms. Twitterfeed currently handles more than 2 million feeds from over 500,000 different publishers and, whilst these tools need optimizing, configuring and setting up, the upside to visibility and traffic that comes from widely distributing content across social platforms can be significant.

Shared content is more likely to be actively processed

The other point of note is that shared publisher content affects how consumers receive the advertising on it. Social media amplification is helping publishers to drive page views (which increases opportunities for monetization), but these socially driven views appear to be of benefit to advertisers too. An international study by CNN titled 'The power of news and recommendation' (POWNAR) set out to evaluate how the process of sharing affects the associated paid media advertising by using a global online survey with 2,300 respondents.

In a post on *The Wall* blog, Gordon MacMillan analysed the results of the POWNAR survey, writing: 'CNN said that the overall uplift for brands who advertise around stories recommended in social media is significant. The survey showed that people who received news content from a friend or associate via social media were 19% more likely to recommend the brand that advertised around that story to others and 27% more likely to favour that brand themselves.'[16]

Social sharing not only drives page views for content, but running paid media advertising on content that is shared appears to enhance favourability for the advertiser – earned media sharing helps paid media placements to work harder.

Integrating Facebook to sites and content via Facebook Connect

Facebook functionality can now be used by site owners and advertisers outside of Facebook too. In December 2008 Facebook Connect launched, and just over a year later in February 2010 Facebook reported that they were nearing a million Facebook Connect installations.[17] Facebook Connect was code that could be added to any website to bring in Facebook functionality. The initial benefit of the service was that it would allow users to log into any Facebook Connect-enabled site with their Facebook details, removing the need to create a username and password for every site that they wanted to be members of. For site owners this helped remove one of the barriers to user registration and conversion.

Facebook Connect offered more than just easy registration, though. It allowed users to take their 'real identity' to any site they went to and allowed actions performed on any Facebook-enabled site to be syndicated into Facebook, with users broadcasting actions to their friends through their Facebook news feed. Facebook users got an easier experience across the web, and site owners benefited from increased traffic generated by the organic impressions that were posted to news feeds. Facebook Connect could therefore be used to enhance existing site functionality whilst creating earned attention in Facebook at the same time.

H&M have used some innovative approaches in their digital market-ing, and in September 2009, when launching their autumn fashion ranges, the main H&M website at **www.hm.com** showcased the new collections. These were then socialized using Facebook Connect, allowing visitors to select outfits and embed interactive images to their blogs or click a button to post them on Facebook to get the opinion of their peers (with everything linking back to the H&M website and the new autumn collection). H&M hosted the new collection on their website, but made it simple for users to share fashion ideas with their Facebook friends, maximizing the visibility for the new ranges by using Facebook Connect to facilitate easy sharing.[18]

Another great example of early Facebook Connect integration was the CNN online coverage of Barack Obama's inauguration. CNN hosted a live video stream on their site, but around this had a live Facebook stream too. This Facebook stream meant that Facebook users did not have to go to Facebook to update their status. They could do it from the CNN site whilst they watched the live video coverage (with all status updates made in this way tagged with the text 'via CNN.com live').

Facebook users watching the CNN coverage could either follow scrolling status updates from friends or follow the updates of 'Everyone Watching'. This socialized the viewing experience, allowing internet users both to watch and to discuss with anyone on Facebook without leaving the CNN stream.

For the inauguration CNN.com saw huge numbers:

- 136 million page views;
- 21.3 million live video streams;
- 1.3 million concurrent live streams at the peak just before the speech started;
- 600,000 Facebook status updates posted through the CNN stream, with 8,500 updates posted in the first minute of Obama's speech and an average of 4,000 status updates per minute across the broadcast.[19]

The Facebook integration encouraged web users to watch the inauguration on CNN.com, and the appending of 'via CNN.com live' created virality that drew even more users to the CNN coverage. Facebook Connect created value for the CNN viewers, but also saw earned driving owned as more and more viewers were pushed to the CNN stream from the links on their Facebook updates.

Facebook integration makes it easier to share and discuss. In a guest post on *Inside Facebook*, Gregg Spiridellis, CEO of JibJab (a site that creates and distributes personalized animated clips), discussed the difference that Facebook Connect had made to his business. He stated that the functionality of Facebook Connect had made it easier for people to sign up to the site and share creations, bringing JibJab

1.5 million new users.[20] The significance of this is only really seen when comparing site figures pre-Facebook Connect and post-Facebook Connect.

JibJab's business is built on viral distribution of content. Before Facebook Connect, the company used e-mail and newsletter sign-ups to recruit site members. Even with occasional hit videos and coverage in mainstream media, such as an appearance on the *Jay Leno Show*, it had taken JibJab eight years to achieve a total of 1.5 million registered users. Using Facebook Connect, it took only five months to gain a further 1.5 million registered users! Facebook Connect integration significantly increased JibJab's viral coefficient, effortlessly pushing content to wider audiences and essentially putting JibJab business growth on steroids.

The increased success came from the ease with which people could share things once Facebook Connect was implemented on the site. According to Spiridellis, before Facebook Connect each piece of content shared by a user through e-mail would generate two to three responses. Sharing through Facebook Connect (where the message is posted to a user's Facebook wall or feed) saw this climb to 12 to 20 clicks back to JibJab – a significant increase. Moreover, when studying the numbers JibJab saw that around 80 per cent of new users were registering using their Facebook details rather than creating an account on JibJab, and this quickly prompted JibJab to adopt the Facebook log-in as their primary registration method. Spiridellis finished his piece by saying through Facebook Connect: 'Your friends will be there with you anywhere and everywhere there is a screen and therein lies distribution gold.'

Social bookmark buttons help content to spread, but integrating Facebook plug-ins through Facebook Connect can improve the viral coefficient further. It's not just about what you make; it's how you build the distribution mechanics too.

Using personalization to boost sharing

The concepts of personalization and social network 'distribution gold' powered the success of an outstanding piece of activity for Radiotjänst, the body responsible for collecting TV licence fees in Sweden. In Sweden, state broadcasting (Sveriges Television, Sveriges Radio and Sveriges Utbildningsradio) is kept advertisement free and, like the BBC in the UK, it has a public service remit that is funded by a licence fee that everyone in the country has to pay. The UK pursues a draconian approach, running advertisements such as the poster with the headline 'London is in our database. Evaders will pay', whereas Radiotjänst have employed a more positive message, encouraging people to pay rather than daring them not to.

The 2009 Radiotjänst activity was centred on a video that positioned the viewer as a 'Swedish hero'. The video is a well-made, powerful film and is based around a press conference with a lead character explaining: 'In times like these... we have to ask ourselves several important questions. How can you, I, our friends and our children really trust that what we see on the TV and hear on the radio is true?'

The press conference continues:

> How do we know that our opinions are really our own? How can we be sure that all the weak voices are heard and not scared into silence? I can tell you how. There is one person we can thank for all of this. We can thank this person for giving us new perspectives. We can thank this person for giving us a choice. This person gives us an alternative to uniformity and short term thinking. We owe this person for making an ordinary day into something special. A day when we rise from the TV couch and say: 'I've changed my opinion.' There's only one word that does full justice to that person: Hero. Thank you.

A standing ovation, applause and celebration then ensue, and the video shows people across the world saying 'Thank you' to the hero – but the face that's appearing on billboards, posters and celebratory placards is your own! (The message is that you are someone to be celebrated simply because you have paid your licence fee.) A page at the end of the film then allows the viewer to pay the broadcast fee, 'Watch Again', 'Make a New Movie' or 'Send the Movie to Someone You Know'. A direct link to your film is also provided, and there is easy functionality to e-mail, post to Facebook, share to Twitter or embed on a blog.[21]

In Sweden the activity was kick-started with well-known movie critics making their own films and reviewing them on the radio. A movie trailer was made for TV and cinema, and movie-style posters were also evident in urban areas. Over the course of the campaign the Hero website had close to 50 million visits, over 115 million page views and approximately 12 million films streamed – the films were watched in every single country and region of the world except for Western Sahara![22]

The personalized 'You are a hero' message made people want to share the film, and the optimization of the content made it easy to do so. The traditional marketing support in Sweden gave the film initial impact, but it was the distribution mechanics that saw it spread so far. (There is more on this example in Chapter 10.)

The expanded range of Facebook social plug-ins

At the f8 conference in April 2010 Facebook expanded Facebook Connect, launching a range of enhancements including Open Graph Protocol, Social Plugins, Graph API, a new Insights Dashboard, Personalization Partnerships and simpler policies.

Open Graph aims to allow site owners to have better, simpler ways to connect to site content, and these connections can then be used 'to provide more personalized, relevant experiences' for visitors. Essentially Open Graph allows Facebook users to take their profile information with them as they travel across the web, allows sites to integrate into Facebook more easily and extends 'the functionality of a Facebook Page to any page on the web'. The most obvious example is in the Social Plugins that Facebook have unveiled. Rather than having a simple button labelled 'Share on Facebook', Social Plugins open the door to a much richer integration.

A website that integrates Facebook's Social Plugins can now allow visitors to like various elements of the site. This also means that, if users are currently logged into Facebook, when they visit a website they can see what their Facebook friends have liked there previously.

Another plug-in enables sites to show a 'Like Box' that lists the content that previous visitors have liked, and it can even display names and profile pictures of friends who have previously visited and liked.

User actions on external sites are now shown both on the site itself and inside Facebook for friends to see, whilst actions taken within the Facebook environment can be highlighted on external sites. This is a social version of 'Most Read', as it draws attention to content by showing not just 'Most Liked', but 'Most Liked *by friends*'. This is a powerful nudge, and it is unsurprising to hear that sites implementing this sort of functionality have seen higher numbers of page views per visitor since installation. As JibJab found, this sort of activity can significantly drive viral coefficients!

Other similar options such as 'Activity Feed', 'Recommendations' and 'Social Bar' also highlight the actions of previous visitors, but the most ubiquitous, and widely used, Social Plugin is the 'Like' button that enables web users to tell their Facebook friends that they like something through just a click of the mouse.[23]

Shortly after the f8 announcement about Social Plugins, it was revealed that over 50,000 sites had implemented 'Like' buttons in the seven days after they were released, and that Facebook Social Plugins received a billion impressions in the 24 hours after launch. These numbers have continued to grow, and Social Plugins have been significantly increasing traffic referrals. Blogging platform TypePad revealed that, since they had made Facebook Social Plugins available to TypePad bloggers, those that had installed them had received a 50 per cent increase in referrals from Facebook, the *Washington Post* claimed a 290 per cent increase in Facebook traffic, and Facebook referrals to *ABC News* and *Gawker* grew by 190 per cent and 200 per cent respectively.

One of the most interesting side effects seems to be that the visits generated from Facebook and Facebook Connect are from users who seem to be willing to engage more extensively with content. Simply Hired found that after activation there were 2.2 times more job searches and 52 per cent more jobs viewed. Personera (a site for creating personalized printing materials) 'found that Facebook users generate 50% more page views, spend 25% more time on site, and have a 20% lower bounce rate'. Canada's *Globe and Mail* newspaper found that installation of Social Plugins had increased Facebook referral by 80 per cent and had also delivered more engaged users – people who had liked their Facebook page 'are more engaged and comment, share, and read more'.[24]

These new Facebook offerings do not automatically install themselves on a site, though. It takes some effort, as code has to be changed and added to in order for them to function (though Facebook have worked hard to make installation as painless as possible). Furthermore, in the same way that the Obama campaign tested combinations of different images and buttons, it is also possible to implement a testing regime around Facebook Social Plugins. What is the best plug-in to use? What is the best position for it on the page? Which version of the 'Like' button should be used? And so on. (Facebook have revealed some data around this, stating that the 'Like' button that includes people's faces results in a click-through rate that is three to five times higher.)[25]

The Facebook range of Social Plugins now enables the people's network to act as a genuine mass-distribution channel. The simplicity of the 'Like' button, or the more recent equivalents such as Google's '+1', coupled with the huge number of socially networked users, means that content can spread quickly and at scale.[26] The changes announced at f8 2011, whereby Facebook apps can automatically post user actions to the news ticker, may fuel spread and scale even further.

Real-world 'Like'

Mobile operators are starting to offer location-based, SMS couponing for users who sign up to the service, with O2 in the UK running with Starbucks and L'Oréal as launch partners.[27] GPS functionality is facilitating powerful call-to-action mobile advertising, but the ever growing number of smart phones is also increasing mobile social network usage in terms of both frequency of visit and time spent social networking. This is bringing social network functionality into the real world, in many cases making it more tangible for brands and businesses – in terms of both couponing and advocacy or loyalty programmes.

Mobile social networkers are now able to 'check in' to physical locations, share their location with friends, earn points or custom badges, and get rewarded by the businesses in question with incentives or loyalty bonuses. The feedback loop then kicks in again, as these businesses get access to enhanced data about their customers derived from their profiles and behaviours. (See Chapter 10 for an example from Radio Shack that shows how Foursquare couponing was able to provide data about the purchasing habits of those who checked in on Foursquare as against the average customer.) Location-based services like Foursquare and Gowalla initially facilitated these types of mechanics, but in recent times they have become a feature of the more generic networks, notably Facebook, where Facebook Places and Facebook Deals make up the location-based offerings. (As Facebook's commerce solution, Facebook Credits, develops, these offerings could become even more interesting.)

Deals, offers, specials or custom assets like badges all need to be set up, but again this is not hard to do and is quickly becoming mainstream. For example, a recent walk down a Swedish high street saw me offered a 20 per cent discount from H&M for checking in on Foursquare, a free gift from sports shop Stadium if I checked in with Facebook Places, and a free milkshake from McDonald's for checking in via Facebook Places (either through Facebook itself or through a multifaceted McDonald's smart phone app).[28]

Brand-related social media conversation and sharing are now happening in real time around real-world locations and can be made even easier with real-world 'Like' functionality – especially if it removes the need for a button altogether! This is exactly where things are headed. Japan's leading social network, Mixi, announced in February 2011 that Google Nexus S phones can now be used to check in to places via Mixi automatically. Using the Near Field Communication (NFC) technology that will soon be included on a wide range of phones, Mixi users simply have to wave their phone in a location and it will automatically post an update to the Mixi user's profile.[29] In May 2011

Foursquare placed NFC check-in points all around Google's I/O developer conference in California (with attendees able to earn a special Google I/O badge).[30] This sort of real-world check-in is starting to happen on Facebook too. For example, in summer 2010 Publicis E-dologic worked with the Coca-Cola Village in Israel to produce a real-world version of the Facebook 'Like'.[31]

The Coca-Cola Village exists for three days every year, aiming to 'integrate music, friends and fun'. For 2010 the organizers set about 'bringing the virtual world of Facebook into the real world of the village', and every village guest was given a wristband that included an RFID chip that contained their Facebook username and password. Exhibits inside the Coca-Cola Village were equipped with RFID receivers, and if these were touched with a wristband a 'Like' would be displayed on the wearer's Facebook profile for the wearer's friends to see. Furthermore, if guests were photographed by one of the official photographers, the RFID technology would automatically tag everyone in the photo and upload it to the relevant Facebook profiles.

This real-world 'Liking' resulted in up to 35,000 posts per cycle, even though the village holds a maximum of only 650 each time, so on average visitors were posting 54 pieces of Coke-branded content each to their Facebook profile for their friends to see! Making it easy for people to post to Facebook generated far more content than would have otherwise occurred, and it all happened in real time.

A similar approach was adopted by Bud Light during the 2011 Super Bowl when they took over the Aloft Hotel in Dallas for five days and rebranded it as the Bud Light Hotel.[32] The Bud Light Hotel hosted four nights of partying, including performances from acts like Snoop Dogg, Warren G, The Fray, Flo Rida, Ke$ha, Nelly and Pitbull, and guests were again equipped with RFID bracelets that enabled them to post updates to Facebook.[33] (Renault and Hyundai also used this type of real-world 'Liking' on their stands at the 2011 Amsterdam Motor Show.)

This is more than just 'checking in' to a place; it is about being somewhere, expressing a real-world preference and then having that syndicated online for everyone to see, in real time, with brands now able to take advantage of various mobile and social offerings both to reward loyalty and to drive advocacy. NFC, RFID, GPS and smart phones have allowed social networks to reach beyond digital realms into the real world and, as smart phone technology further evolves, services like the augmented reality platforms offered by companies like Layar or Metaio (that allow smart phone users to look through their phone cameras and see digital information overlaid on to the real-world physical landscape) may make real-world optimization (RWO) even more interesting. Real-world 'Liking' also gives business greater insight into the profile of their customers and helps with the ROI tracking and measurement of (social) marketing activities.

The energy that social media, and particularly Facebook, can bring to viral coefficients and content distribution efforts is undeniable. Optimizing content gives it the best chance of spreading and maximizes the potential for earned media impressions, with Facebook optimization being a key pillar in driving content spread. Content optimization and social media optimization should therefore be an integral part of the plan, and overlooking them could result in more budget needed for distribution. It's not just about the quality of the content that has been produced; it's also about how easy this content is to find and how easy it is to share.

If you build it they might come, if you optimize they might share, but if you really want success you still need to push – and Chapters 6, 7 and 8 will discuss strategies around this aspect of generating attention.

KEY POINTS

- Discovery strategy is important.
- Search engine optimization (SEO) delivers visibility on search engines, whilst social media optimization helps content to be found on social sites and makes it easier for users to share it.
- The 'test and learn' approach will help to improve optimization over time.
- RSS is the backbone to how things spread.

- Share buttons encourage users to share content through their social profiles, with Facebook's 'Like', Google's '+1' and Twitter's 'Tweet This' being the most prominent.

- Facebook Connect can socialize any web content and improve its visibility and virality.

- Personalization creates a social hook and drives sharing.

- Location-based services can be harnessed for couponing, incentives and loyalty programmes.

- Real-world optimization (RWO) through RFID, NFC and so on is the next phase in optimization and social media optimization.

- RWO is becoming more interesting and important.

Chapter Six
Seeding and viral distribution

Traditionally paid media 'go here now' messages were the only way of attracting attention, but the huge variety of publishing that now occurs online enables advertisers to use seeding and outreach to drive product recommendation, whilst earned media can also be tapped to drive the distribution of content initiatives either through 'natural' outreach or through a range of (paid-for) performance distribution solutions.

Seeding can therefore be used in different ways depending on the objectives. If the aim is to drive product recommendation (advocacy) that leads to sales then a different strategy should be used compared to when the aim is to drive views of content (awareness etc), though there is some inevitable overlap between these. 'Seeding' is therefore a general description that covers different mechanics and techniques.

The 'man in the pub' and the two-step theory of receiving

In many languages there are cultural references that are difficult to translate into English. For example, in the Introduction we saw Karen26 reference the Danish idea of *hygge*, in Holland there is the philosophy of *gezelligheid*[1] and in Germany there is the concept of *gemütlichkeit*, with all of these invoking the idea of cosiness, belonging and sharing quality time with friends. In Germany there is even an additional word,

Kneipenkultur, which can be translated as 'pub culture', and in the UK it is not uncommon for people to have 'coffee mornings' or visit the neighbourhood bar, which is often lovingly described as their 'local'. These are all variations on a theme, but represent the idea that humans are 'social apes' who take pleasure from socializing and being in the company of others, especially friends.

Furthermore, whenever people gather in groups there tend to be individuals who know about different things and are respected as having opinions or expertise in different areas. As a result, socializing can see recommendations sought and received across a range of topics, and the influence of family and friends is frequently cited as the most powerful driver of purchase in many different categories, so much so that in February 2010 *Accountancy Age* in the UK reported that:

> Advisers are warning that the 'man in the pub' could be fined for discussing tax planning, under draft legislation proposals from the taxman. The 'Working with Tax Agents: the next stage' draft legislation could see any individual who gives anyone tax advice that leads to a loss of tax to the Treasury as guilty of a new offence of deliberate wrongdoing, which carries a fine of between £1,500 to £50,000.[2]

The two-step flow of communication

This is indicative of the long-standing influence of personal connections in decision making. In 1955, Katz and Lazarsfeld's seminal text *Personal Influence* analysed 'man in the pub'-type effects as they reported on their research that showed 'the part played by people in the flow of mass communications'.[3]

Lazarsfeld had previously studied the effect of print and radio on voting decisions in the 1940 US presidential election. The research was based on an Ohio community, and the final results 'indicated that the effect of mass media was small as compared to the role of personal influences', with this thinking then becoming the famed 'two-step flow of communication'. *Personal Influence* was based on a follow-up study from Decatur, Illinois, where Katz and Lazarsfeld studied a wider group of people and categories (politics, household goods purchase, movie going and local affairs). They published some, at that time unexpected, results and found that people who wanted to know about something would ask the expert, with the expert deriving expertise from both personal experience and the messages of mass media. Katz and Lazarsfeld found that ideas are received from the media by a select few, interpreted and then passed on by them to a wider audience that is interested and ready to receive.

Interestingly, Katz and Lazarsfeld found no evidence for 'general influencers', as after analysing different categories they found that influencers would vary by topic, and declared that 'each social stratum generated its own opinion leaders'. For movies young people tended to influence older people, in small consumer goods the 'older housewife influenced the younger', 'fashion leadership is strongly related to life-cycle type and gregariousness and somewhat less to social status, while leadership in public affairs is related primarily to social status and to gregariousness, but to a much lesser extent the life cycle'.

Harnessing the two-step flow and helping fans to talk

Brands now can tap into this type of opinion leader advocacy, with customer relationship management (CRM) programmes that allow people to volunteer to be brand ambassadors. For example, Nokia have an always-on outreach programme that is all pulled together at WOMWorld/Nokia.[4] Nokia allow those who wish to be brand advocates to sign up to get involved, with visitors to WOMWorld/ Nokia able to register to give a Nokia device a trial.

This allows consumers to reach in to Nokia (through the ability to volunteer to give a trial) and declare a willingness to be an advocate. Perhaps most importantly, as Emanuel Rosen writes in *The Anatomy of Buzz*, 'if some people have a natural propensity to talk without being triggered to do so, they might talk to even more people when triggered to talk. And that's the idea in a nutshell: find those who talk more about your category, listen to them and help them talk about you.'[5]

Nokia are using WOMWorld/Nokia to engage with people who are positive about their products and likely to speak about them to friends and connections. This initiative is not just about driving awareness of products; it's about driving advocacy and recommendations, with this approach helping the spread of positive product reviews and commentary. (This approach also helps Nokia to create and expand a list of potentially receptive contacts for the future.) Seth Godin agrees with Rosen, saying 'You have to find a group that really desperately cares about what you have to say, talk to them and make it easy for them to tell their friends.'[6]

The content created by those who participate in this style of advocacy programme can also show up in natural search listings. This is important, as searching is how a huge number of people start their internet journeys or their pre-purchase research – the words of fans are accessible to the masses. Links created also deliver a benefit to the natural search ranking of the official sites and official content, and positive presence in organic search benefits paid search activity too, with improved click-through rates (and subsequent lower cost-per-click pricing) resulting from having presence in both natural and paid search listings.

Reaching out to opinion leaders

Katz and Lazarsfeld were concerned with *personal* influence, but in today's society influence can be exerted from both people we know personally and people whom we 'know' through the media. Indeed, this is the basis for programmes like the ad.ly advertising offer, which facilitates celebrity endorsement of brands and products on Twitter. Ad.ly has over 1,000 celebrities registered and, for the right brand, these celebrities will tweet about an advertiser in return for payment. Some of the results reported have been impressive. For example, after acquiring 1 million Twitter followers in just 25 hours, Charlie Sheen was paid to tweet about internships.com, with his tweet offering the chance for a Twitter user to become a 'winning' intern on 'TeamSheen'.[7] Internships.com reported that this tweet produced '95,333 clicks within the first hour, visits from 181 different countries and ultimately more than 74,040 submitted applications'![8] (Interest in this was so high that when a student in Northern Ireland claimed to have been the person selected he was featured on local TV and radio and in newspapers – before it was revealed that he was a hoaxer![9])

Not only do Nokia allow advocates to reach in through WOMWorld/ Nokia, but they also have programmes that reach out, targeting relevant bloggers who they think are respected and listened to, offering selected people trial devices, custom content and the ability to participate in Nokia experiences.[10] Nokia are not alone in pursuing this approach, and official blogger outreach can encompass large, involved initiatives. An outstanding example was seen in June 2008 when blogger Heather Armstrong threw a Wii Fit party at her house after she accepted an approach from Nintendo. Armstrong writes a blog about herself and her family at dooce.com, the perfect target audience for Wii Fit. It's a blog that got her fired from her (then) job in 2001 and a blog she writes professionally now.

Dooce.com has a large readership (it's in the top 15,000 websites globally), and Armstrong has over 1.5 million followers on Twitter. Endorsement from dooce.com is something many brands would aspire to, but Armstrong makes it clear that she will not be a mouthpiece for advertisers. Everything she recommends is either something that she has bought herself or a gift sent by one of her readers that she would have gone out and bought anyway because it fits her 'aesthetic'.[11] This is made clear and appeals to her readership, meaning that Dooce.com offers both a trusted environment and a large reach. The Wii Fit party marked the first time that she had conducted a giveaway or worked with a brand in this way – and the response was exceptional.

Armstrong blogged: 'Some good people from Nintendo came to my house and threw a Wii Fit party. My job was to gather up ten of my friends.' Heather wrote a blog post that discussed the evening, discussed Wii Fit and announced that she had five Wii consoles and five Wii Fit games to give away to five readers. All the readers had to do was leave a comment, 'preferably a comment about Wii Fit and what you think it might do for you or your family'. Forty-eight hours later winners were drawn (Armstrong's mother selected numbers at random), and the corresponding commenters won a Wii and Wii Fit game each.[12]

The competition element created engagement around the post, as, rather than passively consuming the information, readers were encouraged to think about the product and interact with the content. This active audience left a staggering 42,232 comments in all on the Wii Fit party blog post (many talking about how the product will benefit them), and the page has had thousands and thousands of views. Nintendo's only outlay was five consoles, five Wii Fits and the human resource time and agency management costs involved, whilst Heather Armstrong got bonus traffic, increased engagement through the volume of comments and a fun evening with her friends.

The Wii Fit party post was successful, as it generated a huge response and encouraged people to discuss the product positively. However, this style of outreach is difficult to scale, as the effort involved limits the range of sites that can be targeted, and this level of effort may only be worthwhile if a blog with a large readership can be co-opted. Furthermore, the activity is all contained within the blog post itself, and the intimate nature of the event and the level of control that was handed over (Armstrong organized and hosted the party and the write-up) meant there was little opportunity for development of supplementary content that could spread over a wider area.

Blogger outreach can therefore go deeper than just a single e-mail asking someone to post about something, but outreach is a personal area (it tends to centre on approaching individuals rather than organizations), and campaign success often results from quality rather than quantity. Developing an ongoing relationship with a selection of key voices may be more productive than trying to develop a relationship with everyone. This technique harnesses the two-step flow, with consumers coming into contact with an idea after it has been filtered by an expert or someone they trust (rather than simply coming into contact with it directly from an advertiser), and results can speak for themselves.

Diffusion and the role of influentials in helping things to spread

How ideas and products diffuse

Encouraging opinion leaders to talk positively, through either reaching out or allowing them to access information and products, helps to galvanize the two-step flow, seeing advocacy (and hopefully consumer consideration) grow. The two-step theory does not claim to illustrate *how* things spread, though (step one, the message is broadcast; step two, the message is relayed to the audience through an expert), but later explanations of diffusion seem to back up further the idea of engaging opinion leaders.

Katz and Lazarsfeld made little or no reference to chains and pass-on. Their model was based on two steps, the simple idea that pushing messages through opinion leaders would improve receptivity as against pushing messages directly to the audience. However, in his 1962 book *Diffusion of Innovations* Everett Rogers built on the two-step flow.[13] Rogers identified distinct consumer groups and put forward the diffusion of innovations model, which claimed to map how things spread from group to group and diffused into the mainstream.

At the beginning, for any number of reasons, 'innovators' may adopt something, and a trend starts if this is then picked up by a supplementary group known as the 'early adopters' (his equivalent of opinion leaders). He argued that this trend can then diffuse further and become taken up by the 'early majority' and then the 'late majority' before, in some cases, moving into the most resistant sector, the 'laggards'.

The innovators and laggards are small groups in number. The bulk of people are in the early majority or the late majority, with the 'majority' sectors representing the mainstream. As a product, idea or fashion hits these majority sectors it ceases to become a trend; it becomes the norm. As William Higham explains in *The Next Big Thing*, 'Innovators may be the first to adopt a particular behaviour, but they are not necessarily the ones who create a *trend* for it. A trend occurs only when a new behaviour is adopted by a significant number of people.'[14]

The diffusion of innovations model is based on the idea that (in the majority of cases) for a product to enter the mainstream it must have moved along the path from innovators to early adopters to the majority. The model claims that these groups all have distinctive personality traits, and each group can 'influence' the group ahead of it, with the most important group in the model being the early adopter segment.

The innovator category starts things off and may pick up many things, passing only some of them on to the early adopters. The early adopters are therefore the key, as they are connected to both the segment that try things first (the innovators) and the early majority, where critical mass is achieved. As a result, the early adopters tend to be respected by all groups and have an ability to 'translate complexity into accessibility'.

Six degrees of separation and influentials thinking

The findings of Stanley Milgram's 1967 small world experiments have been used to further justify the idea of targeting opinion leaders or early adopters. Milgram found that a package could be sent from one individual and received by another individual (unknown to the sender) by making its way from person to person, from one group to another, via interlinking contacts.[15] The average chain length was six, and this experiment saw the phrase 'six degrees of separation' emerge (though this phrase did not come from Milgram). It is the idea that everyone on the planet is connected to everyone else by an average of six steps.

The world appeared to be a smaller place than people had previously imagined, results that were backed up in 2006 by another small world experiment conducted by Jules Leskovec and Eric Horvitz. They used Microsoft Instant Messenger data to construct a communication network in order to see if the small world phenomenon was relevant in an electronic age and published their results in a paper, 'Planetary-scale views on a large instant-messaging network'.[16] They used a month's worth of data and studied 30 billion conversations among 240 million people to map networks and connections. Their study found that the average shortest 'path length' in the Messenger network is 6.6 (median 6), just slightly more than the path measured by Milgram, but also found that longer paths existed, sometimes up to 29. Leskovec and Horvitz had taken Milgram's idea, scaled it across the planet and still come out with roughly the same result.

Whilst Milgram's small world experiments saw an average chain of six, the majority of the chains that did get completed passed through the same three individuals at the final stage. A small group were consistently responsible for getting something to the target and, no matter where the chain started, these individuals had a network of connections that was strong enough to enable the connections to be found and recruited as capable helpers.

The design of Milgram's experiments saw the three connected individuals who enabled chains to be completed sitting at the end of the chains. In *The Tipping Point* Malcolm Gladwell takes this finding and turns it around, reasoning that these people are important because they can use their 'social power' to connect people and facilitate diffusion. Indeed, Gladwell claims that no social epidemic can occur without their involvement and brings this to life in his idea of the 'law of the few'. In the same way that Katz and Lazarsfeld focused on opinion leaders or Rogers highlighted the early adopters, Gladwell claimed that involvement of hyper-connected influentials allows trends to spread and that without them a trend is dead.[17]

Dreams can come true – the traditional diffusion process

Various stories and examples from everyday culture seem to back up these ideas. It is argued that the long-established US utility clothing brand Carharrt became a fashion brand after first being adopted by US inner-city crack dealers in the late 1980s[18] and that Timberland hit the mainstream after being adopted by hip hop communities,[19] whilst in the early 1990s this sort of diffusion appeared to be responsible for some of the biggest dance music hits.

Before the internet, creators would make a dance music track and circulate test-pressings and 'white labels' amongst key scene innovators in the hope that they would adopt it. If an 'innovator' DJ like Pete Tong picked up on the tune and started playing it in clubs, this could then attract the attention of official record labels, which, rather than trying to prejudge quality and speculate on which tracks would be hits, found that watching club buzz was an easier way of identifying what to sign.

If something was signed by a label then the label tended to implement a pre-release seeding strategy. A promotional copy would be created, and in many cases this would be a double vinyl pack with all the different potential mixes. The Timelords (aka the KLF) summed up this process in their 1988 book *The Manual*:

> There are companies that specialise in mailing out records to clubs [home of the early adopters]. The clubs get the records for nothing and in return have to fill out reaction sheets, reporting back how each individual record is going down with their punters out on their dance floor. Lots of records are initially broken on the dance floor. It's all a cliché now, but it still works. A record is mailed out to the taste-making clubs four weeks before release as a white label or a fake American import (for DJ elitist credibility). Two weeks before release it gets mailed to the rest of the clubs and specialist dance record shops. James Hamilton starts writing about the track in his *Record Mirror* column.[20]

Club dance floors looked to the DJ to give them access effectively to the latest music. In *The Long Tail* Chris Anderson describes the role of a club DJ as a music filter: 'DJs surf the long tail of music and recommend the content their audience is most likely to gain satisfaction from – and dance to.'[21] In *How to DJ (Properly)*, Broughton and Brewster expand this idea, describing the DJ as an arbiter, 'the tastemaker, the discoverer, the champion of a new sound or scene. No musical movement can spread its wings too far without the DJ's approval.'[22] The innovator DJs started the momentum, but the DJs who followed them acted as the early adopters pushing the music to the early majority. Playing the track in question both created pre-release buzz and enabled the record company to use the feedback loop to gain insight into audience reaction, all helping to judge the likelihood of success and calculate how much money to put behind commercial release promotional support.

An extreme example of this was Gabrielle's *Dreams*, which sampled Tracy Chapman's *Fast Car* and originally had a limited release on Victor Trim's Victim Records in 1991. Over the course of the next two years DJs picked it up and buzz grew. After court cases and legal wrangling (involving production rights, ownership rights and use of the sample) the track was eventually re-released on Go! Discs, without the Tracy Chapman bit, though clubs and DJs continued to play the version that included the Tracy Chapman sample. *Dreams* entered at number two in the UK charts, at that point becoming the highest ever new entry for a debut act, and then went on to spend three weeks at number one on the UK singles chart in June 1993, the first hit of a reasonable career. Two years of buzz around both the track and the sample saw *Dreams* cross into the mainstream and launch the career of singer Gabrielle – dreams can come true![23]

Identifying and reaching out to influencers

It is therefore no surprise to see advertisers trying to target influencers in an attempt to get their brands featured in the conversation. However, identifying these people is not easy. In *The Lovemarks Effect* Malcolm Gladwell writes that finding the right voices is difficult, because: 'When they have social skills that don't correlate with education and income, they become a lot harder to find. Now you're trying to find them through their patterns and it's a much trickier game to play – it differs from domain to domain.'[24]

The growth in consumer conversation online and subsequent developments in social computing have in theory made both the identification and the co-option of influencers and brand advocates easier, though. Tools like PeerIndex and Klout seek to provide influence scores for individuals, and the more advanced social listening services can be used to show not only what is being said, but also who is talking and where (with some of them even able to map networks to show who is connected to whom and the size of audience that people posting about a particular topic have).

This space is developing quickly, but it is still early days, as Klout CEO Joe Fernandez noted when he responded to a question on social question-and-answer service Quora: 'There are some major challenges here. The amount of data and all the different ways people interact through social media is staggering. I am proud of what we have built at Klout, but know that we have barely scratched the surface in terms of really understanding the power and importance of influence online.'[25]

Nevertheless the marketing and advertising industry is relentlessly chasing influencers in a quest to gain the earned media grail. As a result someone deemed to be important (it's difficult to find everyone) may receive brand communication and invitations to participate, though as ever relationships are important. 'Dear Blogger' is less likely to work than an e-mail like: 'Dear Nick, hope you are well. I work at X and have been reading your blog recently. I saw you have been writing about X and thought you might be interested in this thing we are doing...'

Communication should also be optimized to make it as easy as possible for bloggers to post, people to tweet and so on. Again, maximize visibility by making sharing easy: no text embedded in images or massive files, just simple, straightforward, keyword-optimized information, wrapped in a personal and polite communication. Relationships help and so do incentives (though in the blogosphere cash payments tend to be frowned upon – gifts are nice, but the most motivating things for a blogger tend to be traffic, kudos and reputation). Following up is also important. Be sure to say thank you, and showcasing the efforts of fans by posting their content to brand social hubs both highlights authentic commentary to a wider audience and rewards the creators by driving traffic to their efforts.

Even though they may be hard to find, identifying and reaching out to a small number of topic influencers can aid product marketing effectiveness (either as part of a specific campaign or as a constituent of always-on efforts), and including outreach within the overall strategy may see products and messaging resonate or penetrate more deeply when compared to the approach of just pumping out paid media advertisements to a mass audience through broadcast channels. It is also an easy concept to understand, and as such the concept of embracing influentials is widely referenced with a selection of great stories (as opposed to theories – more on this later) that seem to show how influencer targeting works in practice. However, whilst it is not unusual to hear the phrase 'early adopters' bandied around in marketing and advertising circles, we need to remember that there is no such thing as a 'general influencer'. Innovators and early adopters vary by category (you may look to IT geeks for technology advice, but would you trust their opinion on fashion?), and the fast-changing nature of today's world also means that the status of 'influential' is not permanent, as things can change rapidly.

The paradox of choice and the changing role of the 'man in the pub'

In Rogers's world and years gone by, information was perishable (for example, the majority of newspaper readership happens on the day of issue), and in many cases access to certain products or content (like the white labels) was limited, so the 'man in the pub' or Gladwell's mavens or Katz and Lazarsfeld's opinion leaders were essential reference points in purchase decisions, as they were the gatekeepers of the required information. (The expert on cars would read and collate automotive information every day, whereas average consumers would be looking for this information only when they were in purchase mode and would therefore be drawn to the expert to provide opinion or access to the information they needed.)

The web has changed the dynamics of these relationships, though. The always-on archive provided by the internet and the ability to interrogate it using search engines has empowered the average consumer, as information is both persistent and searchable and can travel over much larger distances. Furthermore, e-commerce and digital products have improved accessibility. The consumer challenge now is not in knowing how to get something, but in knowing what to choose.

Indeed, people may like the idea of thoroughly researching every decision or option in their lives, but in reality they do not have the time or expertise to do so, and the explosion of choice offered by today's unlimited shelf space may actually have made things harder. Barry Schwartz writes in *The Paradox of Choice: Why More Is Less* that, 'as the number of choices grows further, the negatives escalate until we become overloaded... At this point, choice no longer liberates, but debilitates. It might even be said to tyrannize.'[26]

Chris Anderson explains in *The Long Tail* that 'More choice really is better, but we know that variety alone is not enough; we also need information about that variety and what other customers before us have done with those choices.'[27] Having impartial information from previous buyers therefore increases purchase confidence, and in *Groundswell* Li and Bernoff use examples from companies like eBags to highlight the additional sales and revenue that are seen to be consistently generated as a result of including reviews and ratings on websites and commerce portals.[28] People find comfort and security from reading the opinions of those who have used products previously, and in *Grown Up Digital* Don Tapscott cites another Forrester statistic, reporting that '96 percent of online retailers who offered customer ratings and reviews on their websites said it was effective for improving online conversion rates'.[29]

The 'man in the pub' can still give recommendations (and through the internet has a much wider potential audience), but the power of these recommendations is reduced when the receiver can verify or check them against the experiences of previous customers and other information that can be found through search engines (what is to be more trusted now, the opinion of an expert or the combined opinions of those who have previously purchased?). Indeed, the 'man in the pub' may now be more useful in sense-checking what people have found for themselves rather than by being the key adviser in the path to purchase. Additionally, product-specific online forums allow these experts to congregate, discuss and share their wisdom, with many of these discussions again showing up in search results. The internet has fundamentally changed the mechanics of peer-to-peer advocacy.

Katz and Lazarsfeld spoke of personal influence, the idea that information flows through social connections and that influence travels between people who know each other (either face to face or nowadays from 'celebrity' types who are known through the media), but, with all information searchable and a variety of experts accessible, rather than a single expert loving our product we now need lots of people liking it.

Flow of influence versus flow of information

In 1948 Lazarsfeld, Berelson and Gaudet wrote that 'it is important to distinguish between the flow of *influence* and *information*',[30] and there is a major difference between being provided with information and being persuaded to buy. Clicking 'Like' does not take much effort, whereas acting as a brand ambassador actively advocating a product takes far more effort. We therefore need to start thinking about different earned media strategies for different objectives.

Word-of-mouth advocacy around product recommendation is about having brand ambassadors act as sales agents, verbalizing the message and preaching the benefits of a product through conversation (either face to face or through their actions online). On the other hand, earned media sharing that works through clicking 'Like' buttons, e-mailing links and so on is about the people's network acting as content distribution agents. They are not creating the message; the sales pitch or brand message is delivered by the content that they are passing on.

Ambassador programmes and outreach initiatives that aim to spread influence by targeting opinion leaders and perceived early adopters are therefore difficult to scale meaningfully. Outreach needs to be crafted (events, content, samples, trial products, etc), and the potential for benefits to kudos and reputation is an important motivating factor in whether a recipient decides to participate or post. Receivers need to feel special, need to feel that they have some kind of unique insight or story (think of the way newspapers have traditionally fought each other for the scoop), so exclusivity and a personal touch encourage positive action from those receiving outreach.

Co-opting ambassadors or securing posts in response to outreach is therefore a product of relationships coupled with the right amount of outreach (not too little, not too much). The irony here, though, is that a well-executed outreach programme that gets people posting will invariably not have enough scale to see a message diffuse in a way that is noticeable for the masses (triggering rich-get-richer effects), but an outreach programme that targets a larger list of people is also unlikely to work, as the feeling of exclusivity or being in a 'special club' is lost. Outreach and ambassador programmes that target too many people may actually generate less coverage than the programme that went for quality above quantity!

Furthermore, outreach that aims to spread content should take a different approach to outreach that aims to spread product recommendation. Bloggers can be asked to post (embedding videos and the like), but Facebook fans, Twitter followers and YouTube subscribers can also be used to spread a piece of content. The approach is more of a 'Look at this and tell your friends' than 'Please persuade your audience that this is a product that they should buy.' Henry Jenkins *et al* write in 'If it doesn't spread, it's dead': 'The question now becomes, not how to reach the influencers, but how do individuals choose to behave in a [digitally] networked society and what kinds of social structures best support the spread of content?'[31] Indeed, as we saw in Chapter 5, the optimization of content using social sharing buttons improves the viral coefficient and helps content to spread even further. Anyone can spread to anyone else and, with enough noise, prominent blogs and the media may then feel that they have to write about it, as it's something that everyone else is talking about. The whole cycle starts to become self-fulfilling!

The different strategies required for generating *product* recommendation as against spreading *content* have led some to argue for using a model of paid, owned, earned, shared, splitting our general earned media category into two distinct components, one around product advocacy (earned), one around content spread (shared). This is an interesting idea, but the lines are not clear. If someone leaves a comment on a brand Facebook post that says 'OMG this is so cool!', it is both driving advocacy and helping to spread the message. Is this earned or shared (or both)? Using earned media as a catch-all to cover all the actions of the people's network is less confusing than trying to split everything between earned and shared, but the differentiation between always-on and campaign is useful here (long-term earned initiatives that aim to enhance reputation and drive advocacy will look and feel different to earned activity based around amplifying a specific piece of content or campaign).

How people are connected in a networked world and what it means for the spread of content

Interpersonal connections and how information flows in and between groups

The small world experiments have been used to justify the approach of seeking and targeting influentials, but in writing up the results Milgram and co-author Travers concluded by stating that: 'The study has uncovered several phenomena which future models should explain. In particular, the convergence of communication chains through common individuals is an important feature of small world nets, and it should be accounted for theoretically.'[32]

Since Milgram's time a number of scientific studies have tried to address this and empirically account for how networks function, both understanding how people are linked and how information then flows between connections.

In May 1973 Mark Granovetter published a much cited paper, 'The strength of weak ties'.[33] In accounting for people's connections Granovetter established that individuals have three types of interpersonal tie, defined by elements such as amount of time spent with each other, closeness of relationship and so on. He labelled these 'strong ties', 'weak ties' and 'absent ties', and following Bott in 1957, who referred to a 'close-knit' network versus a 'loose-knit' network, and Epstein in 1969, who used the terminology of 'effective network' versus 'extended network', Granovetter's paper was able to account for the way that groups and networks function.

In the study 'Getting a job', Granovetter looked at the effectiveness of sourcing employment through weak ties.[34] He found that it was about whom you knew rather than what you knew, as the majority of people in his study used their acquaintances or weak ties rather than their strong ties to find their jobs. (This is a foundation stone of professional social network LinkedIn, where both strong ties and weak ties can be formed and secondary and tertiary connections reached through the people users have connected with.)

Information flows freely amongst a group connected by strong ties (a family, a workplace and so on), so all members of the group will tend to have, or have access to, similar information (and all members of the group can also share with one another). An acquaintance is less likely to be connected to other members of a person's immediate group, though, so this weak tie gives access to information that members of the immediate group will not have – hence the number of people finding jobs through acquaintances rather than friends in Granovetter's study. Strong ties carry information reliably over short distances within specific groups; weak ties carry information less reliably, but when they do the information will travel across a further social distance as it passes from one group to another and then potentially on to another. Furthermore, in *Network Models of the Diffusion of Innovations* Thomas Valente noted that speed of diffusion varies according to the strength of tie: 'Diffusion reaches pockets of interconnectivity and spreads rapidly within these dense pockets, but slows between groups.'[35] Strong ties therefore help a message to spread quickly within a specific group, as everyone can spread to everyone else, whereas information spreads more slowly and less reliably via weak ties, as the connections are looser.

Distributing content and models for spread – diseases versus information

The flow of information between people and groups contrasts with the way that viruses spread. If we consider models from epidemiology we find that infectious diseases tend to be modelled using an SIR model. This calculates the theoretical number of people infected with a contagious illness over time, taking into account the number of people infected and the number of people recovered, with these factors acknowledging that a global epidemic can begin with just one person.

On 4 May 2000 the I LOVE YOU computer virus started in the Philippines and within nine days had affected 50 million computers across the world.[36] Four-year-old Edgar Hernandez from La Gloria in Mexico is believed to be the first person to become infected with swine flu in March 2009,[37] and within three months 74 countries had reported a total of 27,737 cases of swine flu and the World Health

Organization raised its pandemic alert to level six (significant transmission of the virus).[38] Whether in the real world or on the internet, viruses don't discriminate. You don't get a choice; you come into contact with it, you get it and you then pass it on to others (whether you know them or not). Outbreaks tend to start from a single person or small group, who then infect others, who in turn infect others. At each stage the virus can spread further because people are 'receiving' it and then 'sending' it to even more people.

In a paper in the *Journal of Theoretical Biology* in 2004, Dodds and Watts present 'A generalized model of social and biological contagion'. They explain that the SIR model of the spread of infectious disease is an independent action model where 'there is no interdependency between contacts; rather the infection probability is assumed to be independent and identical across successive contacts'.[39] You don't need to know people to infect them, and carriers have an equal chance of infecting anyone they come across. Social spread follows a different model, a threshold model, which asserts 'that an individual can only become infected when a certain critical number of exposures has been exceeded, at which point infection becomes highly probable' (our frequency of three idea again!). Furthermore, 'Threshold models are used to explain social contagion where individuals "decide" whether or not to adopt a certain behaviour based in part or in whole on the previous decisions of others.'

Adam L Penenberg thinks about this in *The Viral Loop*, writing that:

> Although the word 'viral' has been co-opted from epidemiology to explain how things spread from user to user over the internet, there is a stark difference between virality online and what is found in nature. Most people do not spread viruses intentionally. Over the web however, users enthusiastically disseminate ideas, information, opinions, links to blogs, photos, videos and web services.[40]

People can assimilate an idea or a message subconsciously (the low-involvement model). However, in order to amplify or spread a piece of content they have to process it actively and then choose to forward it, a process that could have a number of hurdles to overcome. Discoverability is the first step (overcoming the 'noise' and 'interference' highlighted in the Shannon–Weaver model). With

48 hours of video uploaded to YouTube every minute and so much content available online, how will people find your content, let alone feel compelled to share it? We then need to look at the psychology of sharing.

The problem with influentials theory

If people actually receive the message, they then need to decide whether to share it. The *New York Times* 'Psychology of sharing' research published in July 2011 found that there are five relationship-based reasons behind why people share:

1 'To bring valuable and entertaining content to others.'
2 'To define ourselves to others.'
3 'To grow and nourish our relationships.'
4 'Self-fulfillment.'
5 'To get the word out about causes or brands.'[41]

A consistent undercurrent in the responses from participants in the *New York Times* study was that people carefully considered what to share and how the act of sharing it would fit into the categories above. Indeed, this backs up separate findings by Frenzen and Nakamoto that 'The stronger the moral hazard presented by the information, the stronger the ties must be to foster information propagation.'[42] Just because people are linked doesn't mean that a message will travel; just because receivers receive a message doesn't mean that they even process it, let alone automatically become senders and pass it on. In *The Dynamics of Viral Marketing* Leskovec, Adamic and Huberman found that in the recommendation programme that they constructed for their viral marketing experiments 'not all people who accept a recommendation by making a purchase also decide to give recommendations' (even with incentives on offer for doing so).[43]

In Milgram's experiment a similar finding was also noted. The sample size was small, but even then had a fail rate of 71 per cent: the majority of chains did not get completed, demonstrating the weakness of weak ties. Under the right conditions and with the right content, messages can travel over significant distances through person-to-person pass-on, but this is the exception rather than the norm. Weak ties are essential if a message is to have the potential to scale and travel over a large distance, but chances of success diminish as time goes on and there are a number of factors to consider.

People can take precautions against contracting an infectious disease, but ultimately don't have much of a choice about whether they contract it and/or pass it on. In social areas senders and receivers do have a choice as to whether they engage with something and, as with the old-fashioned chain letters, they decide whether it is worth passing on (what do I gain in terms of kudos, reputation, 'friend points', etc?) and then whom to pass it on to. The receiver then goes through the same process and might also pass it on to further contacts, but then again might not.

Influentials driving trends makes a nice story, but it is a story rather than a theory and an explanation that tends to be applied after the event. Influentials explanations don't take into account all the things that could have happened but didn't, and Nassim Nicholas Taleb in *The Black Swan* advises that 'Understanding that little things can lead to large non-random events is more important than trying to look backward and understand the precise causes of large events (which you can't really predict anyway).'[44] Indeed, John Allen Paulos, Professor of Mathematics at Temple University, cautioned about the use of hindsight and reading too much into things that have happened in a 2011 article in the *New York Times*, noting:

> the role of coincidences, which loom large in narratives, where they too frequently are invested with a significance that they don't warrant probabilistically. The birthday paradox [the likelihood of two people in a group having the same birthday], small world links between people, psychics' vaguely correct pronouncements, the sports pundit Paul the Octopus, and the various bible codes are all examples. In fact, if one considers any sufficiently large data set, such meaningless coincidences will naturally arise: the best predictor of the S&P 500 stock index in the early 1990s was butter production in Bangladesh.[45]

After replicating the small world experiments at a larger scale on the web, Duncan Watts uncovered similar findings to Milgram and Travers around chains of connection. The only major divergence in the experiments' results was around influentials. After analysing the much larger dataset, Watts claimed that 'influentials are, at best, modestly better starting points [for chains or cascades] than average people', further noting that 'large cascades are driven by "easily influenced individuals influencing other easily influenced individuals", not "influentials influencing followers"'.[46]

Everyone in a network has a role in influencing everyone else, and it is not just down to 'special people' or 'leaders'. A forest fire analogy is often used to explain this. If the forest is wet then it doesn't matter how good the spark is; if the forest is ready to burn then anyone has the potential to start a raging forest fire. In the words of Watts, 'No one would think that you could attribute the size of the really large forest fires to something about the match that started them or something about the tree that was the first one to burn.'

The unpredictability of using earned media to spread content

With paid media delivery is guaranteed, but with earned media amplification (and all the complexity noted above) spread is hard to predict, let alone guarantee, especially as luck plays a part too. In explaining the unpredictability of 'black swan' or random events, Taleb evokes the concept of chaos theory, an idea that was first put forward by MIT meteorologist Edward Lorenz, who whilst investigating weather systems produced a mathematical model and found that 'small differences in a dynamic system such as the atmosphere could trigger vast and often unsuspected results'. He went on to devise a concept known as the butterfly effect, a term presented in a paper in 1972 entitled 'Predictability: does the flap of a butterfly's wings in Brazil set off a tornado in Texas?'[47]

Lorenz argued that in theory a butterfly flapping its wings in Brazil could start a tornado in Texas, but we would find it difficult to follow the chain of events leading from one to the other. At the same time Lorenz makes it clear that tornadoes in Texas wouldn't always be the result of the actions of a butterfly in Brazil. Essentially Lorenz's findings showed that with any complex system there is unpredictability and a vast array of potential results all depending on the effect of tiny and often random elements. This kind of thinking is useful when we are thinking about how content can spread through earned media or person-to-person sharing.

An interesting early example of the unpredictability of the spread of content online was seen in 1999 when Darude uploaded a new track, *Sandstorm*, to MP3.com.[48] Rather than making the track available to selected individuals and niche groups, Darude made his track available to the world, and internet users across the globe downloaded the track, radio stations and club DJs started playing it, and this in turn then prompted a record company to sign it up – the opposite of the traditional way in which dance records broke into public consciousness. Looking back, Seattle's *CultureMob.com* stated: '*Sandstorm* went on to become one of the biggest selling dance singles in the history of electronic dance music with global sales of over 2 million and featured on over 200 compilations world-wide... as well as receiving phenomenal radio support from national stations in over 70 countries around the world.'[49]

Sandstorm then went on to feature in Hollywood movies and across a range of major sporting events such as the ice hockey world championships and the 2006 Winter Olympics. *Sandstorm* became a regular at American football matches and was even used by Nike in its Kobe Bryant versus LeBron James advertisements.[50]

However, in an interview with Cory Casciato on *Westword*, Darude noted: 'I've realized that the "phenomena" that happened with *Sandstorm* was something more than just a piece of music that I created. The success snowballed, the track had a life of its own for some reason.'

He goes on to say that:

> The thing about *Sandstorm* (or any other big club record) is that there are so many variables in the making or breaking [of] a track that it's pretty impossible [to] just decide and make something like that. If only I knew why this track became the huge success it did, I'd surely make another or five more. There's luck, contacts, hard work, the cycle of the industry internationally – is trance hot? is house hot? is R&B hot? – direction of the wind, position of the moon, etc, etc...[51]

The internet can enable content to find its way to a huge audience, and influentials may have a role in highlighting it, but success is now even harder to plan – the hits can be (much) larger, but results are more unpredictable. Darude realizes that it's probably impossible for him ever to re-create or replicate the factors that were at work with *Sandstorm* and humbly calls the success of *Sandstorm* a 'happy accident'. He has had other hits and makes a living from DJing and producing, but nothing he has made has ever come close to the success of *Sandstorm*. Darude has been able to replicate the *Sandstorm* sound, but not the confluence of social factors that made *Sandstorm* such a huge hit.

Observation not influence?

In 1950 Harvey Leibenstein wrote about this kind of idea. In a paper entitled 'Bandwagon, snob and Veblen effects in the theory of consumers' demand' published in the *Quarterly Journal of Economics* he called this concept 'the bandwagon effect' and described:

> the extent to which the demand for a commodity is increased due to the fact that others are also consuming the same commodity. It represents the desire of people to purchase a commodity in order to get into 'the swim of things'; in order to conform with the people they wish to be associated with; in order to be fashionable or stylish; or, in order to appear to be 'one of the boys'.[52]

Indeed, in *The Next Big Thing*, William Higham describes the thinking of Danish sociologist Henrik Vejlgaard, who 'has questioned whether active personal influence is actually the most influential factor in the diffusion of many trends. He believes many trends today are spread more through consumers' observation of innovators or early adopters, whom he calls "trendsetters", than by the active persuasion of opinion leaders.'[53]

People follow other people, and in a world of infinite choice people don't know the best option or decision for everything. Mark Earls writes in *Herd* that the simplest view of this behaviour 'is that individuals face similar decision problems, by which we mean that people have similar information, face similar action alternatives, and face similar payoffs. As a result, they make similar choices.' This is a major driver for 'herding', and Earls also writes that 'We do what we do largely because of other people and our interaction with them.' So when looking at mass behaviour Earls posits that 'You have to go beyond describing individual experiences of a particular behaviour and see the interactions in a given population.'[54]

Generally this implies that widespread diffusion is more about observation and mimicking than it is about influence flowing from one person to another (though in certain categories, like fashion, trendsetters still have a key role to play). In today's world where everyone can see everyone else and find whatever information they need whenever they need it, then critical mass becomes more important than anything a 'special' individual may have to say.

Maybe, writes James Surowiecki in *The Wisdom of Crowds*, rather than early adopters having distinct personality traits, 'the only thing that made the early adopters of a product more influential was the fact that they were early, and so their actions were the ones that everyone who came after them observed'.[55]

The rich get richer: the influence of critical mass

Various experiments have tested this kind of concept. Whilst Milgram is most famous for his obedience experiments (which assessed how individuals respond to authority) and his small world experiments (which analysed how people are linked), he also looked at conformity and how people react to peer pressure. In a series of experiments known as the 'sidewalk experiments', Milgram placed a pedestrian on a busy street corner, had the person spend a minute looking up to the sky and recorded the actions of passers-by. He then had five people look at the sky from the same corner and finally expanded the group further so that it consisted of 18 people looking up. Milgram then analysed the results of passer-by reaction to each of the different-sized groups. He found that one person staring skywards resulted in one in 25 passers-by stopping to look too, five people looking up saw one in five passers-by stopping to join in, and when faced with a group of 18 people looking to the heavens nearly one in two passers-by stopped and also looked upwards. The more people who were doing the same thing, the more others were tempted to follow and join in themselves, resulting in even more people joining.[56]

Solomon Asch's famous conformity experiments in the 1950s again highlighted the inclination of people to bow to the social pressure exerted by the rest of the group. A volunteer was told that he was taking part in a visual perception test, but what he didn't know was that all the other participants were actors who had been lined up to give the wrong answers. A high number of the volunteers were then seen to answer in common with the rest of the group, regardless of their personal signal that was telling them that they were responding incorrectly.[57]

In many cases people will ignore their own signals in favour of those coming from the crowd, and the larger the crowd the more others are convinced to follow. Nassim Nicholas Taleb in *The Black Swan* thinks that 'The world in which we live has an increasing number of feedback loops, causing events to be the cause of more events (say, people buy a book *because* other people bought it), thus generating snowballs and arbitrary and unpredictable planet-wide winner-take-all effects.'[58] Importantly, he adds that 'We live in an environment where information flows too rapidly, accelerating such epidemics': 'the rich get richer'. This is so prevalent now that Duncan Watts argued in the *New York Times* in 2007 that Justin Timberlake could just be the product of 'cumulative advantage'![59]

Watts has run a number of experiments in this space, notably with Matthew J Salganik. The Timberlake/'cumulative advantage' theory was derived from the Columbia music experiment, an experiment that Watts, Salganik and Peter Dodds ran that aimed to establish whether the key determinant for a hit was actual quality or just the perception of quality. The 14,000 participants registered at the experiment's website were 'asked to listen to, rate and, if they wanted to, download songs by bands they had never heard of. Some of the participants saw only the names of the songs and the bands, while others also saw how many times the songs had been downloaded by previous participants.'

Songs that performed well in the independent world (where participants could not see download counts) tended to perform well in the worlds where download counts were visible, so quality did appear to be a factor in whether a song became a hit. However, the study also found that, in the worlds where the download counts were visible, the most popular songs were much more popular than in worlds where the download counts were not available and, interestingly, the most popular songs also tended to differ from world to world. Where the download counts were visible, people followed other people, and hits were therefore more unpredictable in worlds where social influence was at work or people could judge the opinions of those who had gone before.

The visibility and implied quality that come from featuring highly in rankings and charts really do seem to help the rich get richer. An interesting paradox is: 'On the one hand, by revealing the existing popularity of songs to individuals, the market provides them with real, often useful, information; but on the other hand, if they actually use this information, the market inevitably aggregates less useful information.' The best-selling single is not necessarily the best single. Creating something great does not guarantee success; other social influence factors need to come into play. (This can also be seen to apply on a range of social platforms. The content highlighted as most viewed then gets more viewed as a result.)

The role of mass media in earned media spread

In *Here Comes Everybody* Clay Shirky notes that 'News can break into public consciousness without the traditional press weighing in. Indeed, the news media can end up covering the story *because* something has broken into public consciousness via other means.'[60] Interestingly this seems to apply for bloggers too. They may not have responded to the original outreach, but if something reaches the point where everyone is talking about it then bloggers feel that they will lose kudos if they don't post about it too, which then further adds to the critical mass. This generates additional earned media coverage (and search engine results), though at this point they are posting as a result of what they are seeing rather than in response to an outreach request. Earned media prompts news coverage, which in turn prompts more earned media, which in turn can prompt further news coverage and so on.

This is well demonstrated by a YouTube video entitled *Why Every Guy Should Buy Their Girlfriend a Wii Fit*.[61] Recorded by Giovanny Gutierrez from his couch, it features a back view of his girlfriend doing Wii Fit hula hoop exercises whilst she wears just underwear and a T-shirt. As a result of this video his girlfriend, Lauren Bernat, has become known as the 'Wii Fit girl'. Lauren was not best pleased when the video originally started to spread and said on social conversation site Pownce (a screenshot since posted to her blog):

> Yes, he's in deep trouble. It's amazing what one little video can do and after reading everyone's comments it makes me want to tell some people off. I am not his sister (nor am I 12), this was not a publicity stunt (yes we work at an advertising agency but we do not have Nintendo as a client), I am not a whore or an exhibitionist (... had I known he was recording or that 120,000+ people would watch it on YouTube I would have worn something a little cuter).[62]

Since her posting on Pownce the view count has increased substantially, now standing at well over 10 million! Lauren has written about everything on her personal site in a section called 'Wii Fit journal', noting the different appearances that the video has made in mainstream editorial. It featured in the *LA Times*, on the front page of the *Miami Herald*, in UK newspapers like *Metro*, the *Sun*, the *Daily Mail* and the *Daily Telegraph*, on *Diggnation* and on other sites and publications across the world. *Why Every Guy Should Buy Their Girlfriend a Wii Fit* has also been remade and uploaded by other YouTube users and professional media organizations too.

A duplicate upload (where a user has downloaded and then re-uploaded the original clip) has almost 1 million views, but the remakes and reinterpretations are the things that really drive the additional coverage (particularly when the creator is a mass-media outlet). *Playboy* have uploaded a whole series of 'Wii Fit girl'-inspired YouTube videos, with different models trying different Wii games (all involve being filmed from behind while they gyrate and play). *Playboy Wii Snowboard* has 4 million views, *Playboy Wii Boxing* 2 million, *Playboy Wii Yoga* 1 million and so on. *Zoo Magazine* repeated the formula (model on Wii Fit board) and have attracted over 1 million views, *Obama Girl on the Wii Fit* has over 700,000 views, whilst other male users have filmed their partners using the Wii Fit in the style of the original Wii Fit girl. One user has even uploaded a clip of her boyfriend on the Wii Fit entitled *Why Every Girl Should Buy Their Boyfriend a Wii Fit*!

Nintendo worked hard on the Wii Fit party/Dooce blog collaboration, and it generated positive attention, but the 'Wii Fit girl' video has been viewed far more, has been repeatedly covered in mainstream media across the world and has been shared, remade and shared again by a wide range of other YouTube users. The 'Wii Fit girl' video is centred on a product demonstration, is easily re-enactable and is framed with a (sexist?) call to action to other men – 'Every guy should buy their girlfriend a Wii Fit.'

Dooce is an established blogger, and her Wii Fit party blog post was seen by a large, engaged readership, but the unofficial, unplanned *Why Every Guy Should Buy Their Girlfriend a Wii Fit* video seems to have spread much further. The accidental coverage far outweighs the officially organized outreach. In filming the 'Wii Fit girl', Giovanny Gutierrez became an 'accidental influencer', and it is highly unlikely that Nintendo would have been aware of him before, let alone considered him to be a key 'connector' for spreading Wii Fit information at scale, yet here he is creating a video about their product that has gained global attention and over 10 million views!

Official content can benefit in similar ways if it is set up in such a way as to allow users to reinterpret and remix it. Henry Jenkins *et al* agree in 'If it doesn't spread, it's dead', commenting that 'the repurposing and transformation of media content adds value, allowing media content to be localized to diverse contexts of use', further noting that 'those ideas which survive are those which can be most easily appropriated and reworked by a range of different communities'.[63] It's not enough just to make great content; it's a question of producing a piece of content that lends itself to conversation or reinterpretation – and the easier it is to share the better!

Radiohead commercialized this principle by actively encouraging fans to remix their tracks, first with *Nude* and then with *Reckoner*. They gave fans the opportunity to download the tracks in their constituent parts from download stores, with fans able to purchase the stems for bass, lead vocals, backing vocals, guitar, piano/strings and drums for the total price of a single track. User-generated remixes could then be uploaded to a special Radiohead remix site, and social network functionality was offered to enable fans to embed their remixes in social network profiles (again the easy sharing noted in Chapter 5).

The remix initiative around *Nude* saw 2,252 remixes submitted and 461,090 votes (with the *Nude* remix site getting 29,090,134 page views generated from 6,193,776 unique visits).[64] *Reckoner* is a harder track to remix (and the novelty factor of an initiative is always lower the second time), but it still generated over 1,000 user-generated remixes.

Furthermore, a Radiohead competition on Aniboom, where fans were encouraged to produce their own videos for tracks from the *In Rainbows* album, produced work of such high quality that Radiohead requested that the work of Virtual Lasagne (Clement Picon) become the official video for *Reckoner* (this was after a total submission of 900 storyboards and 236 video clips).[65] These initiatives drove earned media coverage of the tracks and the album, brought fans into closer contact with the band and even lowered official video production and remix costs, as the Aniboom project delivered UGC of sufficient quality to use as official versions.

Planning for earned media amplification

This kind of thinking is important in a world of earned media, as advertiser content has to compete for attention against all content, including other advertisements, publisher content, skateboarding dogs, people talking about their lives and so on.

Additionally, in *And Then There's This* Bill Wasik writes:

> If there is one attribute of today's consumers, whether of products or of media, that differentiates them from their forebears of even twenty years ago, it is this: they are so acutely aware of how *media narratives themselves* operate, and of how their own behaviour fits into these narratives, that their awareness feeds back almost immediately into their consumption itself.[66]

This is the threshold model again: users have to feel a need to share or pass on. Wasik additionally notes that: 'Where TV success was a passive thing, success in viral culture is interactive, born of mass participation defined by an awareness of the conditions of its creation. Viral culture is built, that is, on what one might call the *media mind*.'

Getting attention is one thing; generating sharing is quite another! The public can be willing participants, but they know how the game works. The good news, though, is that, unlike the case with classic chain letters, virality is not based on one huge chain of pass-on that can easily break. Indeed, the average chain length in the small world experiments was around six, and a mix of 'chasms', thresholds and luck all contribute to the fact that large cascades are rare.

Bakshy *et al* set out to analyse this thinking in their paper 'Everyone's an influencer: quantifying influence on Twitter', and again found that large chains of pass-on were unusual: 'Although Twitter is in many respects a special case, our observation that large cascades are rare is likely to apply in other contexts as well. Correspondingly, our conclusion that word-of-mouth information spreads via many small cascades, mostly triggered by ordinary individuals, is also likely to apply generally.'[67]

This research was discussed by a panel at BRITE, and Meghan Keane blogged some of the discussion, posting: 'Almost all "cascades" are small and shallow. A tiny fraction are large and propagate up to 8 "hops", or sharing. But even large cascades only reached thousands.'[68]

This solidifies the idea of using a different approach to generate earned media content spread. It is highly unlikely or improbable that reaching out to a small group of influentials alone will lead to a critical mass of attention around an idea or piece of content that will then spread further (blogger outreach can't be relied upon to deliver reach, and diffusion along weak ties takes time). For something to reach critical mass we need lots of activity in lots of different places at the same time. Instead of just targeting a small number of special people, the alternative approach, the so-called big seed approach, is around targeting a much larger number of potential firestarters. Mark Earls and Alex Bentley summed this up when they wrote in *Admap*: 'If things spread as we have described, it is fundamentally unpredict-able which of the many competing ideas will take off next... Place lots of bets to give yourself the best chance of starting a full forest fire – start lots of fires in lots of promising places.'[69]

Using the lots-of-fires approach to drive critical mass

When Frito-Lay launched their Facebook page in April 2011 they set a Guinness World Record for most 'Likes' gained in a 24-hour period – gaining 1.5 million fans in a single day![70]

When launching a Facebook page (or any kind of content marketing initiative) there are essentially two main strategic approaches. The first is to give the page a push with a bit of marketing and watch it grow organically over time as viral mechanisms kick in and word of the page or content is amplified. The alternative is to employ a big seed approach – if you don't know where fans are going to come from, you place lots of bets, give it a big push and then watch as the resulting critical mass drives coverage and rich-get-richer effects escalate.

To launch their Facebook page Frito-Lay used Facebook advertise-ments and sponsored activity in *Farmville*, which offered game players the chance to harvest sponsored crops that could earn exclusive virtual goods. Additionally, Frito-Lay created an event in Times Square, New York, with chefs giving live cooking demonstra-tions (streamed to the Facebook page), a sweepstake that offered Facebook fans the chance to win all the Electrolux appliances that were used at the event and on the following day then the offer of a coupon for a free bag of Frito-Lay products for 24,000 fans.

This plethora of different activity drove a huge amount of 'Likes' in a short space of time and created widespread coverage, which then drove even more people to like the page. The fan count has grown further since launch day, and the Frito-Lay Facebook page fan base now stands at 2.2 million fans. You can't know for sure what will work, so make a noise, do lots of things well and track accordingly.

Performance distribution – new paid media solutions to drive critical mass

Whilst blogger outreach takes time to build and struggles to scale, it can now be complemented by new (digital) advertising solutions that facilitate this kind of big seed approach. Instead of driving clicks and visits in the traditional way, this form of paid solution is about driving the visibility of content and amplifying user actions. It can be grouped under the heading of 'performance distribution'.

Performance distribution solutions are typically bought through a self-service interface or bid management tool and enable a big seed approach to be adopted, distributing content across relevant areas of the web. These solutions aim to create critical mass for initiatives in a short space of time, and the hope is that as a result they will generate additional impressions or views through earned media.

This type of approach is proliferating. For example, YouTube can be used to host owned media video content, but now offers advertisers a paid performance distribution solution called 'Promoted Videos'.[71] Advertisers buy keywords and, when users search for these, the advertiser's promoted video is shown at the top of the search listings, driving additional views and subsequent potential for amplification. There are also companies that offer guaranteed distribution, primarily around online video content. Companies such as GoViral, the Seventh Chamber or Unruly Media have a large network of partner sites and offer paid solutions to advertisers, with advertisers paying on a pay-per-view basis for a specified number of views delivered through selections of contextually relevant sites.

For the 2011 Super Bowl over 50 per cent of the advertisements were pre-released and seeded online using tools and offerings of this nature. Volkswagen's spot *The Force* was the main beneficiary, and in the four days prior to the Super Bowl it managed to accumulate 15 million views![72] Furthermore, whilst the Super Bowl is a US event, this Volkswagen TV spot became branded content across the rest of the world. The day before the Super Bowl *The Force* was the most viewed YouTube video in a huge range of countries including Canada, the UK, Germany, India, New Zealand, Israel, South Africa, Argentina,

Brazil, France, South Korea and Sweden. Views were delivered through initial seeding and then through person-to-person sharing across the people's network, with Unruly Media highlighting that the 24.1 million views on YouTube had been to a large extent driven by 733,000 Facebook shares. Aside from the fact that this advertisement succeeded in playing on two powerful emotional aspects (father helping son, and *Star Wars*), given the success of the seeding activity it was no surprise to see the advertisement ranking highly in post-Super Bowl advertisement analysis scores.

Aggregator services like BuzzFeed,[73] StumbleUpon,[74] Reddit[75] and Digg[76] also offer the chance for advertisers to pay to highlight content to their users (BuzzFeed's performance distribution offering is presented with the mantra of 'Launch – accelerate – measure'). Following the same kind of principle as search where a mixture of natural and sponsored listings are shown to users, the performance distribution offerings on these sites position sponsored content links amongst the natural links created and posted by users. Advertiser content is therefore highlighted in contextually relevant environments to the audiences that are most likely to be interested. There is no waiting for a piece of content to bubble up naturally; links are positioned prominently in the content lists on the 'Most viewed' pages.

The area of performance distribution continues to grow, and Facebook are active in this space too. We'll look at Facebook paid-for advertising in Chapter 8, but at this point it's worth mentioning the Facebook Sponsored Stories solution.

The dynamic nature of the Facebook news feed, coupled with the Facebook EdgeRank algorithm (discussed in depth in Chapter 3), means that only a percentage of friends and fans will see posts and updates that have been made. Performance distribution solution Sponsored Stories allows for 100 per cent visibility of advertiser-related actions and therefore helps to aid both awareness and engagement.[77]

There are seven different types of Sponsored Stories, but they are all variations on a theme. Advertisers either pay to maximize the visibility of updates they have made to their Facebook pages or pay to maximize the visibility of the actions of Facebook users on their pages or properties (actions are still posted to the feed as an organic impression, but are also highlighted through a Sponsored Stories advertisement site).

Sponsored Stories therefore maximize the awareness for advertiser content whilst potentially increasing the viral coefficient by encouraging more Facebook users to interact with advertiser content more regularly, which then improves EdgeRank standing. The Sponsored Stories advertisement unit needs no creative; it simply amplifies user or advertiser actions and, with fan engagement now being a key objective, it looks as though it will be a powerful weapon in the Facebook marketing armoury!

The final notable solution in this space is the suite of advertising options that Twitter offer with Sponsored Tweets, Sponsored Trends and Sponsored Who To Follow. Twitter's Trending Topics are a key feature of Twitter Search and drive attention for the most featured words or phrases on Twitter at any given moment in time. The Promoted Trend advertising product allows an advertiser to pay for a word or phrase to appear on this Trending Topics list, playing on user curiosity and prompting clicks, exploration and engagement. Sponsored Tweets allow for a tweet that has been previously sent to followers to be pushed out to selected target audiences who are not following, whilst Sponsored Who To Follow, where advertisers can pay for their account to be included as a sponsored result in official who-to-follow lists, is also interesting and paid for on a cost-per-follower basis.

Coca-Cola were the second advertiser to use Twitter advertisements (following Disney Pixar) and bought a Sponsored Trend and Sponsored Tweet during the 2010 football World Cup.[78] Carol Kruse, VP for Interactive Marketing at Coca-Cola, went on record with some of the results, telling the *Financial Times* that Coca-Cola had gained 86 million impressions and an engagement rate of around 6 per cent (significantly higher than the amount of people who click on standard online advertisements, which the *Financial Times* article claimed was 'approximately 0.02%'). The Coca-Cola figures are eye-opening, and other advertisers using Twitter advertisements seem to be similarly pleased with their results. These are in-demand executions!

The benefits of using paid to drive earned

Advertising executions such as Promoted Trends or Promoted Videos are not based on pushing content to a single person or small group of people and hoping that it spreads; they are about pushing content out at scale and positioning it in an environment where users are used to clicking links and submissions. This is a different approach to viral; it's about using strategies that push out to the masses in a way that creates the maximum opportunity to gain additional earned media impressions, hoping that these add up to something significant. (Activity will probably not 'go viral' in the general sense and reach millions of people, but it does have the potential to generate incremental reach through earned media, with this free amplification useful in improving overall campaign performance.)

The most efficient way to drive earned media amplification at scale (at least for distributing content, if not yet for products) is therefore to prompt it through critical mass built out using paid media. Indeed, the conclusion of an article in *Fast Company* magazine, provocatively titled 'Is the tipping point toast?', further expands on this thought: 'Cascades require word of mouth effects, so you need to build a six-degrees effect into an advertising campaign; but since you can never know which person is going to spark the fire, you should aim the ad at as broad a market as possible – and not waste money chasing "important" people.' And: 'If you really buy it [big seed thinking], the most effective way to pitch your idea is... mass marketing. And that is precisely what the wizards of Madison Avenue, presiding over our zillion-channel microniche market, have rejected as obsolete.'[79]

KEY POINTS

- Messages work harder when they are received via an expert – the two-step flow of communication.
- A key principle in generating earned media for brands is to help fans to talk more and ideally talk to a larger audience.
- Experts, fans or influentials can be identified and harnessed for outreach and CRM programmes (though this is not a precise science).
- There is little evidence to support the idea of 'general influencers'. People influence by topic.
- The internet has changed the dynamics of influence, but people still need help in managing choice.
- There is a big difference between the 'flow of influence' and the 'flow of information'.
- Content does not spread like a virus or disease.
- Content can spread quickly in connected pockets, but diffusion between groups is slower.
- The way that content spreads is unpredictable, as explained by Lorenz's chaos theory.
- Observation may be more important than direct influence.
- Critical mass is a key driver, with rich-get-richer effects widely seen.
- Consumers are aware of their role in content distribution.
- It is rare to have large cascades or chains. It is more likely there will be lots of small chains than one big one.
- Placing lots of bets is the best way of securing success and new paid media or performance distribution advertising formats can help.

Chapter Seven
Broadcast

TV versus AV: the medium is the message – different advertisements for different platforms

In his 1964 book *Understanding Media: The extensions of man*, Marshall McLuhan argued that 'all media have characteristics that engage the viewer in different ways... The medium through which a person encounters a particular piece of content would have an effect on the individual's understanding of it.'[1]

The same message is interpreted differently depending on the way it is sent, and brands are realizing the value of tailoring content so that it suits the delivery platform. Paid media messaging is adapted to suit the medium (30-second TV advertisements become five-second spots for pre-roll video advertisements, whilst extended full versions are available through the brand YouTube channel). If mediums all have characteristics that affect the perception of the viewer, understanding the mechanics of particular mediums can therefore enable paid media strategy to be created that becomes more effective or has more impact as it dovetails with audience usage.

A good example of this is around the development of multi-screen viewing. We now need to think in terms of audio-visual (AV) rather than TV, as live web streaming, catch-up services, video sites like YouTube, iTunes, Netflix and mobile viewing are all freeing broadcaster content from the TV set, and consumers can now view professional content across a range of devices. Furthermore, audience composition for a specific show or piece of content will vary according to the screen or device, and this potential for delivering incremental advertising reach is driving advertising spend in the online video medium. A recent piece of research in Spain showed how YouTube worked alongside TV to target 16- to 40-year-old men, the target audience for the launch of PlayStation game *God of War III*. Amongst other things the research found that 44 per cent of those exposed to the YouTube advertisements had no contact with the TV campaign and concluded that YouTube had delivered 9 per cent incremental reach on top of the TV impacts.[2]

Online video is more than just TV online, though. The traditional, lean-back, passive audience is still in evidence, but there is also a growing active audience. With the exception of competitions, reality show voting and the occasional foray into red button interactivity, TV is essentially a one-way medium with content broadcast to the audience, whereas online video has the potential to be two-way, with personalized advertisement targeting and users able to click on the advertisements or even share the advertising content with friends. The majority of online video advertising still seems to mimic its TV equivalent, though, tending to be just a shortened version of TV advertisements served in an interruptive way with low involvement. However, with a small nudge the proportion of the online video audience who are active viewers can be increased significantly.

VivaKi recently pulled together a consortium of advertisers and publishers to test alternatives to existing online video formats in an initiative called the Pool. After extensive research, a format known as the ASq was found significantly to outperform the standard pre-roll approach to online video advertising. Instead of automatically serving an advertisement, the ASq requires viewers to choose one of two or three advertisements to watch before their requested content is served (if no choice is made a default advertisement runs).[3]

In *Nudge* Thaler and Sunstein describe how 'Research shows that subtle priming influences can increase the ease with which certain information comes to mind' and 'If you ask people, the day before the election, whether they intend to vote, you can increase the probability of their voting by as much as 25 percent!'[4] In the same way that asking people about their voting intentions the day before significantly increased the chance of them voting, the action of asking which advertisement the viewer would like to see transforms the advertisement viewing experience from something that is done with low involvement to something that has to be actively processed. This simple idea meant that unaided awareness for advertisements delivered through the ASq format was found to be 288 per cent higher than for the standard automatic pre-roll, but the choice mechanics also created greater engagement, delivering click-through rates that were found to be 204 per cent higher than the pre-roll benchmark.

Returns from paid media can therefore be increased if we can understand how users consume content in different channels, but there are other things to think about too – we have an interlinked landscape of paid, owned and earned to consider!

Broadcast paid media as a content gateway

In a letter to *Wired* magazine in 1993 Nicholas Negroponte wrote: '*Wired*'s patron saint, Marshall McLuhan, was right about the medium being the message in the 1960s and 1970s. But that is not the case today. In a digital world the message is the message, and the message, in fact, may be the medium.'[5]

This speaks to the concept of paid, owned, earned and the idea that the creative execution or content is as important as, if not more important than, the channel selection and method of sending. As a result there are now different ways of thinking about broadcast paid media to deliver messages, alternative options to traditional frequency of three campaigns. Paid media can give the initial push and, if the content is appropriate, person-to-person sharing can then deliver the additional impacts. In Chapter 4, we saw this happen with the Guinness 'Anticipation' advertisement. The advertisement worked on two levels, addressing both active and passive audiences. The TV spot delivered a message, but also worked as a jumping-off point for those who wanted to have a deeper engagement with the brand.

Broadcast advertising can therefore act as a content gateway. Using SMS shortcodes on posters makes it easy for the audience to request further information, tagging TV advertisements with Facebook addresses can help grow the Facebook fan base, and in Japan quick response (QR) codes have long been popular, adorning everything from print advertisements to posters to ambient displays and TV advertisements.

Using QR codes to turn broadcast advertising into a gateway to content

QR codes are a type of mobile barcode and are regularly added to Japanese traditional media paid executions, with smart phone users then able to point their phones at the code in order to be instantly directed to a website or other mobile content.

In recent times QR codes have been rapidly gaining ground in the Western world too. In August 2009 Fendi included a QR code on their *Times* newspaper advertisement in the UK, and this practice has now been widely adopted. An interesting example in October 2010, again in the UK, saw retailer Tesco include a QR code on their posters for *Xbox Call of Duty: Black Ops*, which then led directly to a mobile sales page. Advertisers can track the visits generated in this way using analytics packages, and this Tesco poster campaign drove 3,325 interactions on day one.[6] This is useful information, especially when set against other metrics, as QR codes enable us to assess the effectiveness of the traditional media executions in driving traffic to mobile web pages (we can also track sales).

In Belgium AXA took things further still in March 2011 when they showed a TV advertisement that featured a prominent QR code. The AXA TV advertisement showed a mysterious film of a meteorite crashing into a house, but the story stopped halfway through, and a large QR code was then shown on-screen. Viewers were encouraged to snap it with their phones, which enabled them to watch the second half of the advertisement on their phone, with the advertisement film concluding with the opportunity to download AXA's latest app.[7] (They could have just used a TV advertisement to say 'Download the new app', but the approach taken was more engaging for viewers, made it easier to download the app and generated worldwide PR coverage.)

Indeed, Charles Leadbeater *et al* write in *We-Think* that 'The sociologist Erving Goffman, who studied advertising in the 1960s and 1970s, found that the most sophisticated advertisements were "half-finished" frames which invited the consumer to fill in the remainder of the picture.'[8] Digital content possibilities, particularly through mobile, are making this thinking easier to execute. Google's mobile app, Google Goggles, now even offers the potential for Goggles users to photograph any advertisement from any major US newspaper or magazine and then be taken to the relevant mobile website, regardless of whether there is a QR code or barcode included on the advertisement![9]

The potential for mobile fulfilment of traditional advertising is significant. People don't walk around with a pair of scissors in their pocket (or a printer), but everyone has a mobile. Allowing consumers to use their mobiles to interact with 'traditional' advertising to download coupons and vouchers or connect directly to commerce portals presents some powerful opportunities.

Checking in to TVs to gain mobile rewards

For the 2011 Super Bowl Foursquare created a 'special venue' that was accessible to anyone in the world. Foursquare 'wanted to give the entire Foursquare community a chance to gather together' and created a unique venue that was accessible to anyone in the world – Super Bowl Sunday.

A check-in to Super Bowl Sunday coupled with a shout for one of the teams ('Go Steelers' or 'Go Packers') rewarded Foursquare users with a special virtual badge that they could display on their Foursquare profile. It also unlocked a special offer from the NFL online shop, a promotional code that offered 20 per cent off selected merchandise. Foursquare effectively linked the TV event to mobile and web commerce by providing a combination of reward and coupon for those who were interested and watching the game – and with over 200,000 check-ins (from all 50 US states and 125 countries, including 13 check-ins from the Vatican) the Foursquare activity was an interesting sideshow to the main event![10]

Others are also thinking about the potential for fusing mobile and TV in this way. GetGlue is a mobile service that lets viewers check in to

TV shows, with users rewarded with badges for loyalty, and IntoNow have created a service that lets TV viewers 'tag' a TV advertisement with their phone. Sound recognition technology allows TV viewers to 'capture' or tag the advertisement using their mobile, and this can then be used as a real-world discount coupon in stores.

In April 2011 Pepsi Max were the first advertiser to use IntoNow, and in the United States offered coupons for free drinks from Target or CSV stores. The coupons were available to the first 50,000 people who tagged the advertisement, and IntoNow CEO Adam Chan told *Mashable* that 'This is the first time where consumers can close the funnel between a brand experience on a TV commercial right down to a real world drink you can consume.'

IntoNow launched on 31 January 2011, and by the time of the Pepsi Max promotion had 600,000 users producing 25,000 to 35,000 tags per day.[11] Five days after the announcement of the Pepsi Max promotion IntoNow announced that they had been acquired by Yahoo![12] – from start up to sale in just 12 weeks, perhaps demonstrating that this sort of technology is going to become more pervasive and more prominent.

Fusing TV advertising with mobile apps to create brand experiences

Honda used similar technology to bring their TV advertising for the 2011 Jazz to life. Based around a TV spot called 'This unpredictable life', the 60-second TV advertisement that was rolled out across Europe displayed 'a surreal rolling landscape to depict the journey of life, with all its potential ups and downs', and a range of characters was shown in the advertisement, from children to pets.[13] This advertising execution was more than just a TV spot, though, as it fused together TV and mobile, with the advertisement breaking simultaneously on TV and as an app in the iTunes store.[14]

This campaign saw paid media and owned media fully integrated, as when the Honda TV commercial was shown (or the advertisement was watched on YouTube) mobile users who had downloaded the Honda app could wave their smart phone when a preferred character was on-screen and then 'capture' that character on their handset (sound-syncing technology enabling everything to work). Once characters had been grabbed they could then be interacted with on the phone screen, expanding the narrative accordingly. *Creative Review* even revealed that the 'space monkey character can be made to dance by singing into your phone'!

The TV advertisement was tagged with both 'Search: Honda Jazz' and 'Download the iPhone app to catch the characters as they escape from the screen'. By fusing the broadcast advertisement to a mobile app, viewers were encouraged to engage, and the active audience for the paid media advertising was enlarged accordingly. As one internet commenter wrote, 'That was so much fun to wait for an ad to air and then catch things from it!!! Amazing. Had to watch the whole of *Gypsy Weddings* to do it though!' The advertisements function as a standard brand spot for the passive audience or as a more immersive experience for the active audience who want to participate.

TV driving always-on social hubs

Mass, traditional advertising can now also act as a gateway to an owned media social hub. There are obvious benefits to this. As Jon Burg wrote on his *Future Visions* blog, 'Social is a connective tissue. It ties your upper funnel branding into a real, interactive, human engagement. It makes it real. And at the very least, a social call to action in a branding spot opens the window for community and CRM.'[15]

Indeed, 2011 Super Bowl advertising saw advertisers trying to harness this and, whilst no advertiser featured a social call to action on their Super Bowl TV advertisement in 2010, by 2011 the practice was widespread. Budweiser, Chips Ahoy, Pepsi Max, Skechers, Lipton Brisk and Sony Ericsson Xperia were just some of the brands to tag their 2011 Super Bowl advertisements with Facebook page addresses.

Advertisers also used 2011 Super Bowl spots as a platform to drive earned media conversations. Over 50 per cent of 2011 Super Bowl TV advertisers seeded their advertisements online before Super Bowl Sunday, advertisers like Mercedes-Benz and Budweiser created wide-reaching socialized campaigns, and a number of advertisers opted to use celebrities with large social followings. (Chrysler and Lipton Brisk benefited from Eminem tweeting a link to the advertisements he starred in, whilst Best Buy saw Justin Bieber tweeting about his advertisement to his 8 million Twitter followers and so on.) Audi even included a Twitter hashtag at the end of their TV advertisement, actively encouraging viewers to tweet using the hashtag '#ProgressIs'.

The Super Bowl is a unique advertisement vehicle, but the idea of using TV to drive social hubs is now common practice for many brands. In a number of cases this goes further than just tagging the TV advertisement with a social address. TV creative is being developed with one eye on social in order to facilitate easy extension on to Facebook and social platforms. After Compare the Market launched their Compare the Meerkat spoof spin-off, the central meerkat character (Aleksandr Orlov) grew a Facebook fan base of over 750,000 fans, seeing the main brand smash business targets at the same time. This has inspired a range of others to follow the route of 'TV advertisement with quirky central character will allow campaign to work on Facebook too'. Talking animals, caped Mexicans and the like now regularly adorn our screens in TV advertisements that are made with social media amplification in mind. The TV advertisement drives to the character's social presence, which can then be optimized. (The ubiquity of Facebook, though, means that consumers expect brands to have Facebook pages, so featuring the page address prominently on the TV execution and telling viewers why they should visit is arguably better than just passively showing a Facebook logo or Facebook address.)

How simultaneous channel viewing is creating an amplified present

A number of studies have reported on the fact that consumers are not just using different channels, but are consuming different channels *simultaneously*. In March 2010, the European Interactive Advertising

Association (EIAA) Mediascope research found that 'A rise in laptop ownership is driving greater media convergence with 36% of Europeans using the internet whilst watching TV',[16] all creating what Atlanta-based Moxie Interactive have coined 'the amplified present'.

This passive–active audience dynamic was clearly visible when the founder of online diamond seller Diamondgeezer.com appeared on BBC show *Dragons' Den* in 2008. *Dragons' Den* allows entrepreneurs to pitch for investment from a panel of wealthy dragons and, as Diamondgeezer.com founder Clive Billing started his pitch, the Diamondgeezer.com site suffered an equivalent of the Stephen Fry Twitter effect, receiving so much traffic that it crashed and fell over.

Coincidentally, a blog by an East London blogger also uses the title *Diamond Geezer* (used purely in the slang context rather than the more literal sense) at Diamondgeezer.blogspot.com.[17] His blog posts usually concern London events, but Diamond Geezer the blogger took time out to record the traffic uplift he received as a result of people mistakenly visiting his blog after the Diamondgeezer.com founder appeared on *Dragons' Den*. Diamond Geezer the blogger noted that over the course of three hours he received an additional 3,000 visits compared to his normal traffic – '9:24pm My (ping) blog (ping) is (ping) currently (ping) averaging (ping) about (ping) five (ping) visitors (ping) a (ping) second (ping).' On the following day Diamond Geezer the blogger told me he received a further 2,200 visits, with additional traffic continuing, albeit at lower levels, across the week, and this traffic uplift to the *Diamond Geezer* blog is seen, in real time, whenever this episode of *Dragons' Den* is rerun on cable or satellite channels. Diamond Geezer the blogger can deduce the TV schedule just by looking at his blog analytics and traffic statistics!

Hitwise noted that across the week of this broadcast the phrase 'diamond geezer' was the second-fastest-moving search term in the UK, with traffic increasing '28 fold the day after the program was aired' to the Diamondgeezer.com (correct) website. Hitwise also noted the significantly increased traffic to Diamondgeezer.blogspot. com over this period.[18] Interestingly, at no point did the TV broadcast tell people to go online; the referencing of a website name was all it took.

The amplified present is now seeing simultaneous conversation and sharing too. Broadcast happenings and events in the real world now echo in the online conversation, in real time. Indeed, a new study from Motorola's Mobility unit has found that '42% of TV viewers have exchanged emails, had instant message chats or used a social network to discuss a TV program at the same time they were watching it. Another 22% within the group said multi-tasking via social media is a regular part of their viewing experience.'[19] This will only become more prominent as TVs become internet enabled and tablet computing proliferates.

TV driving conversation on Twitter

Twitter Trending Topics and Twitter Search particularly demonstrate how mass media drives real-time conversation. Social influence at the movies has become more instantaneous through the use of Twitter (Twitter research from Crowd Science in September 2009 showed that 8 per cent of their sample had tweeted live from a cinema *during* a film[20]), and we can also witness TV driving conversation, with one of the first examples of this seen in 2008 during the Eurovision Song Contest. Darren Waters noted that the broadcast saw 'Twitter being used to extend the experience of watching the event together' and further wrote on the *BBC Newsdot.life* blog: 'Arguably all Twitter did was turn an old fashioned mass participation event, viewing Eurovision, into the digital age.'[21] He concluded by writing 'Twitter plus TV = informed viewing' and stated he was 'excited by the potential'.

Fellow BBC blogger (at the time) Robin Hamman also wrote around this combined Twitter and TV Eurovision 2008 experience after participating in the unofficial Eurovision party on Twitter. At the end of his post he offered some interesting thoughts:

> Broadcasters and content providers should take note. What I participated in last night would be almost totally invisible to most viewers. Most people don't know how to find and track conversations on Twitter... but being part of an audience community is a powerful experience for participants and a valuable brand building tool for broadcasters and other content producers. We need to make it as easy as possible for ordinary users to find and participate in

conversations around our content. The way to do that isn't to duplicate the tools and services that are already out there, but to create interfaces, windows, that let people see and join into the conversation.[22]

The subsequent development of Twitter Search and Twitter Trending Topics has made this significantly easier.

In 2009 Twitter started to scale, and Eurovision really took off on Twitter, fuelled by well-followed celebrities getting involved, for example @Wossy (British TV presenter Jonathan Ross) tweeting randomly about every act ('#Eurovision Helloooo Ukraine'). Nine of the top 10 Twitter Trending Topics were Eurovision related as the show progressed, and free Twitter tool Twist showed 9.95 per cent of all tweets across the world included the word 'Eurovision'.

This kind of amplified present or Eurovision effect is now seen more widely. South Korean boy bands like Super Junior regularly hit the Trending Topics list when they appear on TV, the football World Cup match between Holland and Japan generated 3,283 tweets per second, and shows like *The Apprentice* or *The X Factor* consistently feature in Twitter's Trending Topics when they are on air. (The 2011 UK version of *The Apprentice* even saw one episode manage to get the words 'Hip Replacement', 'Bambi', 'Zimmer', 'Covered' and 'Coffin Dodgers' into Twitter's Trending Topics – a long story...[23])

Through Twitter Search and Twitter's Trending Topics lots of people can therefore talk to each other at the same time, and the world can watch. This is not just changing how programme makers are creating content, but changing release schedules for both movies and event TV. Movies are now released on the same day across the world, and the last episode of *Lost* was screened across Europe at 5 am (so that it was shown at the same time as it was shown in the United States).

Another UK syndication of US TV saw the BBC screen Super Bowl 2011 in the UK. The BBC promoted the hashtag #bbcsuperbowl on screen during their coverage, and this encouraged British Twitter users to tweet, with the #bbcsuperbowl hashtag managing to become the second most used term on Twitter during the game build-up and early plays (UK tweeting died down as UK time passed midnight and people headed for bed).

The bulk of Super Bowl tweeting is driven by the US audience, though, and in February 2009 the *New York Times* created a Twitter visualization that showed the location and frequency of commonly used words and phrases in Super Bowl-related tweets as the game progressed. There were tweets about the game and tweets about the half-time show ('Springsteen!'), but throughout the game Twitter users were seen to be tweeting about 'ads' and 'commercials' too.[24] The same phenomenon was witnessed in 2010, with Kevin Weil from the Twitter Analytics team highlighting on the *Twitter Blog* that the most tweeted-about brand was Doritos ('for the minute following the ad, [Doritos] related tweets were 19% of all tweets we saw, eclipsing even the chatter around the Super Bowl itself for a brief period').[25] The 2011 Super Bowl was even larger on Twitter, with a peak of 4,064 tweets per second,[26] surpassing the World Cup record for a sporting event (though not surpassing the levels of Japanese who tweeted 'Akemashite Omedetou Gozaimasu', or 'Happy New Year!', to each other as 2010 moved into 2011[27]), and again the most tweeted-about brand was Doritos.[28]

The TV shows that reach mass audiences therefore become even more important, especially live-event TV like *American Idol*, *The X Factor* or sports coverage, where there is a social imperative to watch the action as it happens. The 2011 Grammy awards got their highest audience for a decade, and as Sue Unerman wrote on her personal blog:

> Would TV pundits and internet soothsayers have predicted that Facebook and Twitter would help to increase ratings and dissuade the audience from waiting for catch up TV or Video On Demand? I can't remember hearing any predictions along those lines. But that's exactly what we've arrived at. If you miss the live show, you miss the best of the chat.[29]

Twitter conversation driving TV viewing

Another thought-provoking example came in February 2011 when HBO in the United States reran Howard Stern's 1997 film *Private Parts* and Howard Stern himself decided to use Twitter to give a live, DVD-style, running commentary about the film to his Twitter followers.[30] 'Private Parts' became a Twitter Trending Topic and, rather than the TV content sparking Twitter conversations, it was Howard Stern's tweeting that drove the audience for the TV broadcast. Again viewers needed to watch it live or miss out on the chat, and one Twitter user summed it up when he simply tweeted 'It's 78 and sunny in LA but @HowardStern's Private Parts Twitter commentary has me glued. Damn you Stern!'

Adam Bain, President of Advertising Sales at Twitter, also tweeted during the live Howard Stern commentary, sending a call-out to TV bosses: 'Every TV producer should be taking note of what @HowardStern is doing live w Private Parts+Twitter. He's new but already broken new ground.' Howard Stern's use of Twitter turned a rerun of a 14-year-old film into must-see, event TV, with the TV audience significantly boosted by the attention of Twitter users. This type of real-time conversation alongside TV content can work for brands too. Perhaps the most astute example of using social around the 2011 Super Bowl TV advertising came from Amazon, a company that weren't even on TV during the game!

Throughout Super Bowl 2011 the Amazon MP3 account on Twitter (@amazonmp3) tweeted live, telling 1.5 million followers the track name and artist of the music that was being used in advertisements and TV montages, including an Amazon MP3 download link for the music being used. Before viewers could even ask themselves what the track was, @AmazonMP3 had tweeted the details of the song and given their followers the opportunity to make an instinctive purchase.[31] Amazon were therefore using Twitter to provide a service, but also to drive sales.

Tom Cunniff wrote: 'This may be the most spectacularly productive use of social media I have ever seen. Commercial break after commercial break, Amazon successfully converted a dozen or so $3million dollar TV buys for other brands into an engine for Amazon e-commerce.'[32]

Robin Sloan on the *Twitter Media* blog suggested that this sort of live tweeting 'turns classic web search on its head by pre-emptively answering viewers' questions', and further stated: 'I think songs in Super Bowl commercials are just the start, this is a technique that can be bent towards plenty of other purposes.'

Reappraising traditional TV planning – how Yeo Valley harnessed the amplified present

Instead of pursuing equally flighted bursts of frequency of three activity, paid media spend can now polarize around broadcast content where the enjoyment comes from participating and watching it live or in real time. These are the programmes to target if we want to stimulate simultaneous social actions and generate conversations, the people's network amplifying our message and delivering additional impacts accordingly.

Impactful mass media is still the fastest way of creating attention or conversation around our messages, and prominent paid media positioning can therefore give a significant boost to earned media. This may just be the echo of the paid media, rather than lasting advocacy, but it's free coverage that can drive action (which may then have deeper effects over the long term).

In the UK contestants' names, judges' names and headline acts regularly appear in the Twitter Trending Topics list, but during the 2010 series of *The X Factor* an advertiser ended up as number one Trending Topic in the UK and number two on the Trending Topic list worldwide!

Yogurt maker Yeo Valley decided to take the first advertisement spot in the first break of the first studio-based *X Factor* show of 2010. However, instead of running a standard 30-second advertisement, Yeo Valley ran a full-length, two-minute version of their latest advertisement. This was the first time that the advertisement had been seen on TV, and it featured rapping farmers appearing alongside their machinery and their animals ('Check out Daisy, she's a proper cow, a pedigree Friesian with know-how' and so on).

The TV advertisement finished with a line telling viewers to 'Search Yeo Valley', and this is where things get interesting. The advertisement ran once a week, only ever appeared in *The X Factor* and, in the same way that *Dragons' Den* drove visits to the Diamond Geezer website, according to Google Insights for Search every time the Yeo Valley advertisement appeared on TV people went online to search for it, searching for both 'Yeo Valley' and 'Yeo Valley advert'. These searches invariably took internet users to the (owned media) Yeo Valley YouTube channel (called *YeoTube*), where they found the TV creative that they could watch again or share with friends.[33]

There was a huge spike in searches around the first appearance of the TV advertisement and, whilst subsequent spikes were lower, it is still easy to see when the advertisement was screened by looking at the Google data. As a result YouTube views grew consistently over the following weeks, with people even leaving comments on the YouTube upload asking for the Yeo Valley track to be made available for download from iTunes (something that Yeo Valley were then able to arrange).

Aside from on-pack promotion and driving a promotional tractor around central London, the weekly TV advertisement was the main manifestation of the campaign. The campaign model saw Yeo Valley (over?-) invest in content and then focus media spend on delivering the single high-impact TV advertisement in *The X Factor* each week, which then drove searches and conversations. Instead of delivering an equally weighted campaign across a different range of stations that aims to achieve an average advertisement exposure frequency of three, it may now therefore be more effective to deliver one very impactful spot that then drives conversation and further engagement. The concentration of paid media maximizes the impact of the creative, maximizes the resulting searches and conversations, and in this case saw Yeo Valley's Live in Harmony campaign manage to deliver a 15 per cent year-on-year uplift in sales.

Crowdsourcing the creative to build pre-launch buzz

Involving the public in the advertisement creation process can also generate beneficial earned media conversation and buzz around a forthcoming advertising campaign, and this was the thinking around T-Mobile's 'Life's for sharing' flashmob activity.

T-Mobile did not start the flashmob idea. That honour seems to belong to Bill Wasik, who created a series of New York City mobs in the summer of 2003. In explaining the mobs he wrote that they harnessed a blend of 'the joining urge' and 'scenesterism' (where the appeal of cultural events is derived from the social opportunities rather than the work itself), but that he also believed that the flashmob concept was a 'vacuous fad' and 'a metaphor for the hollow hipster culture that spawned it'.[34] Wasik stopped organizing mobs suddenly, and in his write-up of the events of that summer he stated that he always felt that advertisers appropriating the flashmob trend would result in its death knell – the Ford/Sony Fusion Flash Concerts of summer 2004 were cited by Wasik as an example.[35] The flashmob did not die here, though; the scaling of earned media brought it back with a vengeance.

The difference between the Wasik-organized mobs and the new versions was in the way that they were put together. The original mobs had no apparent purpose and were essentially gatherings of random individuals organized through viral word of mouth – the concept itself was the only thing that united the group. Recent versions also tended to have little or no pre-promotion and were again designed to surprise onlookers, but the core of the mob was pre-selected and choreographed using advertiser money. These mobs were instigated with the intention of creating earned media publicity. Unlike the Ford/Sony Fusion Flash Concerts, which were all about the event itself, the new mobs were designed to provide a brand experience for those present, create footage and images for use in traditional advertising and, most importantly, aid brand awareness and cut-through by driving conversation and earned media around the brand. The effectiveness wasn't judged by how many people attended the actual event; it was judged by how large the conversation was afterwards.

Flashmobs drove headlines and links that persisted in search engine results (aiding content visibility and site ranking), and this is what saw T-Mobile resurrect the flashmob in 2009. T-Mobile used the mob events to develop owned content that could be used in paid media advertising, on owned media destinations and as conversation currency.

Writing in *AdMap* in February 2010, Gareth Ellis from Saatchi & Saatchi notes that T-Mobile sought to 'broaden appeal and attract high value customers who wanted a relationship, not just cheap price'.[36] The solution was seen to be in developing a stronger brand and brand positioning, and activity was designed to support the idea of 'Life's for sharing', 'a cultural mission' that would 'unite the brand, the employees and our prospective customer base'. (Again, this is the idea that paid, owned, earned marketing is more than about just communicating with consumers; it has wider implications across the business.)

At 11 am on 15 January 2009, music started on London's Liverpool Street Station speakers, and one person started dancing on the concourse. This single person was joined by more and more official dancers and members of the public until there were hundreds dancing. Onlookers phoned and texted friends, and recorded the event on their mobile phones, with many going on to upload content to the web in the aftermath. News organizations covered the Liverpool Street mob as real news, and then 36 hours later a full-length TV advertisement of edited footage was shown on national UK TV. (At the same time a 'Life's for sharing' YouTube channel containing Liverpool Street footage was launched.)

Content captured at the event was used as the basis for advertisements, with TV, outdoor, online, radio, print and point-of-sale executions all using images, video and audio from the Liverpool Street gathering. Outtakes and other video content continued to be uploaded to YouTube and, as the original content spread, more and more people were driven to the 'Life's for sharing' YouTube channel. The campaign content drove traffic and subscribers for the always-on YouTube hub, which facilitated sharing and interaction through the numerous comments left.

The public performance effectively became the advertisement, but the process of making the advertisement was just as important in driving buzz and conversation. People can't resist talking about an event like the Liverpool Street flashmob. At the time of writing *Dance*[37] has had around 30 million views on YouTube and has led T-Mobile's 'Life's for sharing' YouTube channel to be one of the most significant commercial YouTube channels. Most importantly for T-Mobile, *Dance* contributed to a year-on-year sales increase of 52 per cent, with 143,000 new customers (80 per cent of these spending more than £30 per month). Store footfall and brand consideration increased significantly, and the debut advertisement break in *Big Brother* saw the TV audience rise by a further 500,000!

Marketing focused on events that would get people talking and living out the mantra of 'Life's for sharing' and, in the words of Gareth Ellis, 'The brand might create the events, but in the end, the events would create the brand.' The events reverberated through the T-Mobile organization, with Ellis noting: 'It began as a desire to find a more inclusive and differentiated position for T-Mobile, but "Life's For Sharing" soon took on a life of its own – a meme that shaped not just the brand strategy, but also the marketing strategy, the brand communications model, the media strategy and even how the work was produced.'

The success of *Dance* has inspired further T-Mobile activity of this type, such as *Sing* (mass karaoke in Trafalgar Square) and *Welcome Home* at Heathrow Airport, with both again forming the backbone of the creative for traditional paid media advertising. *Dance* has also, unsurprisingly, spawned a host of copycats across the world, from a Belgian TV channel running a flashmob in Antwerp Station, to HTC running a flashmob at Raffles Place in Singapore, to SVT2 in Sweden running a mob in an IKEA store to promote the new series of *Skal vi Danse*.

The advertiser-funded flashmob has been used again and again, popping up on beaches, at transport terminals, in food courts and anywhere else that people naturally gather – though few have the budget to turn these events into mainstream TV advertising. Wasik believed that the flashmob concept would eventually eat itself, and we may be reaching this point for the advertiser-funded flashmob too. Brands continue to use this style of execution, but the novelty (and level of associated earned media conversation) seems to be wearing off, and at some point (as there was with Wasik's original flashmobs) we may see a backlash against the concept.

Paid media advertising can drive content initiatives, and content initiatives can both provide content for and amplify the impact of paid media TV creative. Whilst the look and feel need to be consistent across all platforms, 'trans-media' approaches can be used to build out character stories and plot lines across different media channels and content elements. Everything works together, and this style of thinking can effectively provide content for both passive and active audiences accordingly. As Aristotle said, 'The whole is greater than the sum of its parts'!

KEY POINTS

- Different mediums need different formats.
- We now need to think about AV not just TV.
- Large numbers of people now consume two mediums at once – especially TV and internet or mobile.
- Paid media messaging needs to address both active and passive audiences.
- TV and broadcast media can act as a content gateway, and social media addresses, QR codes and so on can help to fulfil.
- Assets need to be aligned, and channels can then feed off each other.
- Paid media planning should now consider how to deliver the message *and* drive owned and earned media.
- Pre-seeding and crowdsourcing can help drive buzz.
- Events can drive earned media conversation and the volume of active audience for the TV advertisement.

Chapter Eight
Performance

Gorillas going unnoticed – the importance of relevance

In 1907 Austro-Hungarian physician Rezső Bálint documented his observations on a patient who was struggling with perception and vision after suffering brain damage to the posterior parietal lobes. This work is widely known and discussed in neurological circles, and the condition Bálint's syndrome came out of these studies. Husain and Stein published a translation of Bálint's work in 1988, including: 'It is a well-known phenomenon that we do not notice anything happening in our surroundings while being absorbed in the inspection of something; focusing our attention on a certain object may happen to such an extent that we cannot perceive other objects placed in the peripheral parts of our visual field.'[1]

The thinking in this work comes together around the concept of 'inattentional blindness', and this has been the basis for further studies. DJ Simons and CF Chabris from the Psychology Department at Harvard University used Bálint (and other experiments by Neisser and Mack)[2] as reference points when they ran their own series of experiments on inattentional blindness in 1999.[3] In the aftermath they published an enlightening paper about basketball players and gorillas entitled 'Gorillas in our midst: sustained inattentional blindness for dynamic events'.[4]

The experiments were based on asking volunteers to stand by a group of basketball players and watch them passing to each other, counting and recording the number of passes. In the middle of the exercise a gorilla-suited woman walked into the midst of the players and after a few seconds walked out of the game again. In the question-and-answer sessions afterwards, 46 per cent of the 192 observers had failed to notice the gorilla! Observers were so preoccupied with counting passes that they neglected consciously to register a highly visible, yet ultimately irrelevant, interruption.

In *The Hidden Power of Advertising*, Robert Heath references a 1988 study by Langmaid and Gordon, who 'used hypnotism to explore the idea that we absorb far more from advertising than we think we do... What was discovered was that even though most respondents could recall only a trace of an ad when conscious, they recalled *almost every detail* when hypnotised.'[5]

Heath then surmised that 'Advertising can work at a non-conscious level. It *does* have some sort of hidden power which enables it to influence us without our realising it.' (This was also reflected in the ideas of Herbert E Krugman around low-involvement processing, discussed in Chapter 1.)

The low-involvement models discussed earlier would imply that the counters had some cognition of the gorilla, but their noticing had not been actively registered or enough to distract them from the task in hand – and this is an important point. In traditional media, low-involvement processing has been a useful way of building long-term associations (as the hypnotism experiment showed, it registers somewhere in the brain). However, online, and particularly at the moment of searching, this is not enough. There is an immediacy; the person wants the information now and in many cases is ready to click and instantly purchase. To fulfil this need and capture attention the advertising message has to be instant and relevant; the user has to be actively engaged straight away or the opportunity is missed.

How Google advertising taps the feedback loop to reward relevance

The Google AdWords system is based on an algorithm that aims to ensure that the most appropriate advertisement appears in the top spot at the moment of searching – the opposite of the mad dotcom speculation or gorilla creation that was so evident at the end of the 1990s. (The 2000 Super Bowl, the so called 'Bubble Bowl', saw 17 'internet companies spend an average of $2.2million per 30-second spot', with over $40 million spent by dotcoms on TV advertisements around the event in total![6])

AdWords[7] is based on a cost-per-click (CPC) auction.[8] Instead of just offering the top positions to those offering the highest bid price per click (as rival offering Goto.com/Overture did), Google introduced a formula that enhanced user satisfaction and rewarded advertiser relevance, with cost-per-click mechanics meaning that advertisers are charged only if a user processes and acts on the advertisement: no paying for gorillas here!

The relevance reward comes from a secret algorithm, known as 'Quality Score', which influences both the position that advertisers achieve against each search term and the price that advertisers have to pay:

Cost per click × Quality Score = the actual bid price paid

Quality Score is affected by a number of factors, but the key contributory factor is click-through rate (CTR). The more clicks an advertisement gets, the more it is deemed to be relevant, so the better the Quality Score becomes. Quality Score helps to deliver more effective campaigns and better pricing for advertisers, as they are financially incentivized to 'help' the consumer with relevant advertisements or content and penalized for serving advertisements that are less suitable. Quality Score changes over time, and Google effectively uses the feedback loop from the Shannon–Weaver model, constantly judging user receptiveness and rewarding advertisers accordingly.[9] (The importance of the feedback loop will grow further still as Google's '+1' button starts to take hold, with '+1' data filtered into Quality Score and natural search results too.)

Search advertising therefore effectively renders traditional target groups redundant. Traditional segmentation might see labels applied to target groups like 'ABC1 women' or 'main shopper' or 'heavy user', which for advertisement buying purposes would then be translated into a generic trading audience. In contrast, paid search offers an infinite number of audience clusters, all based around what a particular user is searching for at any moment in time.

Searchers can therefore be targeted with different advertisements depending on what stage of the purchase funnel they are in (as indicated by the data that they have made available, ie their search):

- Advertisements can be targeted to people who are starting their purchase journey through searching using generic phrases, for example 'smart phone review'.
- Different advertisements can be targeted to searchers who are further down the funnel, reflected by searching for brand product phrases, for example 'HTC phone review'.
- Yet another advertisement variation can be served to searchers who are close to purchase and searching for a specific phrase, for example 'buy HTC ChaCha'.

Rather than serving a single message to a mass audience, search advertising allows a wide variety of creatives to be developed, directly targeting individuals depending on what they are searching for. Some advertisers run campaigns with hundreds of thousands of keywords triggering advertisements, TV numbers achieved through 1+1+1+1+1 etc, with everything able to be tracked and optimized to produce the most effective return on investment (ROI) (though none of this works unless there is an owned media destination that fulfils the advertisement clicks). Paid search can also be used to drive both always-on spaces and tactical campaigns, with messaging and keyword selection reflecting objectives.

The different motivations behind why people search

Search is particularly powerful against areas of the funnel based on purchase. Search advertisements are effectively point-of-sale displays for the internet, but search can also be used to bring consumers into content initiatives. Search engines are used in one of two ways –

either to fulfil a voyage of discovery (finding out new information) or as a voyage of recovery (knowing what you want at the outset), and recognizing this is important, as it helps in thinking about how to align search activity with wider campaigns.

Searchers on a voyage of discovery will use a search engine to find new information and will often start with a generic (general) search term before refining their searches as they start to learn more and become more specific with their search queries. This creates the idea of a search funnel where a generic term leads to searching on a more refined term before searching on a specific brand or brand product. This kind of behaviour could be around a potential purchase, a problem or even fulfilling the needs of the people who still type into a search engine 'I'm bored'.

Alternatively, on a voyage of recovery searchers will have some idea of what they are looking for. The level of query specificity will vary, but they will start out with something in mind. Research in 2007 by the Telegraph Media Group showed that traditional 'newspaper advertising is a key traffic driver' to online properties. Their findings indicated that in the UK '68% have "used a search engine to find out more about something I have seen written about in my newspaper"', '70% have "visited a website address I have seen printed in an advert in my newspaper"' and '74% have "used a search engine to find out more about something I have seen advertised in my newspaper"'.[10] These findings were based on averages across all respondents, with *Telegraph* readers showing an even greater propensity to be driven online by things they had seen in print.

Prior exposure to messaging (through mass media or word of mouth) can therefore see the generic stage of searching bypassed. Searchers may have seen an advertisement for a product or heard about something that sounds interesting; they are searching because they want to know more. Having a search strategy aligned with activity in other channels (and even the activities of competitors in other channels) can therefore be an efficient way of meeting consumer demand.

A report by GroupM found that this applied to content too, particularly through social media. They found that 'Searchers who engage with social media, especially those exposed to a brand's influenced social media, are far more likely to search for lower-funnel terms compared to consumers who do not engage with social media.'[11] Furthermore, 'The study also showed a 50 percent click-through-rate (CTR) increase in paid search when consumers were exposed to influenced social media and paid search.' This is important, because it demonstrates that social media or earned media activity can save money on paid search campaigns as reliance on generic paid search terms (which tend to be more expensive) is reduced. Everything links together, and the integration can be even stronger if (like Yeo Valley) the TV advertising, poster advertisement, etc can be tagged with a specific instruction such as 'Search for X', as this act of 'nudging' increases the size of the active audience and means that volume of searches against the desired keyword should increase as a result.

Consumers may also be seeking to find a specific piece of content, something that they have seen before or are convinced exists somewhere on the internet. A large number of the Yeo Valley searches were for 'Yeo Valley' as the advertisement instructed, but many were also searching for 'Yeo Valley ad', so having a relevant owned media presence, in this case a YouTube channel that housed the TV advertisement, can help to fulfil these searches.

Paid search advertisements at the top of the page can be useful in ensuring that consumers end up in the right place too. It was interesting to see T-Mobile using paid search in the aftermath of their Trafalgar Square flashmob to direct visitors to the official event content. T-Mobile needed to use paid search against terms like 'Trafalgar Square' to take people to the T-Mobile official YouTube channel, as the 13,000 or so attendees had created so much user-generated content that without paid search people would have found it difficult to locate the official T-Mobile content from amongst the UGC in the natural results!

The T-Mobile paid search advertisements went live around the event, remaining until such time as SEO work had enabled the official content to top the natural search results around relevant queries. Indeed, paid search is a powerful driver of owned and can be activated instantly, a useful quick-response mechanism for advertisers in times of crisis. Whereas natural rankings take some time to change and update, paid search is instant. Advertisements can therefore be served to anyone searching for information and can be used to direct searchers to the official content. Paid search has a reputation for being a direct response or sales-driving medium, but it can also be used for PR activity, and innovative thinking has enabled advertisers to use paid search for branding too.

Using paid search for branding and creativity

In the Google presentation 'Search and brand: the UK horizontal story', research from Comscore and Jupiter was outlined, highlighting that '71% of users expect leading brands to be on top of the Search results page' and that '36% of users link placement to company prominence'.[12] Further research by Enquiro and Ipsos showed that top ranking drove brand recall by 2.5 times, purchase intent by 1.14 times and brand affinity by 1.18 times.[13] Positioning in search results can therefore affect consumer perceptions of brands.

This is an expensive strategy and, whilst getting stand-out using AdWords is hard, as advertisements are text based, this needn't be a barrier to creativity. In 2007 German van and car hire company Sixt were seeking to get a better return from Google AdWords campaigns. They decided to change their approach to Google creative and harnessed Kenneth Knowlton's 1966 ideas about printer art. Knowlton, who was working for Bell Labs at the time, started experimenting with what became known as ASCII art, as at this point in time few printers had graphics capabilities. Knowlton found that pictures could be produced by closely grouping letters and characters, and later in 1966 Knowlton and collaborator Leon Harmon compiled some of their early examples in *Studies in Perception I*, which then became the inspiration for Sixt's 2007 AdWords creative.[14]

Sixt brought this ASCII art to AdWords and created a campaign. Typing 'Mietwagen' into Google Germany served up a Google advertisement that was actually an ASCII picture of two cars followed by a link to the Sixt site. Other ASCII creatives were then used around other keywords.[15]

These Sixt creative treatments worked well in the context of the Google listings, creating both conversation and stand-out. Most importantly, they led to a 47 per cent increase in clicks, with this increase significantly benefiting Quality Score and improving ROI as a result. This particular campaign won a Grand Prix prize at the Eurobest European Advertising Festival awards and represents another example of success from approaching an existing platform in a new way. Since this campaign, though, Google have banned the use of repetitive punctuation, effectively ruling out future advertisements of this nature – no more ASCII pictures in the sponsored links column!

You don't have to draw pictures in search results to start conversation, though. A lift in unaided brand awareness is delivered just from being seen in search results, and in 2010 this principle led UK adult retailer Ann Summers to start using paid search to drive awareness. According to their agency, iCrossing, 'The strategy was not to deliver clicks – it was to leverage the Paid Search mechanic to cheekily insert the Ann Summers brand into unusual places.'[16]

For the 2010 UK Budget announcement, much was made in the morning newspapers of the fact that the Conservative Party were going to advertise their counter-proposals for economic policy alongside Budget-related keywords. When Google users typed in 'Budget' or other financial terms they saw real-time Conservative Party paid search advertising countering the proposals in the Labour government's Budget, but searchers on Budget-related keywords were also exposed to Ann Summers advertising with copy that simply said 'Beat the Credit Crunch – there is no recession in Pleasure! Invest in fun with Ann Summers.'

This campaign was then followed with similarly topical executions running around the British Airways strike, snow and the general election of 2010. Searchers saw the Ann Summers advertisements, but didn't click on them, meaning that, for an overall spend of less than £4,500, 1.5 million impressions were delivered at a cost per mille (CPM) of £3 – with the campaign reported across trade press, featured in national newspapers and blogged about by the BBC. This is a good example of how awareness can be driven through conversation generating search advertisements, the aim being to present a message rather than to generate clicks. The advertisements may not have been to everybody's taste, but using eye-catching advertising copy against high-volume topical keywords enabled Ann Summers to use paid search as a branding tool.

This is the reverse of the original wisdom that display is for branding and text-based search advertisements are for direct response. Indeed, paid search is often thought about as the last stage of the purchase path, the medium that is closest to purchase, but repositioning paid search as a medium that can glue together content campaigns, or even deliver content campaigns, can facilitate interesting and cost-effective results. Regardless, it is still rare for paid search to be used to deliver brand campaigns. If anything, the landscape is moving the other way. Instead of paid search becoming more like a traditional channel, traditional channels are becoming more like paid search. Everything is moving towards greater targeting, performance trading and real-time optimization, though this is perhaps most evident in online display advertising at the moment.

Using cookies and data to enhance the effectiveness of online display campaigns

By entering keywords into a search engine, internet users are flagging up what they are interested in at that moment in time, allowing a creative execution appropriate to the action to be served – right person, right message, right time. On the other hand, display advertisements have traditionally been served against incidental content and have therefore been harder to target so precisely. Search advertisements are based on relevance and are targeted to user activity, whereas display advertisements have always run the danger of being an unnoticed gorilla.

Hotwired sold the first clickable 'banner ad' to AT&T in October 1994, but many believed that internet display advertising would be short lived. In April 1996 Philippe Boutie argued that online display would 'wither', 'stagnate or disappear in coming years' (he believed that 'cyber word of mouth' would replace display advertisements), but online display advertising has evolved considerably since Boutie's prediction. New formats like rich media and online video lean towards the brand space, whilst tracking and optimization systems have transformed targeting approaches, particularly around traditional formats. Rather than high volumes of cheap advertisements being blindly booked in the hope they will work, semi-real-time data coupled with technology have seen optimization and performance become more and more of a feature of online display campaigns – effectively paid search principles applied to display.

In *They've Got Your Number*, Stephen Baker writes: 'Chips are fastidious note takers. They record the minutiae of our lives. Taken alone, each bit of information is nearly meaningless. But put the bits together, and the patterns describe our tastes and symptoms, our routines at work, the paths we tread through the mall and the supermarket. And these streams of data circle the globe.'[17]

The concepts Baker identifies are now used extensively in online display advertising, and the backbone of this ecosystem is ad serving technology, which functions through the use of tags and cookies. Ad servers sit between the advertiser and the publishor and allow the whole online display ecosystem to function efficiently. When a web page is loading, the publisher's ad server talks to the relevant advertiser's ad server, and between them they work out what creative to serve on the page that the site visitor is viewing.

Advertising creatives have descriptions attached to them in the form of tags. These tell the publisher ad server when and where the advertisements should be used. Advertisements can be booked on a run-of-site basis or can be more targeted, on the basis of geography (deduced from IP address) or according to the content of the page (sports advertisements on sports content and so on). Sites that require users to complete a profile at registration can also serve more specific advertisements whenever a user is logged in, enabling advertisements to be targeted to demographics and interests.

The publisher ad server therefore has instructions about what to serve where, but also needs information from the user. This is contained within the browser that a site visitor is using to access the web page, and the information that the publisher ad server needs for correct targeting is all contained within a 'cookie', a tiny piece of code stored on the site visitor's browser.

The cookie is a unique, but anonymous, marker number assigned to an individual. It effectively collates actions and information based on user and browser behaviour. In 2005 Adam L Penenberg wrote on *Slate.com*: 'They're something like virtual license plates, assigned to your browser so a site can spot you in a sea of visitors. Cookies remember your login and password, the products you've just bought, or your preferred color scheme.'[18]

Furthermore, he noted that cookies are useful to advertisers too, as the information they hold 'makes sure a user won't be hit with the same advertisement twice; others guarantee that someone who says they have an interest in sports gets different advertisements than someone who likes gadgets'. Using cookies can enable targeting to be more selective and specific, as users can be targeted on the basis of their prior online behaviour (though users are still not personally identifiable). Cookies and usage data allow interest-based targeting to become easier and the relevance and effectiveness of display advertising to improve.

Using cookie data to re-target potential leads

An even more precise version of this type of targeting is re-targeting, which involves advertisers serving advertisements to users who have previously visited their site or content.[19] Advertisers can therefore gain a data benefit from increased views of their content. The more people who visit or interact with the advertiser's content, the larger the pool of data that the advertiser can develop and the more precise future targeting can be.

Owned media data therefore drive paid media effectiveness, as an internet user who has previously chosen to view advertiser content is statistically a warmer lead than an average internet user who fits a general demographic or behavioural profile, especially if the content viewed was a sign-up or commerce page.

An example of how this can work in practice can be seen from a recent hotel booking experience that I had. I visited a hotel site looking at prices for hotels in Ibiza, but didn't buy. This site captured my information and dropped a marker on to my browser that identified me as someone who was interested in Ibiza hotels. Then as I moved across the web I was 'recognized' and the site I had previously visited served me advertisements across a number of the following sites I visited, all the while trying to tempt me with deals and further offers.

A variety of actions can result in a re-targeting cookie being dropped on to a browser. Visiting an advertiser site, opening an advertiser e-mail, clicking on an advertisement, viewing an advertiser's social content, purchasing and so on can all result in an individual being 'marked'. Cookies expire after a certain amount of time (often 30 days, sometimes sooner), and it's still not perfect, as cookies are based on the computer not the user. (If my wife has been looking at clothes online then when I come to use the computer I may be served corresponding advertisements for women's fashion.) However, returns from these behavioural targeting and re-targeting techniques have consistently been seen to be better than the traditional generic targeting approach for online display.

These approaches change the nature of display buying. Rather than working to the principle of 'If you buy enough and it's cheap enough it will probably work' (with large numbers of cheap gorillas placed all over the internet), these targeting approaches are based on buying audience not impressions. Internet users are served more relevant and useful advertisements (targeted via the data that their actions provide), and this has impact on trading levels and publisher monetization. Instead of advertisers buying large amounts of cheap (remnant) short-term inventory in bulk or making assumptions about audience through buying a particular section of a site, there are now ways of picking out individual impressions against internet users who are deemed useful or interesting. This could be someone who seems interested but has yet to purchase or it could be upselling to an existing customer (I've purchased a flight, and now the airline uses re-targeting advertisements to try to tempt me with a hotel or a hire car).

Every impression therefore has a potential value to an advertiser, and different advertisers are willing to pay different sums for the same impression. Ever increasing page views and ever increasing volumes of remnant inventory were seeing online inventory move to lowest-common-denominator pricing where everything was priced at the lowest cost possible for an eyeball, regardless of the advertiser or desired targets or the quality of the content, but data coupled with the ability to buy on an impression-by-impression basis in real time are fundamentally changing the trading market for online advertising space.

New transactional techniques are quickly evolving, and ad exchanges (automated display buy–sell platforms similar to the Stock Exchange electronic trading systems) are growing in importance. Google delivers scale for AdWords by having search campaigns booked through an interface, with machines doing the legwork. The same is now starting to happen with display through ad exchanges. There are only a certain amount of bookings that a person can make over the phone in any one day, but the automated platforms around ad exchanges are able to handle vast amounts of trades, buying on an impression-by-impression basis and using data (like re-targeting data) to power the decision making around each buy in order to decide what each impression is worth. Buyers now spend their time programming a machine rather than negotiating over the phone.

Using 'network neighbours' to expand targeting pools

To date, the largest barrier to the scale of re-targeting campaigns has been the limited pool of available targets, but growing availability of data is increasing the potential of these techniques (and helping to scale the exchanges). 'Started credit card application, but didn't complete' may be a desirable audience, but it will be significantly smaller than a generic group such as ABC1 women. As time goes on, though, it is becoming easier to collect and/or buy in supplementary data from specialist companies to create 'lookalikes' or 'cookie clones', which can then enhance the size of target lists.

In a paper published in *Statistical Science* in 2006, Shawndra Hill, Foster Provost and Chris Volinsky looked at the adoption of a new telecommunications service and produced three key findings for 'network-based marketing':

1 '"Network neighbours" – those consumers linked to a prior customer – adopt the service at a rate 3–5 times greater than baseline groups selected by the best practices of the firm's marketing team.'

2 'Statistical models, built with a very large amount of geographic, demographic and prior purchase data, are significantly and substantially improved by including network information.'

3 'More detailed network information allows the ranking of the network neighbours so as to permit the selection of small sets of individuals with very high probabilities of adoption.'[20]

Data gleaned from user actions in social media can be used to build out networks and enhance targeting pools, so called cookie cloning. If cookie-based advertising pools are small (there are only a certain number of people who 'look at a car of a certain colour' each month) then the ability to use behavioural advertising and re-targeting at scale is limited, but these cookie pools can be expanded by using this 'network neighbour' idea.

Traditionally list building and direct mail campaigns would harness data from places like the electoral roll (working on the basis that people who live in the same street are more likely to have commonality than people who lived further apart), but, as we saw from the work of Granovetter, individuals are connected to other individuals through either strong ties or weak ties. Strong ties imply similarity (network theorists call this homophily), so through network analysis we are able to use this type of connection information to expand our list of potential targets. We may know about only one person, but that person's network ties enable us to locate and add other similar people to our list. Statistically friends tend to behave alike ('Birds of a feather flock together'), so mining network data and supplementing the cookies of identified users with details of their social network connections can provide a bigger pool to fish in – a larger list of prospects who could have above-average interest in our message.

Various social targeting companies now exist, and experiments have (so far) proved to be effective at raising click-throughs and engagement metrics. Quoted in the *New York Times*, K-Yun Steele, Vice President at Zenith Interactive in New York, says 'The implications for this are pretty amazing... There's a certain traction that you get when you target consumers that you know talk to each other, that you don't get when you advertise like you would in print.'[21]

Advertising networks in this space like 33Across,[22] Lotame and Media6Degrees all help advertisers to harness the social graph for targeting. Each has a slightly different approach, but the underlying principle is the same: use the social graphs of internet users to improve and expand targeting and produce greater campaign effectiveness as a result. 33Across CEO Eric Wheeler states that with these techniques the 'result is large, high-propensity targeting segments consisting of people with similar age, gender, interests, and purchasing behavior'.[23] Advertisements served to these custom clusters are therefore expected to provide a better source of return than just targeting generally, especially when working alongside the behavioural data that advertisers are able to collect themselves.

New technology is not limited just to data and targeting, though. Real-time creative systems can create advertising creative quickly, potentially allowing a huge range of executions. Advertisers load up the building blocks for advertising creative, and systems construct the optimal image for the specific user (for example, a travel company advertisement can be made up of different images, departure airports, destinations, prices and so on, depending on the user, the context and the timing).

These techniques are all about using data to learn about individuals and their friends in order to make commercial messaging more relevant and more effective. As we have seen again and again, in today's world 'relevance' is vital, and data-fuelled targeting greatly improves the chances of campaign efficiency and overall campaign success as a result.

Google text advertisements through AdWords are great for direct response and commerce (someone wants to buy now, so serve them an advertisement), but the display systems that are emerging have the potential to engage the right audience with optimized, more brand-oriented messaging (rich media and so on). However, whilst 'user did x implies that user would be interested in y, so serve them an ad and make it ad copy B' is driven by logic and data, it is still to some extent based on inference and probability. The other key performance channel is Facebook, and Facebook advertisements can be served to individual users, meaning that, rather than inference targeting, advertisements can be served specifically based on the interests that Facebook users have declared on their profiles. (On the same basis Google+ will start to rival Facebook in this area in the not-too-distant future as Google+ user data start to be filtered into Google paid advertising targeting.)

Facebook advertisements

Facebook now has a huge audience of over 800 million worldwide users, who spend a good deal of time using the service regularly.[24] This generates enormous numbers of page views and, where Facebook initially relied on a display advertising partnership with Microsoft for monetization (Facebook provided the audience, and Microsoft sold banner and skyscraper display advertising on to the site), they have now developed their own unique advertising mechanics and sell to market directly.

In 2010 Facebook published research they had conducted with Nielsen into Facebook ad units. Display advertisements on Facebook can be used to drive to another web page or can be used to promote an owned media asset within Facebook, and advertisements driving to other areas of Facebook can include 'social actions' at the base of the ad unit.

Social actions build social proof or nudging into the ad unit itself and in the research project were seen to increase effectiveness as a result. Home page advertisements advertising a Facebook fan page can include a line beneath them stating how many people currently like the page being advertised ('X people like this page'). This footnote can then be further enhanced by using the actual names of friends who already like the page, so instead of showing a number the advertisement shows the actual names of some of your friends ('Tom, Dick, Harry and 10 other friends like this page'). The mass-advertising execution can therefore be personalized for the person who is looking at it.

Additionally, if the viewer engages with the advertisement, for example clicking 'Like', a so-called organic impression is then posted to the user's wall ('Nick likes *x*'). This organic impression is seen by my friends, who then have the chance to engage with the content from their news feed rather than through an ad unit. By using friends' information in the advertising creative, a Facebook paid media placement is therefore able to encourage me to click, and if I do I will then automatically pass on the content organically to my friends – paid media promoting owned and generating earned all at the same time!

Nielsen's BrandLift study analysed survey data from around 800,000 Facebook users across 125 Facebook (home page) advertising campaigns from 70 advertisers.[25] Against a control group, home page advertisements on Facebook were seen to increase advertisement recall by 10 per cent, awareness by 4 per cent and purchase intent by 2 per cent. Advertisements that included personalization or social actions scored higher, though. Home page advertisements including the social advocacy features scored 16 per cent on advertisement recall (against 10 per cent when social actions were not included), 8 per cent on awareness (versus 4 per cent) and 8 per cent for purchase intent (versus 2 per cent for advertisements without the social actions).

Another interesting finding in this research was that 'fan base drives social coverage of advertising campaigns': the more fans a brand has, the more likely a user is to click or like as a result of seeing friends' names attached to the advertisements. Intuitively this makes sense (the law of probability states that the more fans a page has, the more likely that I will know someone who is also a fan), and the Nielsen research properly quantified this for the first time. This produces an interesting paradox, though. The larger the Facebook fan base, in line with rich-get-richer effects, the more fans the page will attract, but, as we saw from the PageLever data in Chapter 3, the larger the fan base, the lower the level of engagement overall. Engagement level affects EdgeRank score and means that, as time goes on, proportionally fewer and fewer fans will see page updates, meaning that brands have to invest in paid advertisements (targeting fans) and Sponsored Stories to maintain engagement levels and visibility.

Facebook paid media targeting options

The majority of Facebook advertising does not come from over the phone or home page reach buys, though. The majority now comes through the Google-like self-service platform. Again we can see the shift from traditional mass-media buying to a performance-based, 1+1+1+1+1 approach, but Facebook performance advertisements work differently.

Behavioural targeting relies on inference and implication, whereas Facebook performance advertisements are targeted to individual users based on their actions on the site and the interests they have listed. When Facebook users set up a Facebook account they fill in a profile page, publishing information about their lives on their personal profiles. Quoted in *The Facebook Effect*, Facebook COO Sheryl Sandberg says: 'It is the first place where consumers have ever said, "Here's who I am and it's OK for you to use it."'[26] The quote from Sandberg stresses that Facebook data are 'real data' rather than cookie-based behavioural data that others collect through actions and implications.

A Facebook profile has sections for:

- basic information (gender, birthday, current location, hometown, 'interested in' (men or women), 'looking for' (friendship, dating, etc), relationship status, political views, religious views);
- personal information (activities, interests, favourite music, favourite TV, favourite films, favourite books, quotations);
- education and work (university, secondary school, employer, location, description).

This is a huge amount of personal information, and Facebook allows advertisers to use any element or combination of elements in aggregate, effectively allowing advertisers to micro-target ads to Facebook users on the basis of their profile information. (Facebook also allow advertisers to use standardized target clusters around particular topics.) Facebook's unveiling of Open Graph applications that let users share what they have read, watched or listened to creates further opportunities for advertisement targeting as advertisers will be able to target Facebook users based on the content that they consume as well as the content and Pages that they 'Like'. (The Inside Facebook blog[27] even revealed that Facebook VP of global marketing solutions David Fischer told them that Facebook are also looking into launching a 'Want' button too which will enable advertisers to target Facebook users who have publicly declared an interest in a product.)

Facebook's sizeable audience therefore creates the opportunity for advertisers to buy mass reach (and include social advocacy in the ad unit), but also allows for platform-based targeting around user interests. Moreover, real-time bidding now allows advertisements to be served in real-time against what a user is typing into their status.

Reminiscent of Google's early days, Facebook advertisers can book through a platform, set daily budgets, buy advertisements on a CPM or CPC basis and run ad campaigns with specific copy targeted to specific users. Advertisers specify what they are going to advertise and then create a simple advertisement with headline, body text and image. Advertisements can then be used to promote either an external website address or 'something on Facebook'. Advertisements can be targeted to everyone in a certain country or city and broken down by sex and /or age and this advertisement targeting can then be further refined using other profile information such as education level, workplace, language or interest. The system then instantly reveals how large the requested audience is. At the time of writing:

- If I want to target 'UK men aged 18–34', the Facebook system tells me that this audience totals 6,219,800.
- If I want to target 'single UK men, aged 18–34, who are university graduates, live in London and support Arsenal', there

is an audience of 2,640 people, and I can serve a message to them accordingly.

- I can even target people on their birthday – 26,100 Facebook users in the UK have a birthday today, and I can serve them a birthday message accordingly.

The size of the Facebook audience, coupled with the data that the audience provides, allows for highly targeted relevant messaging, and for many advertisers this system has been providing better returns than previous display formats. Again, rather than targeting generic TV audiences like 'housewives', Facebook performance campaigns can be the aggregation of huge numbers of strands, with each strand using different copy or images, different targeting and different bid pricing.

This is the difference between Facebook and paid search. Both now offer performance marketing opportunities but, as David Kirkpatrick writes in *The Facebook Effect*, 'If on Google you buy an ad that displays when someone types "digital cameras", on Facebook you display a similar ad to married men in California who have young children, but don't post any photographs.' Search engines primarily serve advertisements when users are in a purchasing state of mind. Facebook primarily serve them further up the funnel. As a result this is leading to rapid growth in the amount of money being transacted on Facebook advertising.[28]

Executing paid advertisements on Facebook

In September 2010 *AllFacebook.com* highlighted 'how one band acquired 3000 Facebook Fans for [just] $0.08 each'.[29] They noted that, 'once you have this initial audience built for your fan page, you will find any updates you do, competitions you run or videos you post will get much better traction and start spreading'. (Again this is paid media being used to build a critical mass, which can then start to trigger organic impressions and earned media spread.) The key tactic identified in this case study was the idea of targeting to specific audiences as defined by their music taste and then deploying micro-targeting or multi-copy techniques learnt through extensive use of paid search.

The other important aspect is the landing page. In Chapter 3 we discussed how more page likes are generated from users landing on a tab rather than the wall. *AllFacebook.com* backs this up by saying:

> When people click on your ad, DO NOT send them straight to your Facebook wall. This is the number one mistake... When you spend money on getting someone to click your ad, make sure they land on a customized landing page which will encourage them to click the 'Like' button. A strong landing page makes the difference between a lasting connection with a fan and money down the drain.

Facebook advertising, though, still tends to be generally classified as 'display'. Facebook has unique advertising formats with optimization techniques deployed that mean they are more closely related to search advertisements rather than to traditional display advertisements. Targeting multiple advertisements or advertisement groups against multiple interests, booking through a platform, setting bids and budgets, and optimizing as a campaign progresses are very different to the original advertising ideas of interruption and 'Irritate, irritate, irritate!'

Data protection and privacy

With the huge amount of public information that internet users are publishing online, paid media systems can now start to use data and the network thinking discussed in Chapter 6 to make paid media advertisement impressions work even harder. Performance paid media can also be effective at driving conversation, and performance paid media is an effective and efficient approach, especially when integrated with other campaign activity and assets.

Advertisers and companies in this space are extremely careful about how data are collected. Major websites all have privacy policies and detailed documents outlining how they collect and use data, stressing that user privacy is important. Concerns over user privacy will continue, so there is an onus on all players in this performance advertising ecosystem to behave ethically and responsibly. Indeed, Google even publish and live by five very public privacy pledges that go across everything they do,[30] and websites, particularly in the social space, allow users to manage their own privacy settings. Online advertising industry actors are also collaborating to find common standards and solutions to allow consumers to opt out of having their data collected through cookies should they so wish, though this is an ever changing area, with regulatory discussion and proposed legislation being mooted and discussed.

KEY POINTS

- With performance media relevance is the key.
- Performance media is based on constant optimization and real-time tweaking to maximize effects.
- Performance media can be used to drive owned and earned media campaigns, but can also be used for branding and buzz generation in its own right.
- Earned media actions can help performance paid media work harder (for example, social actions shown on Facebook advertisements).
- Earned media conversations can improve the efficiency of performance paid media (for example, presence in natural search results can help paid search advertisements work harder).
- Social data can help display campaigns target more effectively.
- Privacy is an ever changing area, but both media owners and marketers are acutely aware of the need to allow internet users to manage and maintain control over their online presence and personal data.

Chapter Nine
Responding

How responding in a socially connected world can drive advocacy and business results

> Ryanair can confirm that a Ryanair staff member did engage in a blog discussion. It is Ryanair policy not to waste time and energy corresponding with idiot bloggers and Ryanair can confirm that it won't be happening again. Lunatic bloggers can have the blog sphere all to themselves as our people are far too busy driving down the cost of air travel.[1]

This was the response from the Ryanair official communications team when it was brought to their attention that a Ryanair employee had engaged a blogger in lengthy discussion and called him 'an idiot and a liar'.[2] In an offline world of telephone calls and letters, customer-to-company and company-to-customer contact was essentially private. In a socially connected internet world it is increasingly happening in the public domain, with bloggers and social media users posting opinions and experiences for all to see, with corresponding responses from the companies in question again seen by everyone (including the search engines that index and highlight content).

Ryanair's response is an exception. The vast majority of businesses are more concerned about their reputations. The long-standing net promoter score (NPS), created by Frederick F Reichheld and identified by him as 'the one number you need to grow', has been widely used and is based on a simple question: consumers are asked how likely it is that they would recommend the company to a friend or colleague. A scoring system groups people into 'promoters', 'passively satisfied' and 'detractors'. Subtracting the detractor score from the promoter score gives the net promoter score, which can then be tracked over time.

Reichheld stated that, 'By asking this one question, you collect simple and timely data that correlate with growth. You also get responses you can easily interpret and communicate.'[3] The importance of this measurement was stressed against statistics such as 'acquiring a new customer can cost 6 to 7 times more than retaining an existing customer' and 'businesses which boosted customer retention rates by as little as 5% saw increases in their profits ranging from 5% to 95%'. Post-purchase, customer satisfaction and advocacy are therefore key elements for customer retention and overall business performance.

Other research has backed up this idea. In a 2005 paper published by the London School of Economics, Marsden, Samson and Upton demonstrated how customer advocacy drives UK business growth. They surveyed 1,256 adult consumers and questioned them about some of the UK's largest businesses. The research revealed that business performance was linked to net promoter scores and negative word of mouth, finding that 'Companies such as Honda, HSBC, O2 and Asda enjoying higher levels of word of mouth advocacy grew faster than their competitors in the period 2003–2004.' The researchers were then able to equate advocacy scores to actual sales and revenue, finding that 'Every 1 point increase in the Net Promoter score correlated with an £8.82 million increase in sales'.[4] Similar findings have been uncovered in the United States. In February 2010, Fornell, Rust and Dekimpe published a paper in the *Journal of Marketing Research* that showed 'that the lagged change in customer satisfaction, which contributes to future demand, has a significant impact on spending growth' (though they noted that this is moderated by consumers' actual ability to spend).[5]

Jeremiah Owyang writes on his *Web Strategy* blog, though, that, whilst NPS has proved to be remarkably enduring, with the message of '"get more promoters and fewer detractors" becoming a clear-cut, actionable, and motivating metric, especially when tied to incentives', it is not sufficient for today's world. He continues: 'NPS, while effective at capturing the intention of advocacy, does not measure actual advocacy or detractions that occur', and this contrasts with 'the social web [which] actually records customers making explicit ratings, rankings, recommendations or warnings about products and services'.[6]

NPS remains a useful tool for measuring customer satisfaction, but this kind of advocacy measure can now be augmented through the use of social listening tools that can supply data on buzz volume, number of mentions and real-time scores on positive versus negative sentiment. A large amount of comment about brands and products is driven by product experience (huge amounts of social conversations are actually in topic-specific forums rather than on general platforms like Twitter and Facebook), and as a result switched-on brands can now context-manage or respond to comments made online, participate in discussions and help to rectify problems – and do this in near real time. The actions of responding can then contribute towards decreasing negative word of mouth and boosting advocacy.

According to *The Retail Consumer Report* published by RightNow in March 2011, '68% of consumers who posted a complaint or negative review on a social networking or ratings/review site after a negative holiday shopping experience got a response from the retailer' and, of those who received a response, '33% turned around and posted a positive review' and '34% deleted their original negative review'.[7]

As social listening technology advances, it is becoming more and more possible to use listening tools to produce a rolling sentiment rating and measure the effects of responding activity, though clearly a rigorous approach to data (outlined in Chapter 2) needs to be deployed. Social listening should be used *in conjunction with* other tracking tools and research rather than *instead of* them. (Remember all the vagaries identified in Chapter 2 – social listening is not yet a precise science.)

Charlene Li aimed to quantify the effects of social engagement (including propensity to respond to consumers online). Taking the '100 most valuable brands' list, companies were bucketed based on their level of social engagement (a range of social activity from publishing to responding to blog posts). The bucket of most engaged companies 'on average grew 18% in revenues over the preceding 12 months', whereas the bucket of the least socially engaged companies 'on average saw a decline of 6% in revenue during the same period'.[8] Clearly this is not as black and white as the above makes it, but, in the same way that Marsden, Samson and Upton found that advocacy drove UK business growth across 2003–04, there is a growing body of data that strongly imply that responding and engaging through social media can drive further value for businesses.

'Engaging the enemy' – creating policies and structures in order to respond effectively

The starting point to earned media or social media responding (or indeed any participation in the social web) has to be the creation of a complete guide that covers every aspect. It should:

- lay out who should be responding to what (including what should be left alone, what should be escalated and whom it should be escalated to);
- specify the tone of voice to be adopted;
- spell out topics that should and shouldn't be referenced;
- give example responses that should be offered;
- establish crisis procedure (potential problems should be discussed and action plans put in place so that unexpected, untoward situations can be dealt with quickly – think about what could possibly go awry, what would be needed to deal with it and who would need to be involved);
- specify the tools to be used;
- determine measurement criteria (this will usually come out of the findings of an initial listening audit and will be married to brand positioning and overall objectives);
- define methods of reporting;
- ideally fix activity review dates in the calendar.

A great example of this is a public document from the US Air Force Public Affairs Agency Emerging Technology Division entitled *New Media and the Air Force*, which spells out social media guidelines for US Air Force personnel.[9] The document recognizes that 'today all Airmen are communicators', stating that: 'The intent of this guide is to educate and empower the PA Airmen who are the trainers for Airmen communication programs. All Airmen are encouraged to use new and social media to communicate about topics within their areas of expertise, or their interests.'

The US Air Force therefore specifies who should be responding (by making responding the responsibility of everyone in the service rather than a specific social media team) and then gives useful guidelines to help personnel understand the parameters and the dos and don'ts of responding. The document ensures that all personnel are taught in the same way and spells out in no uncertain terms that personnel should use online social publishing. The introduction concludes powerfully: 'If the Air Force does not tell its own story, someone else will.'

Responding is often allocated to a specific department, but the US Air Force recognizes that every 'employee' has a role to play.[10] Staff are using social media for themselves, and this has the potential to cause unintentional brand reputation issues if they are uninformed about the mechanics of the new media world. There have been a number of stories about various companies' staff misdemeanours in social media, and the archival nature of the internet means that inappropriate posts and comments can live on. A listening tool can help highlight inappropriate staff activity, but a preferable solution is to harness staff social media enthusiasm in order to drive positive word of mouth about the brand.

This is the route that McDonald's is taking, encouraging employees to talk about the brand online. Heather Oldani, Director of PR for McDonald's USA, is quoted as saying that:

> At the end of the day we absolutely want to recognize that our employees across the world are in the digital space and communicating. And, given our size and given our reach and the number of people who work for the brand on a global basis, we believe that there is an opportunity for our employees to be a positive representation of the brand through social media.[11]

Active employees have an important role to play in social media, but structured training around how to act responsibly and ethically is vital. The US Air Force document does a comprehensive job, going on to discuss how communication flows, and gives detailed blogging guidelines ('No Classified Info', 'Use Your Best Judgement', 'Avoid Copyright', 'Stay In Your Lane' and so on). The guidelines then discuss how various social platforms work, highlight percentages of personnel involved in social media (another example of a statistical nudge) and continue to lay out practical, useful and non-patronizing information. This can help positive words to spread and can correct false information and false stories too. Indeed, the correction of inaccuracies is very important. As former UK prime minister Jim Callaghan famously said, 'A lie can be halfway around the world before truth has got its boots on.'[12] David Kilcullen goes even further in 'Fundamentals of company-level counterinsurgency', writing 'In this battlefield, popular perceptions and rumor are more influential than facts and more powerful than a hundred tanks.'[13] (Thinking in advance about potential crises and how to manage them if they arise improves response times and can help manage or defuse crisis situations before they get out of hand.)

It is essential though that anybody officially responding to online comments and conversations responds in line with the guidelines and tone of voice established at the outset. The US Air Force guidelines are excellent, very readable and a framework that other organizations need have no hesitation in following, though the wording of the rationale might have to be toned down (possibly) – 'The enemy is engaged in this battlespace and you must engage there as well.'

The British government also have a detailed policy on social media, launched in July 2009 when the *UK Cabinet Office Digital Engagement blog* published a 20-page 'Template Twitter strategy for government departments'.[14] Written by Neil Williams, then Head of Corporate Digital Channels at the Department for Business, Innovation and Skills, it contains some useful ideas and frameworks for using social media. The overall paper is more detailed than the US Air Force document and is maybe less readable as a result (words and text versus the US Air Force document's graphics, fonts and photos), but it is again a useful reference.

This starts to have an impact on more than just the function of media or advertising. For large organizations it involves new governance guidelines, restructuring, cultural shifts and so on. This is not easy and is a big task, but many businesses and corporations now have social media guidelines of this nature, and many of them have published public summary versions of their policies.

In Eloqua's 2011 *Social Media ProBook*, Scott Monty, Head of Social Media at Ford, revealed the role that social media plays for Ford. He writes: 'Social media humanises Ford, creating a bond within and between employees and customers and helps to improve our reputation by putting our message in the hands of the people who are most likely to be trusted.'[15] Indeed, Ford have even published a single-page summary of their 'Digital participation guidelines' on *Scribd*, stating:

> In brief, our guidelines for engaging on the social web consist of the following core principles:
>
> 1) Honesty about who you are
> 2) Clarity that your opinions are your own
> 3) Respect and humility in all communication
> 4) Good judgement in sharing only public information – including financial data
> 5) Awareness that what you say is permanent.[16]

For a commercial organization the rules are slightly different to the US Air Force or the UK government (note the explicit attention given to financial data), but the sentiments are essentially the same – particularly around transparency and harnessing both the ears and the efforts of employees.

Furthermore, if we believe in the big seed approach to cascade formation, then inspiring employees to participate and contribute to earned media efforts is important (remember, the more fires we can light, the more chance we have of something spreading), but the role that employees can play in responding is potentially even more valuable. The empowerment of employees to participate can inspire everyone in the organization to pull together, which can then have positive knock-on effects for customer satisfaction and resulting advocacy.

For many, though, this sort of goal is utopian and unrealistic, as few can go down the routes followed by companies like Zappos or Best Buy (with their Twelpforce).[17] To this end the first step is to start responding on a small scale through a small group of well-trained people either internally or via an external agency (though having employees throughout the company, and even the public, aware of social media and customer service intentions can be a useful support tactic).

A small team can often be more nimble when it comes to getting things done and, with responding, speed is essential. If your phone rings you answer it now, not in three days' time. In *Winning the Zero Moment of Truth* Jim Lecinski compares the internet to a 1-800 (Freephone) number: 'You'd never set up a corporate 1-800 number with nobody to answer the phone. (Would you?) You wouldn't build one and just let it ring. The internet is that 1-800 number, and it's been set up for you *even though you didn't ask for it.*'[18]

If someone tweets you (or about you) it should be the same – fast, courteous responding that helps. Both free tools like Twitter Search and paid-for listening tools can be used to highlight conversations and potential issues. Responding can then occur (always in line with the guidelines established at the start) either directly on the sites themselves or through an engagement tool that facilitates real-time and semi-real-time responding. (Some of the better tools offer ticketing to track issues, indexing and archiving of responses and actions, multiple log-ins, built-in approval processes and the ability to respond directly from inside the tool.)

The existence of a document that lays out rights and wrongs therefore becomes incredibly useful, especially in times of crisis. It brings much needed definition, clarity and structure, which gives (the right) staff the confidence to respond in line with overall objectives. It keeps people on-message, but has to be backed up with organizational commitment, the right resource and the right tools if it is to stand a chance of working to the benefit of the organization.

How a proactive approach to responding can change customer perceptions

A *New York Times* article in 2007 titled 'All-stars of the clever riposte' referenced the responding efforts of blog index site Technorati founder David Siffry, claiming that, 'When he learned of a blog post in which he or Technorati was mentioned, he went to that site to leave a comment, a practice that let people know they were being heard.'[19] In the article Siffry states that this can create 'evangelists'. I decided to put this to a test in November 2007. I blogged about the principles of responding, positively referencing David Siffry and Technorati in the process. Even though at this time my blog had (very) low traffic and was not indexed by Google, within 24 hours it was clear that Siffry practised what he preached, as he left a comment for me: 'You're very kind, Nick. I got started blogging because I wanted to get involved in conversations and meet interesting people. Taking criticism gracefully and listening deeply are skills that I'm really grateful I've learned – it's helped me to become a better entrepreneur and a better person (I hope!)... Dave.'

Not only was David Siffry spreading the word about his company, but quick, simple comments were turning web 'publishers' (no matter how small) into people who had positive feelings about him and the company he represented. For Technorati, personal responding was used to help to spread the word and grow the business, whilst Siffry felt that being involved in online conversation made him a better person and a better businessman. Most companies took longer to adopt this kind of mantra or approach (and many have yet to do so), but those who have embraced social have generally seen positive effects.

Interestingly the launch pad to social media responding for many big corporations has been a crisis. Dell were pushed into responding initially by dissatisfaction around customer service (encapsulated in the idea of 'Dell Hell'), but momentum for their social efforts came in response to the 'exploding laptop' issues after an incident at a conference in Japan.[20] Perhaps the most fundamental change in recent years, though, has been the evolution (revolution?) in Comcast's customer service in the United States.

In 2006 a user-generated video appeared on YouTube entitled *Comcast Technician Sleeping on my Couch*.[21] The description of the video detailed what happened when US broadband company Comcast sent a technician to fix a customer's fault and finished with 'I've been in my apartment for three weeks and my internet connection is still non-functional. This is my tribute to Comcast, their low quality technology and their poor customer service.' The video was around a minute long and featured footage of the technician sleeping on the couch interspersed with cutting text comments and the phrase 'Thanks, Comcast'.

This video received over a million views and widespread commentary, but it was the 2007 protest of *Advertising Age* columnist Bob Garfield that really stirred things up, when in October he started a blog that was simply titled *Comcast Must Die*.[22] Garfield stated that he had 'no deathwish for Comcast' but he did have 'an earnest desire for such companies to change their ways'. Customers were urged to post their grievances in the blog comments (including their Comcast customer number). The idea was that if Comcast were serious about customer service they would resolve the issues, and complainants would then come back and record resolution results in the comments.

Unsurprisingly given his connections, Garfield's blog gained attention.[23] He told visitors: 'Congratulations. You are no longer just an angry, mistreated customer. Nor, I hope, are you just part of an e-mob. But you are a revolutionary, wresting control from the oligarchs, and claiming it for the consumer. Your power is enormous. Use it wisely.'[24]

This was no longer individuals suffering customer service issues. An industry opinion leader had created a platform to aggregate customer issues in one highly visible place. Furthermore, in 2008 the *New York Times* noted that Comcast 'ranked at the very bottom of the most recent American Consumer Satisfaction Index, which tracks consumer opinions of more than 200 companies'.[25]

Comcast responded to all the criticism by appointing Frank Eliason as Digital Care Manager in early 2008, and he started to monitor and respond to public comments about Comcast on blogs, forums and Twitter. In the first five months the *New York Times* reported that

Eliason reached out to over 1,000 customers online. The Twitter account @comcastcares was turned into the centre of Comcast online customer care activity, with the account highlighting the different ways that customers could connect with the digital care team and displaying a mission statement: 'The Digital Care team assists Customers throughout the web. It is our goal to listen to our Customers, help where we can, and improve the overall experience for all our Customers.'

By the end of 2008 customer demand had seen Eliason's team grow in size, from one to 10 in a matter of months, and @comcastcares now has over 50,000 followers (whom Comcast religiously follow back, allowing two-way dialogue with customers in both public and private). The efforts of the Comcast digital care team have turned around perceptions of the company's service. Comcast resolved many of the complaints detailed on the *Comcast Must Die* blog, and in September 2009 founder Bob Garfield posted: 'We have declared victory against Comcast, a vast, greedy, blundering, tone-deaf corporate colossus which, in less than two short years, has finally seen the light.'

Comcast were effectively pushed to the point where they had to change, especially as the broadband market was reaching a point of maturity, meaning that customer retention had become more important as an objective. The pressure from the YouTube video, but particularly from the Consumer Satisfaction reports and the *Comcast Must Die* blog, meant that there was a business imperative for Comcast to improve in the way that they dealt with customers – and it's no coincidence to see that the Comcast ranking has improved on the American Consumer Satisfaction Index since the digital care team was put to work.

As systems improve, social media customer service continues to evolve, and customers are expecting more. In his 2007 letter to Amazon shareholders, Jeff Bezos wrote 'Anytime you make something simpler and lower friction, you get more of it', further noting: 'We humans co-evolve with our tools. We change our tools, and then our tools change us.'[26] These quotes were around the launch of Kindle, but they could have applied just as well to customer service (or anything else) online. New platforms are pushing consumers to comment and complain more, but are also allowing companies to respond effectively. This in turn is leading consumers to comment and complain more, and so on. Responding through social media therefore becomes an ever more important (and ever changing) element of a marketer's toolbox. In a very short space of time, changing consumer habits have seen customer service issues move from blogs to Twitter, with ever growing numbers now using Facebook too (though it is worth noting that review sites and forums are still important venues for consumer product discussion and brand responding).

Using Facebook for real-time customer service – SAS and Heathrow

Once an organization has started to use social media to engage in dialogue with fans and customers, it's difficult to stop, but having the infrastructure to deal with customers in real time (and having a predefined framework for responding) can be invaluable, especially during a crisis. One of the best examples I have seen was the response of Scandinavian Airlines (SAS) to the snow chaos at Heathrow Airport in the week before Christmas 2010.

The SAS response to the snow problems is summed up in a poem written by SAS Head of Social Media Christian Kamhaug (published at Christmas on the *SAS blog*). An extract reads:

Twas a week before Christmas at London-Heathrow, The skies darkened over and it started to snow,

And just as they say that it pours when it rains, The snow kept on falling grounding all planes,

Pretty soon all the terminals were flowing over, With passengers wanting to go home to their lover,

For two long days not a plane left the ground, And we brought the old Facebook-team around,

From early morning to late at night, We were on Facebook setting things right.[27]

Heathrow cancelled all planes after the snow of 18 December, and days of chaos ensued. This was the busiest time of the year, and in the face of unprecedented winter disruption the thing people (including me) desperately needed was information. All airlines were affected, and we queued at the SAS transfer desks inside the departure lounge. However, on reaching the front of the queue we were simply told that the only option was to phone a rebooking number. Many of the people in the queue had pre-paid mobile phones that could not access this number, and many non-UK nationals struggled to dial it too. Furthermore, if you did manage to get into the hold system there was a waiting time of at least an hour.

Over the following days more and more flights (from all airlines) were cancelled, the backlog of passengers wanting to fly got larger (especially as passengers who had rebooked after the original can-cellations were now cancelled again), and it was even harder to get through on the phone lines for information. The information on the main website was extremely limited (it just told you if your flight was cancelled or still scheduled to depart) and, whilst SMS text messages were sent when flights were cancelled, in many cases these were sent too late and recipients were already waiting at the airport when they came through.

All through this crisis, though, the SAS social media accounts were staffed, and the airline responded quickly to enquiries from concerned potential travellers. Twitter was used, but the SAS Facebook page was the main source of help.[28] The SAS Facebook page is a promotional vehicle rather than a customer service platform, but during the snow disruption it became a key information source for passengers. Crucially SAS had the infrastructure in place to enable this to happen, and from the beginning passenger queries were responded to in minutes, constant updates were posted regarding the state of play at Heathrow, and passengers were kept informed of extra flights and the ever changing arrangements and contingency plans.

The Facebook page was managed for around 17 hours each day, but, more than this, the team intuitively understood how customers were feeling. This wasn't just a logistical issue, but an emotional one too. This wasn't just about getting home; it was about getting home for

Christmas. Posts therefore ranged from those that gave functional information to upbeat, positive, 'Don't worry, we'll get you home' updates. Some example posts from the SAS Facebook page at the time illustrate this:

- 19 December, 12.01 pm: 'London/Heathrow, Frankfurt and Paris airports are closed until further notice due to bad weather conditions. Passengers booked from LON, FRA and PAR up to and including 20DEC10 may be rebooked.' (The post continued by giving practical information.)

- 19 December, 22.53 pm: 'Dear friends. It has been a long day for all of us, and the SAS Facebook-team is signing off now, hoping to catch a few hours of sleep before we are back online to help get you all home for Christmas (those of you using Spotify, search for Norwegian artist Maria Mena's "Home For Christmas" – it's our theme song).'

- 21 December, 19:08 pm: 'NEWS FLASH: Due to people no-showing, we have right now 40 seats available on the last flight from Heathrow to Copenhagen tonight departing 2035. If you are near Heathrow, hold an SAS ticket from LHR to CPH/ARN/OSL and can make it to check-in at Terminal 3 by 1945, please go to our check-in at Terminal 3 for assistance.'

- 22 December, 16:44 pm: 'More good news: We finally got the OK, and we are adding two extra-flights from Oslo to London tomorrow night to bring the rest of you home! The flights are...'

The posts kept coming throughout the crisis, and the SAS Facebook page did a great job in keeping people informed and responding to comments and questions – evidenced by the huge amount of positive comments posted by Facebook users. For example, on 21 December the first comments on an evening post were 'You are simply the best SAS!', 'Way to go SAS. Great customer-service on Facebook :-)', 'Got to take my hat off to you SAS you should be proud the info is amazin' and 'You're stealing hearts with your Facebook updates! Great job!'

During the Christmas snow chaos the SAS Facebook page helped to take pressure off the call centres, and reassured and informed waiting passengers. At a time of immense frustration SAS were able to use social platforms to interact with customers and generate warmth and good feeling towards the airline (remember, all the comments left would have been visible to the friends of every commenter too).

Using Facebook for customer service is interesting. As SAS found, some people were using Twitter to contact them, but the conversation became centred on Facebook – whether by design or default, that's where their customers were, and questions and responses were not limited by 140 characters. In the United States, Delta Airlines have now even launched a Facebook page tab called Delta Assist, where visitors are presented with a question, 'How Can We Help?', along with a form that allows customers to contact Delta directly for assistance.[29] On launch, a comment by Liz, seemingly a Delta employee, explains:

> You can certainly still share feedback and get help from delta.com. The purpose of this [Facebook] tab is to provide yet another outlet to support customers, especially where we know you're already talking. Plus, it's safe and secure so it allows us to help you right in Facebook, which isn't something we could do before. We hope you find it useful!

Again, this is recognition that it is easier to go to the people than expect people to come to you, and it is an interesting way of approaching Facebook as a customer service tool (though Delta aim to respond within 72 hours rather than the real-time speed with which SAS were responding to comments on their Facebook page before Christmas 2010).

Another attraction of Facebook as a customer service tool emanates from the fact that it is probably the social site with the least vitriol from disenchanted consumers. The requirement to use a real identity, coupled with the fact that comments are spread through a user's network, seems to make Facebook users either think twice before leaving negative comments or at least tone down the language compared to that used on other social sites (where pseudonymous users can be seen to post offensive or bigoted comments from behind their shroud of anonymity). Furthermore, Facebook functionality is based around liking and the 'Like' button. Despite 3.2 million people supporting a Facebook page demanding a 'Dislike' button,[30] only the 'Like' button exists – it's much easier to be positive than negative.

Publishing a code of conduct on the Facebook page ('This page is for... We encourage debate, but offensive comments or spam will be removed') can then help to define what is and isn't acceptable from page visitors. (The standard practice seems to be for pages to post this prominently underneath the profile picture.) Visitors are left in no doubt that moderation is at work and that comments that contravene the page's code will be removed, either by an automated tool or manually, and offenders or persistent offenders risk being barred from the page and prevented from leaving future comments. Spam can also be removed and can be flagged up to Facebook, whilst Facebook users themselves can flag comments as being inappropriate (labelling comments as spam, hate-speech, pornography, etc). It is therefore not just the page owner who can moderate, and encouraging fans to participate in page moderation can be a useful ploy.

Dealing with issues away from the public eye

Issues like the snow delays at Heathrow affect large numbers of people, and the critical thing is up-to-date information. When an issue is an individual one (and certain categories like travel, finance, telecoms and technology invariably have flashpoints or difficulties that prompt customers to react negatively), rather than trying to respond on the wall it is often easier to direct these discussions into another channel. 'Sorry to hear that. Please e-mail us specific details to... and we'll try to help' is often a better way of dealing with things than hosting everything in a public space on the brand Facebook page or through Twitter accounts. Elongated conversations don't look good to other users (remember many more spectate than create), and situations can escalate if other users start to join in. Being available is good, but diverting people off the page gives flexibility to deal with different problems in different ways, where resolution in public could prompt more complaints of a similar nature with everyone expecting the same.

In the UK, restaurant chain Pizza Express are active on Facebook, but try to stop any issues from ever reaching their Facebook page. Customers find that a feedback mechanism is printed on their receipt, with customers encouraged to go to mypizzaexpressexperience.com to fill in a survey about their meal. Powered by RetailEyes, this is a survey that allows customers to give either positive or negative feedback on their dining experience, with problems followed up directly by head office. As the survey says, 'We want Pizza Express to stay high on your list of great places to eat with friends and family, so we need to know when we are getting it right and when we're missing the mark. That's where you come in.' In return for filling in the survey, customers are given a voucher for a free garlic bread or portion of doughballs on their next visit. This not only gives an incentive to fill in the feedback form, but also encourages a return visit. Additionally, this feedback mechanism provides e-mail addresses for the database, supplies data on customer demographics that can be used in future advertising targeting and, perhaps most importantly, gives disgruntled customers an avenue for complaint that is both outside the public domain and in a place that Google's spiders can't see.

The practice of responding is not limited to customer service, though, and public responding around brand activity can see earned media generated in return.

Using responding to drive earned media coverage

In the United States, the Boston Police Department (BPD) use Twitter to increase transparency, 'tweeting to notify the public of incidents and police work'. On 19 May 2009 they notified Bostonites of an incident.

The tweet read: 'INJURED OFFICER: Officer from district 4 transported to Beth Israel Hospital, human bite to arm, suspect in custody.'

Fellow Twitter user Willcady decided to respond to this tweet. Using the @ reply mechanism he sent a public reply: '@Boston_Police if that was a zombie bite, would you tell us?'

Boston_Police don't normally reply to @messages, but this time chose to respond publicly, simply saying '@willcady Yes, absolutely.'

Willcady then blogged about what happened:

> I follow the BPD on Twitter, they send me updates of when people get hit by buses and shoot each other and make bomb threats, etc. It's really depressing, actually. The other night I got a little tweet telling me that an officer was admitted to the hospital to treat human bite wounds. Interesting. Here's what happened after the tweet...[31]

Willcady then linked to a Google Search for 'Boston police zombie', a search that, as a result of his exchange with the BPD, now returns thousands and thousands of results that reference it. As Willcady writes, 'Internet... you never cease to amaze me.'

The initial tweet was not particularly newsworthy. As Willcady says, the stream tends to be dominated by depressing news of crime. The fact that Will responded was not particularly newsworthy either, as many people send @ replies back to public bodies and highly followed accounts. The bit that triggered the conversations, news interest and earned media effect was the Boston Police responding. The organization showed both that it was human and that it had a sense of humour, but most of all it proved it was listening and willing to respond.

Boston Police were simply responding to a question, but in doing so managed to drive huge conversation and coverage, growing their Twitter following accordingly. The action of responding can therefore start to do more than just fulfil customer service or address back-half-of-the-funnel objectives, and similar earned media interest can be generated by responding to complaints.

Tesco showed a human side, and generated positive headlines, when they responded to a complaint received in September 2009 from Daniel Jones, who wrote to the grocery retailer claiming he was 'humiliated and victimised for his [religious] beliefs following an incident at a store in Wales'.

Daniel Jones heads up the 500,000-strong International Church of Jediism and claimed that the religion states that he has to wear a hood in public. The *Guardian* reported: 'Tesco has been accused of religious discrimination after the company ordered the founder of a Jedi religion to remove his hood or leave a branch of the supermarket in north Wales.' After a confrontation he left the store and was seeking legal advice. However, Tesco defused the negative potential by replying: 'He hasn't been banned. Jedis are very welcome to shop in our stores although we would ask them to remove their hoods. Obi-Wan Kenobi, Yoda and Luke Skywalker all appeared hoodless without ever going over to the Dark Side and we are only aware of the Emperor as one who never removed his hood.' A final comment stated that: 'If Jedi walk around our stores with their hoods on, they'll miss lots of special offers.'[32]

The Tesco situation here is reminiscent of the Ryanair response at the beginning of this chapter. However, Tesco use a typically Tesco tone of voice and manage to present things differently. Their light-hearted tone saw their response turn the situation into a story that positioned them in a positive way. Rather than spelling things out in black and white, the tone and the words used allowed readers to make up their own minds about the person in question, generating earned media coverage as a result.

These are easy wins, though. It's a bit like a comedy double act. The joke has been laid; the sidekick just needs to listen and deliver the punch line at the right time – and the punch line is the bit that attracts attention, makes people laugh and causes the joke (in this case the content) to spread. In many cases the initial context or content frame-work has already been set up (the zombie scenario or the idea of Jedi shopping); the brand just needs to respond quickly and appropriately.

If done well, responding can therefore be a powerful driver of earned conversation, in the process not only turning a negative into a positive, but also contributing to areas in the front half of the funnel like awareness, consideration or preference, as seen by Tesco using the Jedi opportunity to mention special offers!

Responding as part of a branded content strategy

The Jesus shot – using video to respond

Boston Police simply typed a tweet, and Tesco issued a press release, but it is possible to spend more time and budget producing content for responding – and generate further cut-through and conversation as a result. In August 2007 YouTube user Levinator25 uploaded a video that showed a glitch in the *Tiger Woods PGA Tour 08* Xbox game. The video shows what Levinator25 calls the 'new feature, the Jesus shot, where he can stand on the water'.[33] Game play features Tiger Woods 29 yards from the pin, but standing on the surface of a lake! From this position Woods takes his shot and sends the ball straight into the hole, making his par in the process. The video finishes with Levinator25 heard saying that 'Jesus prevails!'

This video slowly accrued views, and the watch count increased to around 50,000. However, since then the view count of Levinator25's video has increased to over a million. Instead of ignoring the problem with the game and the video that highlighted it, EA Sports went the other way and embraced (and highlighted) it by publicly responding.

EA contacted Bryan Levi (Levinator25) and paid him for the worldwide usage rights of his film.[34] EA then went to an actual golf course with Tiger Woods and a film crew and made a real-world re-creation of the Levinator25 work!

The EA response video shows a brief clip of Levinator25's original, before cutting to the real-life action. Real-life Tiger Woods is seen to hit his ball into the centre of a lake, where it comes to rest on a lily pad. We then see Tiger sit down on the bank, remove his shoes and socks, before calming walking across the water. He reaches the ball, plays it as it lies and sends it straight into the hole! A simple message is then displayed – 'It's not a glitch. He's just that good.'[35]

The EA film is posted as a response to the original, meaning that the two films are linked together, and the real-life Tiger Woods film has now attracted over 5 million views and around 10,000 comments: a piece of branded content is created as a response to a consumer. Again the framework has already been established and, in the same way that Tesco highlighted 'special offers' in their Jedi response, the EA response film promotes the Tiger Woods game. The novelty of it being addressed directly to a YouTube user, rather than the public at large, then helps it both to spread and to deliver value to the original creator, by driving views for the UGC version too – advertising dollars give back to an individual.

The following year EA reprised the real-life Tiger Woods film, but this time used Rocco Mediate as the central character. Again the ball lands on a lily pad in the middle of the pond, again there is a scene with the player sitting on the bank and removing shoes and socks, but shortly after starting his water walk Rocco disappears into the lake. He climbs out and, soaking wet and shoeless, takes a drop and then chips straight in. The film finishes with the message 'Rocco Mediate. He's not Tiger. But he's close.'[36]

This sort of responding can prompt conversation and earned media attention, but real-time responding has been seen to be even more effective at driving conversation.

Real-time video responding

In without doubt the most talked-about social execution of 2010, Wieden + Kennedy took the idea of video responding (they had created 'the Jesus shot' video) and dovetailed it with the concept of real-time marketing. The work that was subsequently produced for Old Spice Body Wash has spurred a worldwide conversation and a revival for the product as a result.

In the original Old Spice film, Isaiah Mustafa is cast as 'the man your man could smell like' and, topless, he proceeds to move from one fantasy setting to another. Starting in the shower and talking quickly, 'Old Spice man' starts to deliver his lines: 'Look at your man, now back to me, now back at your man, now back to me. Sadly he isn't me.' The shower disappears and suddenly 'You're on a boat with the man your man could smell like.' He then produces an 'oyster with two tickets to that thing you love'. This then changes into diamonds. Finally, 'Anything is possible when your man smells like Old Spice and not a lady. I'm on a horse.'[37]

This original Old Spice TV advertisement was broadcast during the Super Bowl (a fact that seems to be missing from most of the unofficial social media case studies and discussion around this work!). Critical mass was driven by TV placement, and the video was then uploaded to the Old Spice YouTube channel, where it continued to attract views from the (active) audience, who wanted to watch again and share. At the time of writing *The Man Your Man Could Smell Like* has had over 18.5 million views and over 24,000 comments, and has been shared through Facebook 271,471 times, tweeted 7,000 times and blogged about in 3,114 posts.

Supplementary activity in July 2010 (five months after the advertisement first aired during the Super Bowl) then expanded the reach and discussion around Old Spice. This second phase of activity was kicked off with performance distribution paid media and saw real-time responding used as 'the Old Spice guy' personally responded to individual web users.[38]

Personalized Old Spice video responses were created to answer related comments and posts that had been made on Twitter, Facebook, MySpace and Yahoo![39] A staggering 183 personalized videos were made and distributed across a three-day period, and *Fast Company* interviewed project supervisor Ian Tait, who detailed the process involved. He stated that:

> In the studio we have a team of social media people, we have the
> Old Spice community manager, we have a social media strategist,
> a couple of technical people, and a producer. And we've built an
> application that scans the Internet looking for mentions and allows us
> to look at the influence of those people and also what they've said.
> They're working in collaboration with the creative team that are there
> to pick out the messages that: 1. Have creative opportunity to produce
> amazing content; or 2. Have the ability to then embed themselves in
> an interesting or virally relevant community.[40]

As a result, personalized messages were created for internet celebrities like Perez Hilton, Demi Moore and Guy Kawasaki, as well as for less known people like Rose ('Rose asks on Yahoo.com, how many teeth do sharks have? Well my dearest Rose, it's funny you should ask as I spent my younger years as an apprentice in a shark dentistry practice on a distant island...').

Old Spice video responses were pushed out across the three-day period. By the end of this burst the responding videos had had a total of just under 11 million views, and the views of the original film had increased significantly too. Old Spice distributed the content, but the users targeted also embedded the response videos on their blogs and helped drive further attention. Discussion of the responses was then high across other social platforms. For example, on day one the responses campaign prompted Twitter users to generate 61,626 tweets, and on day two (the peak) 96,364 Old Spice-related tweets were posted by Twitter users. Interestingly, 26 per cent of these were 'retweets', people passing someone else's content to their own followers – indicative of content spreading.

Post-campaign, Nielsen point-of-sale scanning data have pointed to success, showing that, 'Over the past three months, [Old Spice Body Wash] sales jumped 55 percent and in the past month [July 2010], they rose 107 percent.'[41] (However, heavy couponing across this period helped to boost these figures; the video activity was not the only contributory factor.[42]) This campaign, and the videos used for responding, generated earned conversation by targeting a personalized message to prominent internet users, with the public nature of the messages allowing anyone to get involved.

Responding for Old Spice was about driving buzz and traction for the brand films. The more responses they sent out, the more attention they attracted – turning the 'man your man could smell like' into what has been positioned as a great example of social media success.

Context management and responding are therefore the foundation stones of social media campaigns, epitomized through the process of listening and then answering questions, responding to comments and complaints, and encouraging sharing and advocacy. Participating in and responding to conversations on brand websites, on social network pages and channels, and directly on blogs and forums drives the back-half of the funnel, the customer service-type areas that build relationships and drive advocacy. However, the connected web of sender and receivers means that responding can also now drive attention for content and deliver against objectives in the front half of the funnel, with Old Spice and Tiger Woods showing the way!

KEY POINTS

- Social media responding and customer service can have an impact on brand reputation that contributes to business performance.
- Guidelines and social policy should be in place across the whole company.
- Responding should be fast and courteous.
- Staff are a key asset to harness for earned media.
- Responding starts with a robust approach to listening and a structure that can then act on the findings.
- Facebook and Twitter can be used for customer service as well as advertising.
- When faced with frustrated customers it is preferable to try to deal with them in private (ie e-mail, phone, etc) rather than on a public social space.
- Responding can be used in brand content activity to gain additional coverage or exposure.

Chapter Ten
Measurement

Calculating the value of marketing

Frank Davidson, Strategic Resources VP at ZenithOptimedia in Boston, argues that the value of any marketing effort is essentially a function of three elements:

1 the change in the number of people with an interest in the company's products;
2 the change in the amount of money these people would ultimately spend with the company if they were to make a purchase;
3 the change in the likelihood of these people purchasing (or similar, eg subscribing, contracting with, etc).

He notes that, 'Ideally, these factors need to be accounted for over time – for example, a brand campaign doesn't necessarily increase immediate sales, but over time sales should increase as the awareness and affinity to the company increase.'

Davidson believes that it is possible to rewrite these points in the form of measurement-oriented questions:

1 'Did this or will this marketing effort increase the number of people aware of the company's products, and, if so, by how many?'
2 'Did this or will this marketing effort make people want to buy more from the company, eg cross-sell, up-sell, if they were to buy?'

3 'Did this or will this media effort increase the likelihood that a person will ultimately buy?'[1]

These three questions create a framework for evaluation, and everything should refer back to them, but, even if we can answer these questions satisfactorily, success or failure can be judged only if clear objectives and goals have been established at the outset.

Setting objectives and goals

The overarching strategy plan will define the strategic objectives and campaign goals in response to listening and research around the business, the brand and the consumer. Different companies have different approaches, but a useful concept is to ensure that objectives are SMART – specific, measurable, achievable, realistic and timely. (However, it is interesting to note that a UK NHS paper from 2004 suggests that 'M-A/R-S-T is often the best way to write objectives.'[2])

Young and Aitken write in *Profitable Marketing Communications* that: 'Metrics drive the entire marketing process, and what it is trying to achieve, whether it's acquiring new customers or retaining existing ones. The ability to judge the success of a particular marketing activity in fulfilling a specific business objective is vital if the objective is ever going to be achieved.' They further note that 'the return on investment will differ according to the brand and its objective' and stress that meaningful ROI measurement will ultimately 'always need to be a metric that is readable and attributable to a business metric'.[3]

As the media marketplace fragments and gets more complicated, it is all too easy to jump on to the latest fads and create a social network page, application or augmented reality solution without really asking the key questions – 'Why?', 'What for?', 'For whom?', 'How does this fit with everything else we are doing?' and, crucially, 'How will we judge and measure success?' With so many channels and different areas now, it is more important than ever that objectives and goals are clearly defined and clearly measurable!

Furthermore, a sensible approach is to have long-term objectives for the always-on presence (against the three questions posed above translated into more specific goals such as 'How many fans are we aiming to acquire this year?', 'What is the ratio of paid media to owned media to earned media that we want to achieve?' and so on). This long-term tracking or measurement can then run concurrently alongside measurement of campaign-specific activity. We need to think about the always-on overall picture as well as individual campaigns.

On his *MetricsMan* blog, Don Bartholomew goes into detail around measurable objectives. He claims that 'Most objectives today are either not measurable as written or are strategies masquerading as objectives.' He gives examples of best practice, writing:

> In order to be measurable, objectives must contain two essential elements:
>
> - Must indicate *change in metric of interest* – from X to Y
> - Must indicate a *timeframe for the desired change* – weeks, months, quarter, year, specific dates tied to a campaign (pre/post)
>
> Therefore, properly stated, measurable objectives should look more like these:
>
> - Increase awareness of product X from 23% to 50% by year-end 2012
> - Increase RTs per 1000 Followers from 0.5% in Q1 '12 to 10% by the end of Q2 '12[4]

Essentially, if objectives and goals are properly in place at the outset, the most appropriate measurement processes and tools can be adopted. We can then focus our efforts on evaluating success against the specified objectives and goals and, perhaps even more importantly, the contributory factors and the reasons for the success, with these learnings valuable for future activity.

The need for multi-channel metrics

In a world of limited advertising channels, ROI calculations and quantification of advertising effectiveness were fairly straightforward. Companies advertised using paid media and then mapped effects on to sales figures. If we go back to the 1947 Clark Gable film *The Hucksters* we can see the client, Mr Evans, talking about the marketing of his product. He argues that 'Sales principles are not theories; they're proven facts' and cites advertising as a reason for market leadership: 'The difference is in selling and advertising. We sell soap twice as fast as our nearest competitor. Why do we outsell them? Because we out-advertise them.'

Broadcast paid media was traditionally used to achieve maximum coverage for the lowest possible cost – Mr Evans's 'Irritate, irritate, irritate!' or interruption method of advertising. Share-of-voice and share-of-market calculations were the guiding principle, with effectiveness judged by the resulting changes against our three questions, particularly against objectives around share of market and number of sales.

Mr Evans with his beauty soap only had to measure the effects of advertising from a single channel, though. He could look at sales, map them on to advertising spend and then come to conclusions, but, fuelled by the evolution of the internet, the proliferation of channels and advertising options has seen campaigns become very much more complex. Effective measurement has become more challenging, as multi-media campaigns are now the norm, and it is much harder to isolate the effect of any one part of them.

In the past paid media, direct response advertising could use unique telephone numbers or coupon codes, but every element of an online campaign can now be measured with constant tracking and measurement fuelling campaign optimization. Various different methods are used to collate the data, and technological developments have vastly improved both the potential scope of measurement and the speed of data availability. As a result online marketing has many more dimensions that can be used to evaluate performance, such as reach and frequency metrics (reach, frequency, GRPs, targeted rating points, impressions and unique impressions) and direct response metrics (clicks, click-through rates, cost per click, cost per action, derived from post-click and post-impression measurement data).

Throughout the campaign data from the above can be used to help tweak and optimize performance. Bid prices can be changed, positioning can be amended, copy can be altered and selected sites can be dialled up or down on the basis of performance. Much of this happens in real time or semi-real time and, if anything, the difficulties have been in having too much that can be measured rather than too little, especially now that the internet fulfils a large amount of offline advertising too. Writing in *Admap* in October 2010, Bryan Smith expands on this idea: 'The growth of the internet has proved to be a double-edged sword for judging media effectiveness. While providing hard sales response data, it has also made the sales contribution of offline media harder to evaluate as its interaction with, and contribution to, online response has to be measured across an increasingly diverse range of channels.'[5]

The problem with just measuring the last click

Since the inception of the internet, percentage and number of clicks have been perhaps the key online metrics, predominantly because they are arguably the easiest things to measure. However, this has led to a tendency for the last click before a sale to be credited with being responsible for it. This disproportionately skews in favour of channels like paid search and affiliates and is a continuing issue, with these performance channels consistently overrated as sales drivers compared to more traditional advertising approaches.

The introduction section of GroupM's 2009 Interaction report drew attention to the flaws of last-click attribution: 'This is unsatisfactory for advertisers and publishers. The market cannot be sustained by an obsessive focus on the last click, typically referred to as the "bottom of the purchase funnel".'[6] And backing this up the 2009 Google presentation 'Search and brand: the UK horizontal story' highlights research showing that '67% of online search users are driven to Search for information about a particular company, product, service, or slogan by an offline channel'[7] (effectively confirming the findings of the *Telegraph* research discussed in Chapter 8).

The last click has been the easiest thing to measure, but it is clearly not the only consideration in measuring campaign effectiveness. Understanding the path to purchase rather than just the last click is important. Channels work together at the same time, so focusing on the last click tends to overlook the interplay between different areas and distorts the view of the effectiveness of individual channels.

The Internet Advertising Bureau (IAB) in the UK even argue that, outside search, clicks may be the wrong metric entirely! They highlighted a study from 'United International Media – Germany's biggest digital sales house – who found, the average heavy clicker is aged 40–59 and has a low/medium education and income level'. In a separate paper, they draw attention to Eyeblaster research that has shown that 'internet users interact with nearly 10% of all rich media ads, compared to less than 0.4% they click on'.[8] Again, the advertisement delivers value, even if users don't click on it.

Furthermore, a revised version of the 'Natural Born Clickers' study released by ComScore and Starcom USA in October 2009 'indicated that the number of people who click on display advertisements in a month has fallen from 32 percent of Internet users in July 2007 to only 16 percent in March 2009, with an even smaller core of people (representing 8 percent of the Internet user base) accounting for the vast majority (85 percent) of all clicks'.

In the press release for this updated study Starcom USA Director (Research and Analytics) John Lowell further commented:

> A click means nothing, earns no revenue and creates no brand equity. Your online advertising has some goal – and it's certainly not to generate clicks... you want people to visit your website, seek more information, purchase a product, become a lead, keep your brand top of mind, learn something new, feel differently – the list goes on. Regardless of whether the consumer clicked on an ad or not, the key is to determine how that ad unit influenced them to think, feel or do something they wouldn't have done otherwise.[9]

There are a number of approaches to remedy last-click bias. For example, there are some clues in user actions. The principle of the paid search funnel is based around the idea that users will start with a generic search like 'family car'. Then, as searchers become more informed, they will start searching for more specific terms that most likely include brand or product names. Some searchers, though, will start a search with a specific term or will go directly to the website without searching at all. In these cases it is likely that searchers or direct website visitors got their prompt or initial information from somewhere else first, and analysis of the campaign data may provide the answers. Thus conversions resulting from specific searches or direct visits should not be held 100 per cent responsible for the sale; other areas need to be credited too.

The obvious solution to this is therefore to measure and report on all paid media online activity from one place. Pulling activity into a central reporting and analysis platform will enable everything to be evaluated side by side. Most importantly it allows analysts to ensure that sales are not double-counted. When working with a mix of different metrics (for example, display looking at those who have been exposed to a message in the last 30 days versus paid search daily clicks versus affiliate advertising, which has an even longer window), it is all too easy to attribute a single sale to multiple sources, effectively counting it more than once. So-called 'de-duplication' allows clearer understanding of the factors that led to a sale and the relative importance of each aspect.

In this sort of set-up it can also be possible to look at exposure-to-conversion reports, which map out the impressions that were served to a user in a time period prior to purchase or the desired action. This moves things on considerably from the last-click model by allowing impressions from perhaps the previous five stages to be analysed (a huge amount of data is produced by these reports, but anything more than five steps prior to purchase tends to be completely unmanageable). There may be commonality in the path, and these placements are therefore significant. Every sale may have come from a different site, but further up the chain everyone seemed to visit (for example) nickburcher.com. In the last-click model nickburcher.com would have been downplayed, or at worst ignored, whereas exposure-to-conversion data indicate that it is vitally important in the consumer path to purchase. In a world where small changes can make big differences, this sort of information is important!

Looking at the last 30 days or the last five site visits may lead to incremental improvements in campaign performance, but still doesn't take into account longer-term exposure, brand sentiment or the effect of offline channels. Any contact with a brand at any point in time may contribute to the purchase, even observational influences, for example seeing cars on the road. We are still not at a point where we can know with certainty the role of each impression, but analysing path to purchase can help improve campaign performance, and we can employ further techniques to aid understanding.

Apportioning value across the purchase path is known as 'attribution modelling', and this can start to help in understanding how things fit together. Forrester define attribution modelling as 'the practice of using business rules to allocate proportional credit to any marketing communications, across all channels, that ultimately lead to the desired consumer action'.[10] Rather than allocating 100 per cent of the sale or impact to the last click, attribution modelling seeks to widen understanding of the path to conversion and include some of the wider or longer-term influences, allocating proportions of the sale to different areas of the purchase path depending on their perceived contribution to the sale. Weighted values are therefore added to each element of the activity, and we start to be able to account more effectively for things such as researched online, bought offline and so on.

For online display it is also possible to look at 'beyond the click' metrics, factoring in general advertisement interaction rates (percentage of expansions, number of roll-overs and so on), and more complexity can be added by looking at longer-term, more subjective brand-oriented metrics such as unaided brand awareness, aided brand awareness, message association, brand favourableness, brand attributes, advertisement recall and purchase intent. The methodology invariably looks at the difference in pre- and post-campaign results between those who were 'exposed' to the campaign and control groups who were not, and these brand effects tend to be measured through online surveys and panels (and can be expanded to include owned and earned activity).

Across all media, though, the only way to know for sure what is driving what is to use testing, either gauging the opinions of controlled groups made up of members representative of our target audience prior to going live or running advertising in certain channels in one area and switching them off or using alternatives in others. A/B splits, dark regions and so forth have all been practical ways of testing different content or creative in paid media, but there is inherent difficulty in persuading advertisers to turn off something that may be driving sales, as it puts targets at risk. It is then extremely difficult, if not impossible, to apply this sort of on-and-off approach with any reliability or consistency in owned or earned spaces. It may be possible to route different people to different pages or web destinations, but it is impossible to control conversations in this way!

Measuring owned and earned media

Owned media is a key contributor to campaign performance, and data pulled from analytics tools such as Site Catalyst or Google Analytics, or platform-specific tools like Facebook Insights or YouTube Insights, can inform the advertiser and allow optimizations to be made, driving owned media efficiency and overall campaign effectiveness.

As with paid media, there is a large variety of different data points that can be measured (and optimized) around owned media. On-site information like number of visitors, unique visitors, returning visitors, time spent on-site, bounce rate and content viewed can all be considered, whilst search engine natural search ranking can be tracked (and manipulated through SEO). Furthermore, as we saw with the Obama conversion optimization in Chapter 5, conversion rates can be measured (and subsequently improved), and average basket size per visitor can also be tracked.

Owned media analytics packages can highlight traffic sources too, so it is possible to see where visits come from, and these data can be used to determine the proportion of visits delivered from paid media against the proportion of visits delivered from owned and earned media (though we have to temper this with the factors around attribution discussed above). Moreover, overlaying site visits on traditional media schedules can help in understanding the amplified present or dual consumption effects, for example site visits driven by a TV advertisement as opposed to site visits driven by search, etc.

For earned media things are different again, and the key measurement constituent is a listening tool. Understanding the volume of conversations, topics of conversations, tone of conversations (positive or negative) and so on can provide data and show effects of paid, owned or earned initiatives – either at promoting positive conversations or at negating or reducing negative ones (the mechanics of listening are discussed extensively in earlier chapters). Additionally, the listening data can be combined with traditional research and surveying to provide a more complete picture, which can then be used across an organization (marketing and advertising, product development, customer service, training and so on).

The guiding currency across paid, owned and earned disciplines has traditionally been 'opportunity to see', but as the world has moved to the web the potential for deeper insight and measurement has grown – if we can untangle the channels. We need to account for returns from each individual element of the media trinity, and we need to understand the links between the different segments. We need to understand how consumers behave in different spaces and the value of these behaviours in driving returns – especially on Facebook.

Establishing the value of a fan

In *The Facebook Effect* David Kirkpatrick references 'unnamed Facebook sources', writing: 'Once an advertiser establishes some sort of connection with a user it gets a tremendous amount of what Facebook calls "derivative value." Executives say that once a brand makes a connection with a consumer, it leads to an average of about 200 free additional "impressions" – occasions when people on Facebook see information about that brand.'[11]

Early calculations around the quantification of the value of a Facebook fan (or Facebook 'Like', to use the latest terminology) tended to focus on an equation based on this idea of derivative media value – an equivalent of the frowned-upon PR practice of looking at average value equivalent (AVE).

In April 2010 Vitrue produced analysis and claimed that the value of a fan was $3.60 per annum based on a fan page following of 1 million.[12] This figure was calculated on the basis of the media value of the free impressions served into a Facebook fan's news feed. Vitrue's maths translated two posts each day to the 1 million fan page into approximately 60 million free impressions per month. Using a $5 CPM rate, Vitrue equated these free Facebook impressions to $3.6 million worth of media value each year. However, these calculations were made pre-EdgeRank and are based on the assumption that every post has 100 per cent visibility.

The Facebook EdgeRank algorithm, coupled with frequency of user log-in, now means that visibility of any single Facebook update is significantly lower than 100 per cent (though, as we saw in Chapter 3, this can vary). If we use a visibility figure of 10 per cent (for ease of working out, although the real figure will probably be lower), reworking Vitrue's figures against this sees the number of free impressions reduced to 6 million per year, with the average media value of free impressions against a 1 million fan base changing to $0.36 per fan per year as a result. Pass-on rates may see the total media value of free impressions increase slightly, but it all depends on the viral coefficient for each update, and pass-on levels will vary depending on the content posted.

These free impressions may be used to drive traffic to an original owned content area, and for many sites Facebook is a significant traffic driver, but the real value of a Facebook fan is in more than just free impressions. The power of an owned media social media profile comes from having an active audience, rather than just a large one.

After Bing recruited 400,000 new Facebook fans through their *Farmville* activity (discussed in Chapter 3) Paul Adams raised some interesting points about this activity on his *Think Outside In* blog. He wrote: 'The quality of those fans is questionable. Are those people really fans of Bing? Or are they fans of *Farmville*?... Before you try and collect as many fans and followers as possible, think long and hard about who you want as a fan/follower, and what value you're going to give them when they follow you.'[13]

Fan or follower numbers are not everything, and a much cited paper, 'Measuring user influence in Twitter: the million follower fallacy' by Cha *et al*, demonstrates that large amounts of followers on Twitter do not necessarily equate to large amounts of engagement.[14] The same thing is true on Facebook, and using Facebook Insights (or some of the new third-party tools) it is possible to calculate ongoing engagement levels. Social management tool provider Conversocial use a formula called interactions per thousand (IPM):[15]

**(Across a 30-day period) Number of comments
+ number of likes ÷ number of posts ÷ number of fans = IPM**

At the time of writing Skittles and Red Bull both have large fan bases, 18.6 million and 21.4 million respectively. Both have posted 24 times in the last 30 days, but Skittles have generated more 'Likes' and more comments. As a result Skittles have an IPM of 0.59 compared to Red Bull's IPM of 0.34, and their EdgeRank figure will benefit accordingly.

Engagement level is important, so much so that Forrester's Augie Ray went so far as to declare in a provocative and attention-seeking blog post: 'the Value of a Facebook Fan? Zero!' His argument was that Facebook fans are worth nothing unless they can be put to use. This headline is too sensationalist, though. We have seen from things like the derivative value and free impressions or the effects of social advocacy in ad units that there is a clear value in having a fan base, but if the fan base can be mobilized then the value of a fan potentially increases. Ray clarifies his position along these lines, writing in the body of the post:

> consider the difference between potential value and realized value. There is an appropriate and interesting corollary in the world of high school physics: If you lift the ball off the ground and hold it stationary, it has no kinetic energy but it does have potential energy; drop the ball, and the potential energy becomes kinetic energy. Facebook fans are like that – all potential energy until you introduce something that creates kinetic energy. As such, the operative question isn't, 'What is the value of a Facebook Fan?' but 'How do I make my Facebook fans valuable?'[16]

As Adams says in the conclusion of his Bing blog post, 'You don't want the most fans. You want the best fans.' We still need to equate engagement to business outcomes, though, and matching up data from owned media on social platforms like Facebook or Twitter with other sources of information can start to give us more understanding of the value of a fan base.

Experiments comparing growth in Facebook fan levels for Facebook pages across a vertical sector to real-world brand preference tracking data have, in some cases, found interesting correlations where increases in numbers of fans have been seen to correlate with increases in brand preference, whilst *eMarketer*, in a paper on social media measurement in February 2010, declared: 'Marketers should develop clever ways to assign monetary values to so-called soft metrics, such as number of fans, friends or followers, as a means to measure ROI.' They highlight the example of Papa John's pizza and quote Jim Ensign, VP of Marketing at Papa John's: 'We [Papa John's] look at the percentage [of Facebook fans] that convert to customers, the percentage increase in their frequency [of visits], projected increases in their average ticket and what their tenure is with us... We can project their future value. Are we 100% right? No. But are we directionally correct? Absolutely.'[17]

This idea of equating social media and Facebook fan base to real-world purchasing is being investigated by a number of marketers. At the 2011 *Ad Age* Digital Conference, Wendy Clark, SVP for Integrated Marketing Communications at Coca-Cola, told the audience about research that they had conducted around Coca-Cola Facebook fans in Colombia and the UK.[18] In comparing fans against non-fans, they found that Coca-Cola fans had twice the consumption frequency and 10 times the purchase intent. Coke also looked at the effects of fan page activity on the existing fan base and found that, when the fan page was activated, there was a 7 per cent lift in daily consumption and 10 per cent increase in purchase intent amongst the existing fan base (though there were clear differences between audience reaction in the UK and Colombia).

At the same conference, CMO of Radio Shack Lee Applbaum told attendees that Radio Shack had been able to track the activity of Foursquare users (primarily through using Foursquare couponing via 'Specials') and found that 'Foursquare users at Radio Shack generally spend three-and-a-half times more compared to what non-Foursquare users [spend].'[19] When social behaviour can be tied to sales it's interesting and makes for compelling investment arguments.

Social as a transactional medium is interesting many brands, and social commerce is evolving quickly. Groupon grew into a huge company in record time through harnessing earned media to spread knowledge of its Daily Deals and, as Facebook commerce functionality evolves, a growing list of brands (Starbucks, easyJet, Asos, Heineken, P&G and so on) are experimenting with using Facebook as a store front or transactional platform (F-commerce). Furthermore, Dell continue to push out Twitter coupons, and location-based offerings like Foursquare Specials are being used by a range of businesses to push offers and incentives pegged to real-world locations. Advertisers are not using platforms like Facebook solely to drive fan numbers and 'have a conversation'; they are using Facebook to solve audience needs, which can then develop into trackable revenues.

So after all of this, what's the value of a fan? It depends who you are and how you are using Facebook and other social platforms. Ultimately it all comes back to having measurable objectives and goals – the value of a fan will be very different to a pizza company compared to a luxury car brand! The only way to know how much a Facebook or Twitter presence is really worth to a business is to test and learn and build up models and benchmarks over time. Working to assumptions like Papa John's can help, and Don Bartholomew (*MetricsMan*) is a strong advocate of 'hypothetical ROI models', which 'help you think through the data requirements your research approach must address in order to actually measure the ROI of the program after implementation'.[20] (The model is based on logic and assumptions at the beginning, but becomes more useful, as actual data rather than predicted data can be used.)

Expressions not impressions

As far back as 2002, in a paper titled 'Pathways to measuring consumer behaviour in an age of media convergence', Koerner *et al* had an alternative idea for measuring and assessing media value. They put forward thoughts around the idea that: 'Traditional media measures, such as impressions or reach and frequency, provide a very limited ability to estimate value in this emerging interactive world. At best, counting impressions provides an enumeration of those who have been exposed, but hardly gives any indication of the likely range of consumer actions and responses to that content.'

The authors of this 2002 paper argued in favour of judging campaigns on the basis of 'expression' rather than the traditional 'impression', stating that:

> The determination of true communication value has more to do with the effect that the message has on the consumer than the absolute number of exposures. Understanding the intrinsic power of the medium is now as important as simply understanding the number of people reached by the vehicle. Therefore, in this new research environment the idea of an expression would serve as a supplemental measure to provide an additional impact dimension to the impression.[21]

On the one hand this thinking can be taken as a validation of the click-through being an important measure (low-involvement impression versus actively engaged click), but it is not limited to this, and in a socially connected world the idea of 'expression' can also be taken as meaning talking or sharing. Conversation (including sentiment scoring) can be measured through listening tools, which again reflect the sum of all activity, and this type of idea is powering a new approach to measurement at Pepsi.

In the October 2010 issue of *Admap* Joe Mandese goes into detail, writing that Pepsi is 'advocating a new model for planning, buying and posting conventional media buys based around the amount of social media they generate'.[22] PepsiCo are now championing an idea called 'impression-plus', and in explaining this the article states: 'Instead of simply paying for impressions generated by an advertising buy, [Pepsi] advertising deals should now factor in the impressions generated by shared media, or what social media and PR pros call "earned" media generated by consumers on social media outlets.'

Shiv Singh from Pepsi is quoted in the article too, saying 'Don't just tell me about impressions – tell me about what the sharing capability is. That's the model to think about.'

In a world where OTS meant 'opportunity to see', the media strategy was about the numbers who had the possibility of seeing the paid media placements, but now we can look at the actual impact of campaign communications on consumer sentiment and behaviours.

Clearly not all product categories are going to be tweeted and discussed, and this approach downplays low-involvement impact, but it is an interesting way of assessing campaigns and speaks to the idea that paid and owned can drive earned and effective measurement needs to cover all three areas simultaneously. In a world where OTS can be reinterpreted as 'opportunity to share', with the right measurement approaches Pepsi are betting on planning and trading based around homing in on those in the target audience who will consume *and* share the message.

In the same way that TV activity can be overlaid on to searches to understand the link between the two (looking for a Diamond Geezer effect), if we run listening at the same time that paid media is on air we can map correlations between advertisements being shown and people talking online. Mapping conversation development (or fan base growth) against a schedule can therefore give us another view on the effectiveness of paid media placements by allowing us to identify which spots most prompted people to talk and share, which spots drove the largest uplift in new Facebook fans, and so on. We can also look at the effects of traditional media in driving visits to owned media and the impact of different media channels on fan counts.

Business outcomes, not virality measures – Hero revisited

While the approach of 'expression' is interesting, it doesn't fully answer the questions around business outcomes unless it is matched to a more substantive, real-world dataset. We looked at the 'Swedish hero' personalized video in Chapter 5, and Paul Adams highlights this campaign in another post on his *Think Outside In* blog. He noticed that the footnote at the bottom of the video page had a clickable question, 'How did we create the most successful global interactive viral film ever?' On clicking this footnote more information was given, explaining that the film had had millions of views in just eight weeks.

In the same way that he questioned the value of the Bing/*Farmville* activity, Adams had an issue with this statement on the 'Swedish hero' video, writing:

I'm going to assume that the client's metric for success was not to create the most viral video out there. After all, the audience is people living in Sweden. I'm assuming the success metric was the number of people who went on to pay their broadcasting fee. So why is that not the metric being promoted? Surely a better promotion is: 'Find out how we motivated 21% of people in Sweden to pay their broadcasting fee (and created the most successful global viral interactive ever).'[23]

Adams concludes, 'Virality is not a success metric. How many times something gets shared or forwarded is only ever a means to an end... We need to get better at measuring and promoting the metrics that matter.'

A good example of how this plays out in practice can be seen around the evaluation of Evian's record-breaking Roller Babies campaign in 2009.[24] By 9 November 2009, this complex matrix of interlocking paid, owned and earned activity had seen Evian's Roller Babies film record over 45 million views on YouTube, in the process becoming recognized by the *Guinness Book of Records* as 'the most viewed online advertisement' to date (excluding music videos and film trailers). Unruly Media found that sharing and views generated from earned media were a crucial part of the view count, with analysis finding over 6,000 blog posts, 16,481 tweets and 655,000 Facebook shares (driving over 400,000 new Facebook fans).[25]

Not content just to report on view counts, wider research was undertaken against the campaign. Findings recorded why the video was shared and discussed so much and also evaluated the effects on consumer attitudes towards the brand as a result of the activity. It was found that 72 per cent of respondents agreed that the Evian Roller Babies advertising 'is an ad I will tell other people about', against a Nielsen norm of 50 per cent, and 48 per cent of respondents agreed that 'I will send a link to this ad to other people so they can see it', against a Nielsen norm of 44 per cent. 'Evian ad recall increased by 27% overall and 55% at two exposures' and 'Purchase consideration for Evian increased by 4 percentage points.'

The industry still has a tendency to celebrate the soft metrics, but the more compelling headlines are around campaigns that are proved to deliver actual business advantage.

Bringing it all together

As all media becomes social in theory it is starting to get easier to see what drives digital views and fulfilment. The above discussion should give some ideas as to how to measure different channels, but whilst significant advances have been made we still have some way to go before we will be able to know anything definitively. We saw how offline media is driving searches and, with couponing and commerce, the lines of sight, particularly from digital, are becoming more obvious. We now have a world within which it is possible not just to measure the impact of activity through survey responses and so on, but also to evaluate the actions of the active audience in terms of clicks, tweets, shares, conversations and so on. The paths to purchase are more visible than they have ever been before. We no longer have to rely on gut feel or implication, as data management tools are becoming simpler, yet more comprehensive.

Being able to track and optimize quickly is important while the campaign is active (and helps support a 'test and learn' approach). Additionally, measurement processes and structures are vitally important for post-campaign analysis, which provides learnings and benchmarks that can be fed into the next activity.

The key, though, is in taking a helicopter view of everything – whether this is done through econometrics, bespoke research or just looking at channels side by side and de-duplicating where appropriate. Using 'systems thinking' when looking at the outcomes and effects of advertising is the only way to understand things properly. Peter Senge writes: 'Systems thinking is a discipline for seeing wholes. It is a framework for seeing interrelationships rather than things, for seeing patterns of change rather than static snapshots.'[26]

In a multi-channel world of paid, owned and earned, this sort of mindset is crucial if we want to understand how things work together. We should be looking at paid, owned, earned performance by campaign and also from the big picture perspective (allowing us to see the effects of campaign activity on our always-on hub performance too). There is no fixed campaign approach, no consistent formula for success and no standardized measurement criteria, as every campaign will be different and aiming to achieve different things. However, if SMART objectives and goals are set up at the outset and married to a structured approach that enables data to be analysed and used effectively, then the advertiser is placed favourably. Perhaps Carl Warner, Executive Creative Director at JWT in Atlanta, best summed things up in *Adweek* when he reworked the classic measurement quote:

> The science of analytics when used poorly is like the old adage of how a drunk uses a lamp post – for support rather than illumination. Metrics can illuminate things we couldn't dream of being able to see 25 years ago, but the science should complement the 'art' in a decision, not supersede it. Because, according to the saying, some things that can be measured don't count. And some things that count cannot be measured.[27]

KEY POINTS

- The setting of pre-campaign, SMART objectives and goals is important for effective post-campaign measurement.
- Measuring the last click only can confuse and corrupt measurement.
- Centralized data management makes multi-channel measurement easier to conduct.
- Paid media data come from tools such as the ad server; owned media data come from site analytics packages; and earned media data primarily come from listening tools.
- Platform-specific data can also be used (eg Facebook Insights).
- There are a number of ways of looking at the value of a fan – from advertising value equivalency (AVE) to engagement to sales tracking.
- A number of companies are looking at expressions, not impressions, as a key metric.
- Business outcomes are more important than social outputs.
- Systems thinking and a helicopter view are the only way of bringing things together, as we want to know not just what happened by channel but also how each affected the others.

Conclusion

The arrival of the internet fundamentally changed the marketing landscape, and since the end of the last century digital connectivity has infiltrated into more and more of society. It's no longer a question of going to a computer to use the web; the web surrounds us and everything is becoming connected. Technological advance in areas like broadband penetration, Wi-Fi, 3G, 4G and mobile data and the hardware needed to take advantage of all of this continues to change society. We don't access the web just from our home, office or college PC; we access it through our phones, our game consoles and our iPads and, more and more, through everyday devices. In 2011 Samsung unveiled a tweeting fridge, the Chevy Cruze now has Facebook built into it, and even PepsiCo's latest vending machines come equipped with the ability to access social community Pepsi Refresh or record a video message and give a beverage to a friend.

We are entering an era when we will no longer have to 'go online'; we will just be always on. We will be connected to the internet by our computers, our phones, our TVs and our everyday devices, and when this is then wired into social networks like Facebook and Twitter the possibilities become mind blowing, especially when location and commerce are also factored into the mix. The changes in technology are also changing human behaviours, the way that people connect with each other – from basic communication to sharing content to collaborative consumption. The implications for advertising and marketing are enormous, and if the industry thinks that the last 10 years have been a rollercoaster then hold tight, because things are going to go faster!

Vastly expanded streams of data, real-time targeting, everything connected, everything searchable, everything tagged and everyone everywhere able to create and find an audience, all set against a backdrop of the ever increasing speed of technological innovation, will challenge even the most on-the-pulse practitioners.

Near field communication (NFC) technology, virtual wallets, social and mobile commerce, gesture-based interfaces, robots, Wi-Fi everywhere and more are all on the way. For marketers and advertisers the ability to monitor and piggyback trends is going to become increasingly important and, whilst no one can say certainly where this is all going to end up, one thing is certain – in Rishad Tobaccowala's words, 'The future doesn't fit in the containers of the past.'

Everything is now joined up, and nothing can work in isolation. It's about paid *and* owned *and* earned.

Notes

Introduction

1. 'Hi, my name is Karen', video, **http://www.huffingtonpost.com/ 2009/09/15/danish-mother-seeking-den_n_287483.html**

2. 'Most successful viral advertising', *Politiken* in English, **http://politiken.dk/newsinenglish/article788087.ece**

3. 'Story telling in spirit of HC Andersen', *Adland*, **http://adland.tv/ commercials/karen26-karen-denmark-seeking-augusts-father-2009-denmark**

4. 'Broadminded country', *Politiken* in English, **http://politiken.dk/ newsinenglish/article788087.ece**

5. *Politiken* in Danish, **http://politiken.dk/indland/article787965.ece**

6. **http://wallblog.co.uk/2010/06/02/fired-grey-stands-by-pulled-visit-denmark-viral/**

7. **http://adland.tv/content/will-karen26-please-cannes-jury-it-did-after-all-go-viral**

8. Fox News, *The O'Reilly Factor*, **http://video.foxnews.com/v/3940320/ desperately-seeking-daddy**

9. *Swedish Father Seeking Danish Mother*, **http://www.youtube.com/ watch?v=YuiqlFXTTiE**

10. *Brooklyn Father Seeking*, **http://www.youtube.com/ watch?v=MXdbNWJaif4**

11. *Danish Mother Seeking (The Father's Story)*, **http://www.youtube.com/ watch?v=Amsk2ixS_cc**

12. *Danish Mother Seeking – I'm Not a Bimbo Remix*, **http://www.youtube.com/watch?v=U15NurVy5bg**

13. *I Am Your Father, August*, **http://www.youtube.com/ watch?v=EU5XT-64Tbs**

14. *Danish Mother Seeking, Part 2*, **http://www.youtube.com/ watch?v=sJcDgz5uCwM**

[15] http://foreigndispatches.typepad.com/dispatches/2009/10/ditte-arnth-translated.html

[16] http://www.brandrepublic.com/news/605760/Surge-Kazakh-hotel-searches-thanks-Borat-effect/

[17] Frank Rose, 'Entertainment and ads are being blurred', *WiredUK*, Ideas Bank section, May 2011

[18] 'Paid, owned, earned', *eMarketer*, http://www.emarketer.com/Reports/All/Emarketer_2000686.aspx

Chapter One   How the world of paid, owned, earned works

[1] 'A mathematical theory of communication', http://plan9.bell-labs.com/cm/ms/what/shannonday/shannon1948.pdf

[2] http://en.wikipedia.org/wiki/File:Shannon-Weaver_model.png

[3] Thomas Smith (1885) *Successful Advertising*, 7th edn, http://en.wikipedia.org/wiki/Effective_frequency

[4] Herbert E Krugman (1965) *The Impact of Television Advertising: Learning without involvement*, http://ctl.scu.edu.tw/scutwebpub/website/DocUpload/CourseTeaching/mywang200626121254_1.pdf

[5] Jean-Marie Dru, extract from *Disruption*, http://www.campaignlive.co.uk/news/787134/Hotline-Thought-Leaders-series/

[6] 'The brand effects of adwords', April 2008, slide 16, http://static.googleusercontent.com/external_content/untrusted_dlcp/www.google.co.uk/en/uk/intl/en/advertisers/pdfs/searchandbrand.pdf

[7] Valerie Lopez, 'Blending paid, owned and earned media in today's landscape', 7 July 2011, http://blog.us.cision.com/2011/07/blending-paid-owned-and-earned-media-in-todays-landscape/

[8] Bob Thacker, quoted in Jim Lecinski, *Winning the Zero Moment of Truth*, http://www.zeromomentoftruth.com/

[9] Joe Mandese, 'Media goes organic', *Admap*, October 2010

[10] http://www.iabuk.net/en/1/automotivecarconsumersonline.html

[11] Jim Lecinski, *Winning the Zero Moment of Truth*, http://www.zeromomentoftruth.com/

12   Rishad Tobaccowala, 'A new marketing mindset', slide 22,
     http://www.slideshare.net/NikiHirschmann/rishad-tobaccowala

13   Tim Broadbent, 'Channel planning: effectiveness lies in channel
     integration', *Admap*, January 2011

14   US Congress Office of Technology Assessment, 'Global
     communications: opportunities for trade and aid', September 1995,
     http://www.princeton.edu/~ota/disk1/1995/9535/9535.PDF

15   Jay Rosen, quoted in 'The people formerly known as the audience',
     Economist, July 2011, **http://www.economist.com/node/18904124**

16   Philip Rayner, Peter Wall and Stephen Kruger (2004) *Media Studies:
     The essential resource*, Routledge, London

17   John Fiske (1989) *Understanding Popular Culture*, Unwin Hyman,
     Boston, MA

18   Jonah Peretti, 'The hidden secrets of social media and viral advertising',
     slide 23, **http://techcrunch.com/2011/03/30/buzzfeeds-jonah-peretti-
     on-why-the-facebook-media-world-view-wins/**

19   Philippe Boutie, 'Will this kill that?', *Communication World*, April 1996,
     http://www.thefreelibrary.com/Will+this+kill+that%3f-a018512266

20   Kevin Roberts (2006) *The Lovemarks Effect: Winning in the consumer
     revolution*, Powerhouse Books, Brooklyn, NY

21   Kirk Cheyfitz, 'Advertising's Future is 3 simple words: paid. owned.
     earned.', *Huffington Post*, 27 October 2010,
     **http://www.huffingtonpost.com/kirk-cheyfitz/advertisings-future-
     is-3_b_774821.html**

22   Sean Corcoran, 'Defining earned, owned and paid media', *Forrester.com*,
     **http://blogs.forrester.com/interactive_marketing/2009/12/defining-
     earned-owned-and-paid-media.html**

23   Daniel Goodall, 'Owned, bought and earned media', *All That Is Good*,
     http://danielgoodall.com/2009/03/02/owned-bought-and-earned-media/

24   Daniel Goodall, 'Owned, bought and earned (redux)', *All That Is Good*,
     http://danielgoodall.com/2009/05/20/owned-bought-and-earned-redux/

25   Jeffrey Graham, 'Getting the correct mix of paid owned earned',
     **http://www.brandrepublic.com/news/article/1075978/
     initiative-challenges-assumptions-paid-earned-owned-media/**

26   **http://www.nickburcher.com/2011/05/paid-owned-earned-on-star-
     wars-day-vw.html**

27   Jeffrey Graham, 'Virtuous cycle of involvement',
      http://www.brandrepublic.com/news/article/1075978/
      initiative-challenges-assumptions-paid-earned-owned-media/

28   G Franz, quoted in Tony Yeshin (2006) *Advertising*, Thomson Learning,
      London

29   Arto Joensuu, 'Working the non-working', *Working in Digital*, **http://**
      artojoensuu.wordpress.com/2009/02/04/working-the-non-working/

30   Andrew Walmsley, 'Media's added dimensions', *Marketing* magazine,
      http://www.allbusiness.com/marketing-advertising/marketing-
      techniques-media/13338699-1.html

Chapter Two   Listening

1   'O brother, where art thou?', *The Simpsons*,
     http://www.thesimpsons.com/recaps/season2/#episode15.htm

2   **http://bedrebustur.dk/default.asp?page=tekst.asp&id=3370**

3   **http://youtu.be/xgOyTNtsWyY**

4   'Bus driver becomes internet sensation', *Copenhagen Post*, 21 May
     2010, **http://www.cphpost.dk/component/content/**
     49047.html?task=view

5   John Battelle, *The Search*, **http://battellemedia.com/archives/2003/11/**
     the_database_of_intentions

6   Bill Tancer (2009) *Click: What we do online and why it matters*,
     HarperCollins, London

7   Google Eurovision predictor, **http://www.google.com/landing/**
     eurovision/index.html

8   Facebook Lexicon Correlations group, **http://www.facebook.com/**
     group.php?gid=12455359236&v=photos

9   Facebook 'Campaign to get Brian Blessed to do a voiceover for my sat
     nav' group, **http://www.facebook.com/group.php?gid=16221530186**

10   Brian Blessed sat nav mock-up video, **http://youtu.be/-JpKuYbJQK4**

11   Brian Blessed TomTom thank-you message,
     http://youtu.be/BOicbYFq4C0

12   Brian Blessed TomTom recording, **http://youtu.be/FMiLQwKLSQM**

13   Brian Blessed TomTom, **http://www.tomtom.com/brianblessed**

14 Stephen Baker (2009) *They've Got Your Number: Data, digits and destiny – how the numerati are changing our lives*, Vintage, London

15 Andrew Keen (2007) *The Cult of the Amateur: How blogs, MySpace, YouTube and the rest of today's user-generated media are killing our culture and economy*, Nicholas Brealey, London

16 Laura P Naumann, Simine Vazire, Peter J Rentfrow and Samuel D Gosling, 'Personality judgments based on physical appearance', *Personality and Social Psychology Bulletin*, 17 September 2009, **http://psp.sagepub.com/content/early/2009/09/17/ 0146167209346309.full.pdf+html**

17 Johannah Cornblatt, 'Making a digital first impression: why you can't fake your Facebook profile', *Newsweek* summary of *Psychological Science* paper, **http://www.newsweek.com/blogs/the-human-condition/ 2009/11/10/making-a-digital-first-impression-why-you-can-t-fake-your-facebook-profile.html**

18 Steven D Levitt and Stephen J Dubner (2009) *Superfreakonomics: Global cooling, patriotic prostitutes and why suicide bombers should buy life insurance*, William Morrow, New York

19 Charlene Li and Josh Bernoff (2008) *Groundswell: Winning in a world transformed by social technologies*, Harvard Business School Publishing, Boston, MA

20 Kevin Roberts (2006) *The Lovemarks Effect: Winning in the consumer revolution*, Powerhouse Books, Brooklyn, NY

21 Baker, *They've Got Your Number*

22 **http://news.bbc.co.uk/1/hi/uk/8116869.stm**

23 Dan Hurley, 'The science of sarcasm (not that you care)', *New York Times*, 3 June 2008, **http://www.nytimes.com/2008/06/03/health/ research/03sarc.html**

24 'Facebook speak: teenagers create secret language', *Telegraph*, 26 April 2010, **http://www.telegraph.co.uk/technology/facebook/7632133/ Facebook-speak-Teenagers-create-secret-online-language.html**

25 **http://www.idea.gov.uk/idk/core/page.do?pageId=14523988**

26 Converseon white paper, 'Listening 2.0', **http://converseon.com/us/ news/listen20.html**

27 'HMU – the status update sweeping Facebook like wildfire', *Guardian*, **http://www.guardian.co.uk/technology/2010/dec/15/ facebook-fastest-growing-status-update**

28   http://www.nytimes.com/2007/08/27/technology/27brands.html?_r=1

29   WARC Word of Mouth Marketing Awards 2008

30   Robert Cialdini, 'Influence', **http://www.rickross.com/reference/brainwashing/brainwashing20.html**

31   **http://www.nickburcher.com/2010/03/wispa-newspaper-ads-drive-traffic-to.html**

32   'First Direct bank launches pioneering digital campaign [Sep 09]', **http://www.madebypi.co.uk/ourwork/work-items/first-direct-bank-launches-pioneering-digital-campaign.aspx**

33   'An honest banker', *Blogstorm*, **http://www.blogstorm.co.uk/an-honest-banker/**

Chapter Three   Content hubs and communities

1   Clay Shirky (2009) *Here Comes Everybody: How change happens when people come together*, Penguin, London

2   Mark Earls (2007) *Herd: How to change mass behaviour by harnessing our true nature*, John Wiley, Chichester

3   Peter L Berger and Thomas Luckmann, 'The social construction of reality', **http://books.google.co.uk/books?id=MzGV9A5qLzgC&lpg=PA42&ots=3Dt0E8oPky&dq=berger%20luckmann%20social%20construction%20of%20reality&lr&pg=PA42#v=onepage&q=berger%20luckmann%20social%20construction%20of%20reality&f=false**

4   James J Sempsey and Dennis A Johnston, 'The psychological dynamics and social climate of text-based virtual reality', **http://web.archive.org/web/20050430232422/www.brandeis.edu/pubs/jove/HTML/v5/sempseyjohnston.htm**

5   Bernard Cova and Véronique Cova, 'Tribal marketing: the tribalisation of society and its impact on the conduct of marketing', **http://venus.unive.it/vescovi/cova-tribe-2001.pdf**

6   Henry Jenkins *et al*, 'If it doesn't spread, it's dead', **http://www.henryjenkins.org/2009/02/if_it_doesnt_spread_its_dead_p.html**

7   Martin Czerwinski, personal conversation

8   **http://www.zynga.com/about/numbers.php**

9 http://www.imediaconnection.com/content/22997.imc

10 http://www.insidefacebook.com/2010/03/03/bings-facebook-page-gets-400000-new-fans-in-a-day-through-ad-offer-in-farmville/

11 http://www.lunaticgames.com/blog/?p=184

12 http://cartownaddicts.com/2011/01/10/new-prius-and-money-tree/

13 http://cartownaddicts.com/2011/01/24/new-car-2012-toyota-prius-plugin/

14 http://www.zenithoptimedia.com.cn/publication/vol46/en/case_02.html

15 http://www2.chinadaily.com.cn/china/2007-07/11/content_5432238.htm

16 Primark Appreciation Society, **http://www.facebook.com/group.php?gid=2210213021**

17 Personal interview with student involved

18 'Primark bucks Facebook', *Brand Republic*, **http://www.brandrepublic.com/News/766273/Primark-bucks-Facebook/**

19 Rubicon, 'Online communities and their impact on business', **http://rubiconconsulting.com/downloads/whitepapers/Rubicon-web-community.pdf**

20 **http://www.forrester.com/rb/Research/global_update_of_social_technographics%26%231/4%3B/q/id/57523/t/2**

21 **http://www.insidefacebook.com/2010/05/20/facebook-creates-removes-restriction-on-landing-page-tabs/**

22 Robert Cialdini, 'Influence', **http://www.rickross.com/reference/brainwashing/brainwashing20.html**

23 **http://www.insidefacebook.com/2011/06/22/unique-page-views/**

24 Comscore, 'The power of like', **http://www.comscore.com/Press_Events/Presentations_Whitepapers/2011/The_Power_of_Like_How_Brands_Reach_and_Influence_Fans_Through_Social_Media_Marketing**

25 *The Cluetrain Manifesto*, **http://www.cluetrain.com/**

26 Matthew Creamer, 'When it comes to Facebook, relevance may be redefined: to create conversation, simple, random and banal may be a brand's best bets', *Advertising Age*, 29 November 2010, **http://adage.com/article/digital/marketing-a-brand-s-bet-social-media-randomness/147272/**

27 AT Kearney, 'Socially awkward media', **http://www.atkearney.com/index.php/Publications/socially-awkward-media-volume-xiii-number-2-2010.html**

[28] 'The Betfair Twitter mystery solved', Business Diary, *Independent*, 11 January 2011, **http://www.independent.co.uk/news/business/news/ business-diary-the-betfair-twitter-mystery-solved-2181294.html**

[29] **http://www.creativereview.co.uk/cr-blog/2009/august1/ tuning-in-to-radio-maliboom-boom**

[30] Robert Cialdini, 'Influence', **http://www.rickross.com/reference/ brainwashing/brainwashing20.html**

[31] Jason Kincaid, 'EdgeRank: the secret sauce that makes Facebook's news feed tick', *TechCrunch*, 22 April 2010, **http://techcrunch.com/ 2010/04/22/facebook-edgerank/**

[32] **http://www.allfacebook.com/more-detailed-patterns-in-status- updates-found-2010-12**

[33] **http://www.google.com/logos/**

[34] '10 ways to engage your fans', Buddy Media white paper, **http://forms.buddymedia.com/rs/buddymedia/images/ WhitePaperEngageFans_v2.pdf**

[35] Tourism Australia, **http://www.youtube.com/watch?v=h62dxLDzzUY**

[36] Porsche, **http://www.porsche.com/microsite/facebook/ international.aspx**

[37] Matthew Adell, 'Becoming "One": anatomy of a #1 hit', *BeatPortal*, 6 July 2010, **http://www.beatportal.com/feed/item/ becoming-one-anatomy-of-a-1-hit/**

[38] W Samuelson and RJ Zeckhauser (1988) 'Status quo bias in decision making', *Journal of Risk and Uncertainty*, **1**, pp 7–59

[39] Richard H Thaler and Cass R Sunstein (2009) *Nudge: Improving decisions about health, wealth and happiness*, Penguin Books, London

Chapter Four　Content

[1] Perez Prado biography, **http://www.allmusic.com/cg/amg.dll?p=amg&s ql=11:dpftxqe5ldde~T1**

[2] 'Anticipation' TV advertisement, **http://youtu.be/S5HU5axz6GI**

[3] Guinness 'Anticipation' screensaver, **http://youtu.be/qBcdAOw9V-k**

[4] Carl Lyons's blog, **http://www.talkablelikeable.com/tag/ guinness-screensaver/**

5   Ciar Byrne, 'Rappers sell their lyrics (and their souls) to the highest
    corporate bids', *Independent on Sunday*, 30 March 2005,
    **http://www.independent.co.uk/arts-entertainment/music/news/
    rappers-sell-their-lyrics-and-their-souls-to-the-highest-corporate-
    bids-530444.html**

6   **http://knowledge.wharton.upenn.edu/article.cfm?articleid=1093**

7   Byrne, 'Rappers sell their lyrics (and their souls) to the highest corporate
    bids'

8   Andrew Keen (2007) *The Cult of the Amateur: How blogs, MySpace,
    YouTube and the rest of today's user-generated media are killing our
    culture and economy*, Nicholas Brealey, London

9   2010 USC Annenberg Digital Future Study, **http://www.digitalcenter.org/
    pdf/2010_digital_future_final_release.pdf**

10 **http://mashable.com/2011/04/04/angry-birds-rio-stats/**

11 **http://boxofficemojo.com/movies/?id=rio.htm**

12 Bob Thacker, quoted in Jim Lecinski, *Winning the Zero Moment of Truth*,
    http://www.zeromomentoftruth.com/

13 **http://youtu.be/CHtyQJzTy70**

14 **http://news.bbc.co.uk/sport1/hi/cricket/9340921.stm**

15 **http://news.bbc.co.uk/sport1/hi/cricket/tms/9339769.stm**

16 *JK Wedding Entrance*, **http://youtu.be/4-94JhLEiN0**

17 *JK Divorce Entrance*, **http://youtu.be/zbr2ao86ww0**

18 'The moment William and Kate dance down the aisle (but don't worry,
    this is a mobile phoney Royal Wedding)', *Mail Online*, 16 April 2011,
    **http://www.dailymail.co.uk/femail/article-1377166/T-Mobile-Royal-
    Wedding-advert-Prince-William-Kate-Middleton-dance-aisle.html**

19 **http://www.wired.com/politics/law/news/2000/04/35670**

20 Don Tapscott and Anthony D Williams (2007) *Wikinomics: How mass
    collaboration changes everything*, Atlantic Books, London

21 Chris Anderson (2007) *The Long Tail: How endless choice is creating
    unlimited demand*, Random House Business Books, London

22 Henry Jenkins *et al*, 'If it doesn't spread, it's dead',
    **http://www.henryjenkins.org/2009/02/if_it_doesnt_spread_
    its_dead_p.html**

23   'I now pronounce you monetized: a YouTube video case study', *YouTube Biz Blog*, 30 July 2009, **http://ytbizblog.blogspot.com/2009/07/i-now-pronounce-you-monetized-youtube_30.html**

24   **http://youtu.be/MYheMAO_Sqs**

25   **http://danielgoodall.com/2009/05/20/owned-bought-and-earned-redux/**

26   **http://bundesliga.theoffside.com/teams/werder-bremen/the-dietmar-hamann-bridge-phenomenon.html**

27   **http://www.lda.gov.uk/server/show/ConWebDoc.1071**

28   **http://www.dmbootdesign.com/designs/**

29   **http://www.dmbootdesign.com/designs/peoples-winner**

30   **http://digital-examples.blogspot.com/2008/09/dm-boot-design-winner-problem-with-ugc.html**

31   **http://digital-examples.blogspot.com/2008/05/design-boot-for-dr-martens.html**

32   **http://www.kaboodle.com/reviews/the-official-dr.-martens-usa-store--1914**

33   Jonah Peretti, quoted in Bill Wasik (2009) *And Then There's This: How stories live and die in viral culture*, Viking Penguin, New York

34   Greg Verdino, 'The problem with the paid isn't the "paid"', **http://gregverdino.typepad.com/greg_verdinos_blog/2009/04/the-problem-with-paid-media.html**

35   Hugh MacLeod, 'The trick to marketing', *GapingVoid*, **http://gapingvoid.com/2007/09/08/the-trick-to-marketing/**

Chapter Five   Optimization

1   Michael Wolff, 'Not the Antichrist again!', British *GQ*, January 2011, **http://www.gq-magazine.co.uk/magazine/2011/january**

2   Joost de Valk, 'SEO for newspapers', *Yoast*, **http://yoast.com/seo-newspapers/**

3   Malcolm Coles, 'How newspapers SEOed Patrick Swayze's death', *Online Journalism Blog*, 16 September 2009, **http://onlinejournalismblog.com/2009/09/16/seo-patrick-swayzes-death/**

4   Malcolm Coles, 'SEOing Patrick Swayze's and Keith Floyd's death', **http://www.malcolmcoles.co.uk/blog/seo-swayze-floyd/**

5   Wolff, 'Not the Antichrist again!'

6   **http://rohitbhargava.typepad.com/weblog/2006/08/5_rules_of_soci.html**

7   Jeremy Liew, 'Viral marketing, randomness and the difficulty of controlling growth in social media', *Lightspeed Venture Partners*, 13 September 2007, **http://lsvp.wordpress.com/2007/09/13/ viral-marketing-randomness-and-the-difficulty-of-controlling-growth-in-social-media/**

8   Craig Lambert, 'The marketplace of perceptions', *Harvard Magazine*, March–April 2006, **http://people.hbs.edu/nashraf/ marketplaceofperceptions.pdf**

9   **http://www.marketingsmartt.com/making-data-driven-business-decisions-with-google-website-optimizer/**

10   Fiona Mackay, 'Business schools respond to demand for use of social media', *New York Times*, 30 March 2010, **http://www.nytimes.com/ 2010/03/31/education/31iht-riedmba.html**

11   **www.feedburner.com**

12   Chris Anderson, 'The web is dead. Long live the internet', *Wired*, 17 August 2010, **http://www.wired.com/magazine/2010/08/ff_webrip/ all/1**

13   **http://weblogs.hitwise.com/sandra-hanchard/2009/09/government_ sites_receive_more.html**

14   **http://blog.textwise.com/2010/01/08/how-informative-is-twitter/**

15   **http://searchenginewatch.com/article/2092682/ Google-1-Button-on-More-Homepages-than-Tweet-Button**

16   Gordon MacMillan, 'Shared news and advertising matters more says CNN social media study', *The Wall*, **http://wallblog.co.uk/2010/10/07/ shared-news-and-advertising-matters-more-say-cnn-social-media-study/**

17   **http://www.allfacebook.com/2009/02/facebook-connect-users/**

18   **http://www.nickburcher.com/2009/09/h-social-fashion-new-interactive.html**

19   **http://mashable.com/2009/01/20/cnn-facebook-inauguration-numbers/**

20   'Connect brings JibJab 1.5 million Facebook viewers', *Inside Facebook*, 10 November 2009, **http://www.insidefacebook.com/2009/11/10/ connect-brings-jibjab-1-5-million-facebook-users/**

21   **http://youtu.be/-I7EOs3WAlI**

22 Figures from Swedish hero case study film made by agency
(no longer online)

23 'Social Plugins', *Facebook Developers* blog,
http://developers.facebook.com/docs/plugins/

24 'After f8: personalized Social Plugins now on 100,000+ sites', *Facebook
Developers* blog, **http://developers.facebook.com/blog/post/382**

25 'Some early data shows Facebook plugins increasing web sites' traffic',
**http://www.insidefacebook.com/2010/05/05/
some-early-data-shows-facebook-plugins-increasing-sites-traffic/**

26 'What "Like" buttons mean for web traffic (stats)',
http://mashable.com/2010/09/29/facebook-like-stats/

27 **http://gigaom.com/2010/10/14/o2-turns-on-geo-
fencing-for-starbucks-loreal-in-uk/**

28 **http://www.paidownedearned.com/2011/07/facebook-places-on-
swedish-high-street.html**

29 **http://mixi.co.jp/press/2011/0209/4324**

30 **http://blog.foursquare.com/2011/05/09/experimenting-
with-nfc-check-ins-for-google-io/**

31 **http://www.contagiousmagazine.com/2010/08/coca-cola_15.php**

32 **http://www.anheuser-busch.com/media/email2/index.html**

33 **http://www.businessinsider.com/bud-light-rents-entire-hotel-2011-2**

Chapter Six   Seeding and viral distribution

1 **http://www.dutchamsterdam.nl/155-gezellig**

2 Kevin Reed, 'Concern over "man in the pub" caught under tax advice law',
Accountancy Age, 15 February 2010, **http://www.accountancyage.com/
aa/news/1809935/concern-pub-caught-tax-advice-law**

3 Elihu Katz and Paul Lazarsfeld ([1955] 2006) *Personal Influence: The part
played by people in the flow of mass communications*, Transaction, New
Brunswick, NJ

4 **http://www.womworld.com/nokia/**

5 Emanuel Rosen (2001) *The Anatomy of Buzz: Creating word of mouth
marketing*, HarperCollins Business, London

6 'Seth Godin on standing out', *TED*, April 2007,
http://www.ted.com/talks/seth_godin_on_sliced_bread.html

7 'Charlie Sheen's Twitter account breaks more records', *Los Angeles Times*, 9 March 2011, **http://latimesblogs.latimes.com/technology/ 2011/03/charlie-sheens-twitter-account-breaks-more-records.html**

8 Arnie Gullov-Singh, 'Charlie Sheen: data beats emotion', *Ad.ly*, 9 March 2011, **http://adly.com/2011/03/charlie-sheen-data-beats-emotion/**

9 Matthew Thompson, 'Charlie Sheen internship hoax by NI man Jonny Campbell', *BBC News Northern Ireland*, 30 March 2011, **http://www.bbc.co.uk/news/uk-northern-ireland-12899356**

10 **http://www.womworld.com/nokia/14930/big-unboxing-for-n97-mini/**; **http://www.womworld.com/nokia/13148/another-chance-to-see- some-mariachi-madness/**; and **http://www.womworld.com/nokia/ 12786/extreme-e72-unboxing/**

11 **http://www.dooce.com/2008/06/30/my-hearts-beating-rabbit**

12 **http://moblogsmoproblems.blogspot.com/2008/07/case-study-dooces- nintendo-wii-giveaway.html**

13 Everett M Rogers ([1962] 1983) *Diffusion of Innovations*, Free Press, New York

14 William Higham (2009) *The Next Big Thing: Spotting and forecasting consumer trends for profit*, Kogan Page, London

15 Jeffrey Travers and Stanley Milgram, 'An experimental study of the small world problem', **http://bit.ly/e0YilV**

16 Jules Leskovec and Eric Horvitz, 'Planetary-scale views on a large instant-messaging network', **http://research.microsoft.com/en-us/um/ people/horvitz/leskovec_horvitz_www2008.pdf**

17 Malcolm Gladwell, 'Six degrees of Lois Weisberg', **http://www.gladwell.com/1999/1999_01_11_a_weisberg.htm** (included in *The Tipping Point*)

18 **http://www.nytimes.com/1992/11/29/style/ thing-the-carhartt-jacket.html**

19 **http://www.nytimes.com/1993/11/07/style/out-of-the-woods.html**

20 'KLF – The manual: how to have a number one the easy way', **http://www.kirps.com/web/main/resources/music/themanual/**

21 Chris Anderson (2007) *The Long Tail: How endless choice is creating unlimited demand*, Random House Business Books, London

22 B Brewster and F Broughton (2006) *How to DJ (Properly): The art and science of playing records*, Bantam Press, London

23   http://www.songfacts.com/detail.php?id=8005

24   Malcolm Gladwell, in Kevin Roberts (2006) *The Lovemarks Effect: Winning in the consumer revolution*, Powerhouse Books, Brooklyn, NY

25   http://www.quora.com/What-determines-influence-Is-it-a-calculated-score-fan-numbers-or-something-else

26   Barry Schwartz, quoted in Virginia Postrel, 'With so many choices, no wonder you need help', *New York Times*, 7 December 2004, http://www.nytimes.com/2004/12/07/business/businessspecial/07POST.html

27   Anderson, *The Long Tail*

28   Charlene Li and Josh Bernoff (2008) *Groundswell: Winning in a world transformed by social technologies*, Harvard Business School Publishing, Boston, MA

29   Don Tapscott (2009) *Grown Up Digital: How the net generation is changing the world*, McGraw-Hill, New York

30   Paul Lazarsfeld, Bernard Berelson and Hazel Gaudet (1948) *The People's Choice*, Columbia University Press, New York

31   Henry Jenkins *et al*, 'If it doesn't spread, it's dead', http://www.henryjenkins.org/2009/02/if_it_doesnt_spread_its_dead_p.html

32   Jeffrey Travers and Stanley Milgram (1969) 'An experimental study of the small world problem', *Sociometry*, **32** (4), December, pp 425–43, http://www.cis.upenn.edu/~mkearns/teaching/NetworkedLife/travers_milgram.pdf

33   Mark Granovetter, 'The strength of weak ties', http://www.stanford.edu/dept/soc/people/mgranovetter/documents/granstrengthweakties.pdf

34   Mark Granovetter, 'Getting a job', http://faculty.babson.edu/krollag/org_site/org_theory/granovet_articles/granovet_job.html

35   Thomas Valente, *Network Models of the Diffusion of Innovations*, Chapter 6: 'Network models and methods for studying the diffusion of innovations', http://homes.chass.utoronto.ca/~wellman/gradnet05/valente%20-%20DIFFUSION%20OF%20INNOVATIONS.pdf

36   http://en.wikipedia.org/wiki/ILOVEYOU

37   http://www.timesonline.co.uk/tol/life_and_style/health/article6182789.ece

38   http://en.wikipedia.org/wiki/2009_flu_pandemic_timeline#cite_note-MMWR-58d0430a2-4

39 PS Dodds and DJ Watts, 'A generalized model of social and biological contagion', **http://research.yahoo.com/files/d_w_JTB.pdf**

40 Adam L Penenberg (2009) *Viral Loop: The power of pass-it-on*, Sceptre, London

41 'The psychology of sharing', *New York Times*, **http://nytmarketing.whsites.net/mediakit/pos/POS_PUBLIC0725.php**

42 J Frenzen and K Nakamoto, quoted in Tony Yeshin (2006) *Advertising*, Thomson Learning, London

43 Jure Leskovec, Lada A Adamic and Bernardo A Huberman, 'The dynamics of viral marketing', **http://www.hpl.hp.com/research/scl/papers/viral/viral.pdf**

44 Nassim Nicholas Taleb (2007) *The Black Swan*, Allen Lane, London

45 John Allen Paulos, 'Stories vs. statistics', *New York Times*, Opinionator, 24 October 2010, **http://opinionator.blogs.nytimes.com/2010/10/24/stories-vs-statistics/**

46 Duncan Watts, **http://youtu.be/AtnR5H6AVVU**

47 Edward Lorenz, **http://web.mit.edu/newsoffice/2008/obit-lorenz-0416.html**

48 **http://dancemusic.about.com/cs/interviews/a/IntDarude.htm**

49 **http://culturemob.com/events/5724478-unity-2009-w-darude-blake-lewis-live-full-band-ryle-hyperfunk-35-locals-wa-seattle-downtown-98121-king-cat-theater**

50 **http://newsflash.bigshotmag.com/?p=3634**

51 Cory Casciato, 'Q&A with Darude', *Westword*, 4 June 2008, **http://blogs.westword.com/backbeat/2008/06/qa_with_darude.php**

52 Harvey Leibenstein (1950) 'Bandwagon, snob and Veblen effects in the theory of consumers' demand', *Quarterly Journal of Economics*, **64** (2), **http://areadocenti.eco.unicas.it/mbianchi/LEIBENSTEIN.50.QJE.pdf**

53 Higham, *The Next Big Thing*

54 Mark Earls (2007) *Herd: How to change mass behaviour by harnessing our true nature*, John Wiley, Chichester

55 James Surowiecki (2005) *The Wisdom of Crowds: Why the many are smarter than the few*, Abacus, London

56 **http://www.washingtonpost.com/wp-dyn/content/article/2007/12/16/AR2007121601472.html?nav=rss_nation/science**

57 **http://www.bbc.co.uk/programmes/p00f8mzr#synopsis**

58 Taleb, *The Black Swan*

59 Duncan Watts, 'Is Justin Timberlake a product of cumulative advantage?', *New York Times*, 15 April 2007, **http://www.nytimes.com/2007/04/15/magazine/15wwlnidealab.t.html**

60 Clay Shirky (2009) *Here Comes Everybody: How change happens when people come together*, Penguin, London

61 *Why Every Guy Should Buy Their Girlfriend a Wii Fit*, **http://youtu.be/v31qxrXsxv0**

62 **http://laurenbernat.com/category/wii-fit-journal/**

63 Jenkins *et al*, 'If it doesn't spread, it's dead'

64 **http://www.wired.com/listening_post/2008/05/radiohead-nude/**

65 **http://www.aniboom.com/Radiohead**

66 Bill Wasik (2009) *And Then There's This: How stories live and die in viral culture*, Viking Penguin, New York

67 E Bakshy *et al*, 'Everyone's an influencer: quantifying influence on Twitter', **http://research.yahoo.com/files/wsdm333w-bakshy.pdf**

68 **http://www.newhousesocialmedia.com/brite-influence-on-twitter-cant-be-purchased-0**

69 Mark Earls and Alex Bentley, 'Forget influentials, herd-like copying is how brands spread', *Admap*, November 2008

70 **http://www.pepsico.com/PressRelease/Frito-Lay-Fans-Set-Guinness-World-Record-for-Most-Fans-on-Facebook-In-24-Hours-W04282011.html**

71 **https://ads.youtube.com/pdf/YouTube-Promoted-Videos.pdf**

72 **http://youtu.be/R55e-uHQna0**

73 **http://www.buzzfeed.com/about/advertise**

74 **http://www.stumbleupon.com/ads/**

75 **http://blog.reddit.com/2009/12/self-serve-advertising-on-reddit-is-now.html**

76 **http://about.digg.com/blog/ads-you-can-digg%E2%80%A6or-bury**

77 **http://voices.washingtonpost.com/fasterforward/2011/01/facebook_sponsored_stories_tur.html**

78 **http://www.ft.com/cms/s/0/6726ef4e-805a-11df-8b9e-00144feabdc0.html?ftcamp=rss#axzz1CqV0hB4L**

79 'Is the tipping point toast?', **http://www.fastcompany.com/magazine/122/is-the-tipping-point-toast.html**

Chapter Seven   Broadcast

1   Marshall McLuhan (1964) *Understanding Media: The extensions of man*, Routledge & Kegan Paul, London

2   **http://bit.ly/oiwX8s**

3   **http://vivaki.com/view/?post=698**

4   Richard H Thaler and Cass R Sunstein (2009) *Nudge: Improving decisions about health, wealth and happiness*, Penguin Books, London

5   Nicholas Negroponte, 'Repurposing the material girl', *Wired*, November 1993, **http://www.wired.com/wired/archive/1.05/negroponte_pr.html**

6   **http://2d-code.co.uk/tesco-qr-code/**

7   **http://www.moxieinteractive.com/pulse/2011/03/07/ qr-code-makes-tv-interactive/**

8   Charles Leadbeater *et al* (2008) *We-Think*, Profile, London

9   **http://googlemobile.blogspot.com/2011/01/google-goggles-gets-faster-smarter-and.html**

10   **http://blog.foursquare.com/2011/02/10/super-bowl-recap/**

11   **http://intonow-blog.com/blog/2011/04/20/special-offer-from-pepsi-max-and-intonow/**

12   **http://intonow-blog.com/blog/2011/04/25/12-weeks-and-yahoo/**

13   **http://www.creativereview.co.uk/cr-blog/2011/january/ honda-jazz-this-unpredictable-life**

14   **http://www.psfk.com/2011/02/iphone-interacts-with-new-honda-tv-ad.html**

15   **http://jburg.typepad.com/future/2010/02/dear-agencies-why-didnt-we-see-social-calls-to-action-in-the-superbowl.html**

16   **http://www.eiaa.net/news/eiaa-articles-details.asp?lang=1&id=216**

17   **http://diamondgeezer.blogspot.com/2008_07_01_archive. html#8043344823072327871**

18   **http://weblogs.hitwise.com/robin-goad/2008/08/fast_moving_search_terms_british_gas_fallout_beatrix_potter_diamond_geezer.html**

19   **http://connectedplanetonline.com/residential_services/news/ Motorola-survey-see-social-media-changing-TV-1118/**

20   **http://pub.crowdscience.com/Twitter-Summary.pdf**

21   **http://www.bbc.co.uk/blogs/technology/2008/05/tv_becomes_social_again.html**

22 http://www.cybersoc.com/2008/05/twitter-europar.html

23 http://www.paidownedearned.com/2011/06/tv-as-content-gateway-paid-owned-earned.html

24 http://www.nytimes.com/interactive/2009/02/02/sports/20090202_superbowl_twitter.html

25 http://nms.com/docs/NMS-Super_Bowl_Snapshot_Report_2-2-09.pdf

26 http://blog.twitter.com/2010/02/super-data.html

27 http://blog.twitter.com/2011/01/celebrating-new-year-with-new-tweet.html

28 Twitter Blog – http://blog.twitter.com/2011/02/superbowl.html

29 http://sueunerman.com/2010/11/appointment-to-view-tv-is-back-and-this-time-it%E2%80%99s-hashtagged/

30 http://allthingsd.com/20110212/howard-stern-and-twitter-just-made-me-watch-private-parts-again/

31 http://media.twitter.com/1273/amazonmp3-superbowl

32 http://www.mediabizbloggers.com/media-biz-bloggers/How-Amazon-MP3-Won-The-Social-Media-Super-Bowl--Tom-Cunniff--MediaBizBloggers.html

33 http://www.nickburcher.com/2010/10/yeo-valley-rap-becomes-twitter-trending.html

34 http://www.andthentheresthis.net/mob_email_1.html

35 http://harpers.org/archive/2006/03/0080963

36 Gareth Ellis 'Mobilising consumers', *Admap*, February 2010

37 http://youtu.be/VQ3d3KigPQM

Chapter Eight   Performance

1 M Husain and J Stein, 'Reszö Bálint and his most celebrated case', http://www.ncbi.nlm.nih.gov/pubmed/3276300?log$=activity

2 http://viscog.beckman.illinois.edu/flashmovie/15.php

3 http://viscog.beckman.illinois.edu/djs_lab/demos.html

4 http://www.wjh.harvard.edu/~cfc/Simons1999.pdf; and http://www.scribd.com/doc/4958384/Gorillas-in-Our-Midst-Sustained-Inattentional-Blindness-for-Dynamic-Events-Simons1999

5   Robert Heath (2001) *The Hidden Power of Advertising: How low involvement processing influences the way we choose brands*, World Advertising Research Centre, Henley-on-Thames

6   http://www.msnbc.msn.com/id/6877753/

7   http://www.google.com/press/pressrel/pressrelease39.html

8   http://www.google.com/press/pressrel/select.html

9   https://adwords.google.co.uk/support/aw/bin/answer.py?hl=en-uk&answer=10215

10 http://www.mediaweek.co.uk/news/637332/New-research-boosts-credibility-Telegraph-brand/

11 GroupM, 'The influenced social media search and the interplay of consideration and consumption', http://www.scribd.com/doc/20703026/The-Influenced-Social-Media-Search-and-the-Interplay-of-Consideration-and-Consumption

12 'Search and brand: the UK horizontal story', http://www.google.co.uk/intl/en/advertisers/pdfs/searchandbrand.pdf

13 Duncan Parry, 'Research into search and branding: a recap', *Search Engine Watch*, 27 August 2010, http://searchenginewatch.com/3641276

14 http://www.knowltonmosaics.com/pages/HKnewd.htm

15 http://blog.mindvalleylabs.com/using-ascii-art-on-google-adwords-brilliantly-innovative/336/

16 http://www.icrossing.co.uk/fileadmin/uploads/Case_studies/Ann_Summers_iCrossing_Case_Study_01.pdf

17 Stephen Baker (2009) *They've Got Your Number: Data, digits and destiny – how the numerati are changing our lives*, Vintage, London

18 Adam L Penenberg, 'Cookie monsters: the innocuous text files that Web surfers love to hate', *Slate.com*, 7 November 2005, http://www.slate.com/id/2129656/

19 Joanna Lord, 'Retargeting: what it is and how to use it', *SEOmoz*, 5 April 2011, http://www.seomoz.org/blog/retargeting-basics-what-it-is-how-to-use-it

20 Shawndra Hill, Foster Provost and Chris Volinsky (2006) 'Network based marketing: identifying likely adopters via consumer networks', *Statistical Science*, **21** (2), http://arxiv.org/PS_cache/math/pdf/0606/0606278v2.pdf

21 Stephanie Clifford, 'The online ad that knows where your friends shop', *New York Times*, 25 June 2009, **http://www.nytimes.com/2009/06/26/ business/media/26adco.html**

22 **http://33across.com/advertisers.php**

23 Jodi Harris, 'Branding through the social graph', *iMedia Connection*, 8 December 2009, **http://www.imediaconnection.com/summits/ coverage/25296.asp**

24 **http://www.digitalstrategyconsulting.com/intelligence/2010/09/ time_spent_online_facebook_ove.php**

25 **http://blog.nielsen.com/nielsenwire/online_mobile/ nielsenfacebook-ad-report/**

26 David Kirkpatrick (2010) *The Facebook Effect: The inside story of the company that is connecting the world*, Simon & Schuster, New York

27 **www.insidefacebook.com/2011/09/22/what-F8-means-for-advertisers- the-ability-to-target-users-based-on-media-consumption**

28 'Facebook to top Yahoo! in US display market, as Google looms', **http://www.emarketer.com/PressRelease.aspx?R=1008259**

29 'How one band acquired 3000 Facebook fans for $0.08 each', *AllFacebook.com*, **http://www.allfacebook.com/ band-facebook-fans-2010-09**

30 **http://www.google.com/intl/en/corporate/privacy_principles.html**

Chapter Nine   Responding

1 Steve Keenan, 'Ryanair and the "idiot bloggers"', *Times Online*, 24 February 2009, **http://www.timesonline.co.uk/tol/travel/news/ article5797990.ece**

2 'Ryanair: "Lunatic bloggers can keep the blogosphere"', *Guardian*, 25 February 2009, **http://www.guardian.co.uk/media/pda/2009/feb/25/ ryanair-socialnetworking**

3 Frederick F Reichheld, 'The one number you need to grow', **http://www.netzkobold.com/uploads/pdfs/the_one_number_you_ need_to_grow_reichheld.pdf**

4 Paul Marsden, Alain Samson and Neville Upton, 'Advocacy drives growth', **http://www2.lse.ac.uk/intranet/LSEServices/**

divisionsAndDepartments/ERD/pressAndInformationOffice/PDF/
AdvocacyDrivesGrowth_5-9-05.pdf

5 C Fornell, RT Rust and MG Dekimpe (2010) 'The effect of customer satisfaction on consumer spending growth', *Journal of Marketing Research*, **47** (1), **http://www.atypon-link.com/AMA/doi/abs/10.1509/jmkr.47.1.28**

6 Jeremiah Owyang, 'The problem with Net Promoter score', *Web Strategy*, **http://www.web-strategist.com/blog/category/social-media-measurement/**

7 RightNow, *The Retail Consumer Report*, March 2011, **http://www.rightnow.com/files/Retail-Consumer-Report.pdf**

8 'New study: deep brand engagement correlates with financial performance', **http://www.altimetergroup.com/2009/07/engagementdb.html**

9 US Air Force Public Affairs Agency Emerging Technology Division, *New Media and the Air Force*, **http://www.af.mil/shared/media/document/AFD-090406-036.pdf**

10 **http://www.web-strategist.com/blog/2008/12/31/diagram-how-the-air-force-response-to-blogs/**

11 **http://www.employeefactor.com/?p=2658**

12 **http://news.bbc.co.uk/1/hi/uk_politics/3288907.stm**

13 David Kilcullen, 'Fundamentals of company-level counterinsurgency', **http://www.smallwarsjournal.com/documents/28articles.pdf**

14 **http://www.scribd.com/doc/17313280/Template-Twitter-Strategy-for-Government-Departments**

15 **http://socialmediagovernance.com/policies.php?f=0**

16 **http://www.scribd.com/doc/36127480/Ford-Social-Media-Guidelines**

17 **http://theinspirationroom.com/daily/2010/best-buy-twelpforce/**

18 Jim Lecinski, *Winning the Zero Moment of Truth*, **http://www.zeromomentoftruth.com/**

19 Allen Salkin, 'All-stars of the clever riposte', *New York Times*, 30 September 2007, **http://www.nytimes.com/2007/09/30/fashion/30commenters.html?pagewanted=1&_r=1**

20 **http://www.engadget.com/2006/06/29/dell-looking-into-flaming-laptop-incident/**; and **http://www.theinquirer.net/inquirer/news/1042700/dell-laptop-explodes-japanese-conference**

21 http://gizmodo.com/182440/comcast-tech-falls-asleep-on-guys-couch

22 http://www.comcastmustdie.com/

23 *ABC News*, http://www.youtube.com/watch?v=1a2R8wKfmHM

24 http://comcastmustdie.blogspot.com/2007/10/how-to-use-this-blog.html

25 Brian Stelter, 'Griping online? Comcast hears and talks back', *New York Times*, 25 July 2008, http://www.nytimes.com/2008/07/25/technology/25comcast.html

26 http://www.scribd.com/doc/29295346/April-2008-Letter-to-Amazon-com-s-shareholders

27 http://love.flysas.net/blog/2010/12/23/seasons-greetings-from-sas-social-media-team/

28 www.facebook.com/sas

29 www.facebook.com/delta

30 http://www.facebook.com/pages/Dislike-Button/102038567018

31 http://www.thehelphouse.com/blog/band_blog/entry/?id=11

32 Helen Carter, 'Jedi religion founder accuses Tesco of discrimination over rules on hoods', *Guardian*, 18 September 2009, http://www.guardian.co.uk/world/2009/sep/18/jedi-religion-tesco-hood-jones

33 http://www.youtube.com/watch?v=h42UeR-f8ZA

34 'Levinator25 gets a paycheck for his Tiger Woods glitch video', *Los Angeles Times*, 25 August 2008, http://latimesblogs.latimes.com/webscout/2008/08/levinator25-get.html

35 http://www.youtube.com/watch?v=FZ1st1Vw2kY

36 http://www.youtube.com/watch?v=yWUdsy2kGUc

37 http://www.youtube.com/watch?v=owGykVbfgUE

38 http://wearesocial.net/blog/2010/07/spice-videos-viewed-11-million-times/

39 http://wearesocial.net/blog/2010/07/social-media-buzz-advantage-spice/

40 Mark Borden, 'The team who made Old Spice smell good again reveals what's behind Mustafa's towel', *Fast Company*, 14 July 2010, http://www.fastcompany.com/1670314/old-spice-youtube-videos-wieden

41 http://www.brandweek.com/bw/content_display/news-and-features/direct/e3i45f1c709df0501927f56568a2acd5c7b?pn=2

42 http://adage.com/article/viral-video-charts/spice-killing-youtube-sales/229080/

Chapter Ten   Measurement

1   Frank Davidson comments from personal correspondence and discussion

2   NHS, '10 steps to SMART objectives', 3 August 2004, **http://www.natpact.info/uploads/Ten%20Steps%20to%20 SMART%20objectives.pdf**

3   Antony Young and Lucy Aitken (2007) *Profitable Marketing Communications: A guide to marketing return on investment*, Kogan Page, London

4   'Social media measurement 2011: five things to forget and five things to learn', *MetricsMan*, **http://metricsman.wordpress.com/2010/12/30/ social-media-measurement-2011-five-things-to-forget-and-five-things-to-learn/**

5   Bryan Smith, 'Media measurement: online and offline connectivity', *Admap*, October 2010

6   GroupM, 2009 Interaction report

7   'Search and brand: the UK horizontal story', **http://www.google.co.uk/ intl/en/advertisers/pdfs/searchandbrand.pdf**

8   IAB Europe, 'Brand advertising and digital', **http://www.iab.fi/assets/ Tiedotteet/iab-europe-white-paper-brand-ad.pdf**

9   ComScore and Starcom USA, 'Press release: ComScore and Starcom USA release updated "Natural Born Clickers" study showing 50 percent drop in number of U.S. internet users who click on display ads', **http://www.comscore.com/Press_Events/Press_Releases/2009/10/ comScore_and_Starcom_USA_Release_Updated_Natural_Born_ Clickers_Study_Showing_50_Percent_Drop_in_Number_of_U.S._ Internet_Users_Who_Click_on_Display_Ads**

10 'Untangling the attribution web', Forrester, **http://www.forrester.com/ rb/Research/untangling_attribution_web/q/id/58173/t/2**

11 David Kirkpatrick (2010) *The Facebook Effect: The inside story of the company that is connecting the world*, Simon & Schuster, New York

12 Brian Morrissey, 'Value of a "fan" on social media: $3.60', *Adweek*, 13 April 2010, **http://www.adweek.com/aw/content_display/news/ digital/e3iaf69ea67183512325a8feefb9f969530**

13 Paul Adams, 'The fans + followers arms race', *Think Outside In*, 17 April 2010, **http://www.thinkoutsidein.com/blog/2010/04/ the-fans-followers-arms-race/**

[14] Meeyoung Cha *et al*, 'Measuring user influence in Twitter: the million follower fallacy', **http://an.kaist.ac.kr/~mycha/docs/icwsm2010_cha.pdf**

[15] Conversocial, Facebook Page Profiler, **https://app.conversocial.com/profiler/**

[16] Augie Ray, 'What is the value of a Facebook fan? Zero!', Augie Ray's blog, *Forrester.com*, **http://blogs.forrester.com/augie_ray/10-07-08-what_value_facebook_fan_zero**

[17] 'Seven guidelines for achieving ROI from social media', *eMarketer*, **http://www.scribd.com/doc/48228865/eMarketer-Social-Media-ROI**

[18] **http://adage.com/article/special-report-digital-conference/coca-cola-s-wendy-clark-liquid-linked-key/226836/**

[19] Christopher Heine, 'Radio Shack says Foursquare users spend 3.5x more', *ClickZ*, 11 April 2011, **http://www.clickz.com/clickz/news/2042629/radio-shack-foursquare-users-spend-35x**

[20] 'Social media measurement 2011: five things to forget and five things to learn', *MetricsMan*

[21] SL Koerner *et al*, 'Pathways to measuring consumer behaviour in an age of media convergence', ESOMAR: Television Audience Conference, Cannes, June 2002

[22] Joe Mandese, 'Media goes organic', *Admap*, October 2010

[23] Paul Adams, '"Virality" is not a success metric', *Think Outside In*, 17 March 2010, **http://www.thinkoutsidein.com/blog/2010/03/virality-is-not-a-success-metric/**

[24] 'Evian "Live Young" ad effectiveness: UK', **http://static.googleusercontent.com/external_content/untrusted_dlcp/www.google.co.uk/en/uk/intl/en/advertisers/pdfs/evian_uk_brand_research.pdf**

[25] **http://www.slideshare.net/UnrulyUK/star-wars-the-force-vs-evian-roller-babies-infographic**

[26] Farid A Muna, 'The helicopter view and strategic thinking', *Meirc*, January 2010, **http://www.meirc.com/meirc-consultants/992-the-helicopter-view-and-strategic-thinking-.html**

[27] Carl Warner, 'The science of the art of advertising', *Adweek*, 17 November 2010, **http://www.adweek.com/aw/content_display/news/digital/e3i156046bdea3250cec573d096c6f735e0**

Index

NB: page numbers in *italic* indicate figures or tables